'Nick shares from a long  levels of professional cons perspective and conclusi invaluable. Essential r entrepreneur.

'*Risk, Reward and Values* draws from history, experience and timeless truth to remind you of the point and purpose for your business. Every founder, owner and manager in companies of any size or scale will find this book to be a vital asset in the years to come.'

Stephen K De Silva, CPA (retired), Author of Money and the Prosperous Soul

'In these conflicted times, where there is a void of values and virtues, arises a need for true entrepreneurs who reflect the values and culture of the kingdom of God. Nick Nicholson has penned the book for these new times of resilience in which he has captured with brush strokes of wisdom and years of experience the attributes associated with the character of a true kingdom entrepreneur. *Risk, Reward and Values* is a challenging invitation to dare to impact communities and nations through a renewed mind and a godly character. Enjoy!'

Humberto Martuscelli, Senior Pastor at El Almendro Church, and CEO of CCA Community Business Center, Mexico City

'Over many years Nick Nicholson has successfully led both an international company and a church, alongside being a husband of one and father of three. Nick is always open to learning, and the challenges, joys, ups and downs that he has experienced have developed in him an ability to guide and advise others with the ambition to become kingdom entrepreneurs.

'Written in the style of autobiographical storytelling, the book distills and communicates Nick's experience of entrepreneurial leadership linking with his understanding of where God resides in that process.

'Each chapter covers his experience of the nuts and bolts of building and sustaining an organisation that advances the kingdom of God. At the end of each we are then invited to Pause for reflection, Pray to ask what area of the subject God wants to minister to us and then put our learning into Practice.

'Nick has personally helped me to understand what it takes to build an organisation with kingdom values, and I admit I was one of the many people advising him to write about his expertise and wisdom to help others. This book succeeds in doing that and I thoroughly recommend it.'
Dr Clive Colledge PhD FRSA, Academic and TEDx speaker

'I have known Nick for a number of years and have seen first-hand the high level of integrity and wisdom in everything he does; it has been inspirational for me. *Risk, Reward and Values* further highlights how ordinary people like you and I (and Nick) can successfully navigate life and its challenges when our foundational principles are firm and rooted in truth. This benefits not only us and our enterprises (be they business or otherwise) but also the people around us, thereby creating an upward spiral of value and shared success.'
Jonathan Canning, International Legal Director

RISK, REWARD AND VALUES

THE CAUSE AND CHARACTER OF THE KINGDOM ENTREPRENEUR

Nick Nicholson

instant
apostle

First published in Great Britain in 2021

Instant Apostle
104 The Drive
Rickmansworth
Herts
WD3 4DU

British Library Cataloguing-in-Publication Data

A catalogue record for this book is available from the British Library.

This book and all other Instant Apostle books are available from Instant Apostle:

Website: www.instantapostle.com

Email: info@instantapostle.com

ISBN 978-1-912726-44-8

Printed in Great Britain.

Let your light shine before others, that they may see your good deeds and glorify your Father in heaven. (Matthew 5:16)

To Helen.
Thank you for your love and support while journeying with me in this unexpected venture. I couldn't have done it without you.

Contents

Foreword

Over the last twenty or thirty years, there has been a renewed emphasis in the evangelical church on the importance of the truth of the kingdom of God and its outworking in all facets of the lives of believers. This has gone alongside a recognition of the need for evangelicals to be involved in serving our communities through social action projects, etc. Understanding the truth of the kingdom of God has helped us see the priority of living for Jesus through our secular work, through the arts, through our family life and in other spheres of life in the public square rather than only facing inwards towards our personal faith and church activities.

Risk, Reward and Values: The cause and character of the kingdom entrepreneur follows this prophetic theme and focuses helpfully on the outworking of the truth of the kingdom of God for entrepreneurs. Entrepreneurs are essential for our nations' economies, and more Christian entrepreneurs need to rise up to take their part for the benefit of society and as an opportunity to demonstrate both Christian character and risky faith initiatives.

Nick Nicholson is well qualified to write on this subject, having been a successful entrepreneur himself as well as having taught and mentored others in accordance with the principles found in this excellent book. His emphasis on godly character as a foundation for Christian entrepreneurship is absolutely essential. It is a challenge for us in whatever our line of work to display the character of Jesus and the fruit of the Holy Spirit rather than living 'double-minded' lives where we are displaying one set of values in the church but others in our secular lives. Nick brings out this important point for the subject of entrepreneurship, but it applies in other contexts too.

I first observed Nick's passion for spreading this message when he accompanied my wife and me on one of our frequent visits to Russia more than fifteen years ago. Nick conducted seminars on the subject for Russian churches and was well able to contextualise his teaching appropriately, and also to create a desire for godly entrepreneurship within the churches we served there.

Having served the Lord both in business and church leadership, Nick is able to draw from his experience of both to present an attractive and compelling vision of the call upon many to take initiatives as 'kingdom entrepreneurs'.

I enthusiastically commend *Risk, Reward and Values* to you.

David Devenish, Newfrontiers Together Team

Introduction

Imagine that you are going on a journey, a trek, an adventure. It's not a short journey; there are places that you will need to stay before setting off on the next stage. You have a starting point, where you are right now, and you probably have a destination in mind, or at least you have an initial destination planned. But a journey also has way points, those places we pass through and which mark out the steps on the journey. That's how you can imagine the way that this book is structured. You're invited on a journey of discovery via way points – a journey to explore our character, motivations and mindsets, our purpose and our calling, and to encounter God whose kingdom we have entered as his sons and daughters.

We'll start by considering our purpose and position as a kingdom entrepreneur. We'll journey on, checking out the foundations of our lives, through to the key characteristics of humility and integrity, pausing to admire the view at creating culture and our wealth and power mindsets, before descending into the place of contending and rising again to examine success and failure, finishing at being lighthouses in dark places. We'll not have arrived at our final destination, but at the place where our hearts are refined, ready for God to take us deeper and further. It's not the complete guide but a particular viewpoint, an important viewpoint, an exploration of the heart of the kingdom entrepreneur.

It's not an easy journey. The path is rarely flat and uncluttered, but it is exciting and never boring! There are times of riding the rapids when you feel that you dropped the paddle on entry, losing sleep as you seek God for a clear way forward, or interceding for an answer to a problem client, or feeling becalmed when there seems to be no wind of the Spirit[1] to fill the sails, and needing to press on to provide the impetus. That's why knowing that we are called by God along that path is so important.

It's not a book primarily about managing businesses; there are many books and blogs available, written by great authors who are more experienced in leading global businesses than me. It's not a book about Christians in business or the marketplace; there are fine examples of those to be read. The book doesn't give lists of three rules to achieve this, or ten principles to achieve that. These are helpful, and I've read some myself. It's a book honed from my own experience of being determined to see the kingdom of God demonstrated and advanced in my entrepreneurship and in pioneering and running small businesses and in co-leading churches over many years.

Kingdom entrepreneurs are not just those who own, develop or run for-profit enterprises. They are just as likely to develop and run not-for-profits, charities, churches and community groups. The model adopted is not so much my concern as the purpose for its existence – its vision, values and outputs. Through being involved with church leadership in the not-for-profit sector as well

---

[1] See John 3:8.

as directing a for-profit enterprise, I realised that leading both requires very similar skills, competences, character, faith and love; in short, people who passionately love Jesus, are filled with the Holy Spirit and seek to live their lives from a biblical worldview. So, although I write often here from the perspective of a for-profit entrepreneur, I believe that the messages are valid no matter what form your entrepreneurship takes.

My motivation above all others is to pass on what I wish I had known when I started on this journey thirty years ago. It's written with the young entrepreneur in mind – young in experience if not in age – either setting out or considering whether to do so. It could be that you are a more seasoned entrepreneur exploring faith and wondering how faith in Jesus Christ impacts your entrepreneurship. This book will help you too. Over the course of these years, I have learned wisdom to pass on; to help to prevent unwise actions, pitfalls and shipwrecks, and to encourage godly character and to reflect the glory of God through us, even as earthly vessels who don't always 'get it right'. If this book helps, then my goal will have been achieved.

It is my prayer that the Holy Spirit will use these words, written with humility but knowing that this is a part of my calling, and that they will help to inspire, motivate, teach and cheer you on from the terraces/bench/royal box/ dressing room/prayer room (please delete according to your culture and favourite sport)! God loves you and His favour is upon you. You are someone who is saying 'yes and amen' to the prayer of Jesus that His kingdom may come on earth as His kingdom is in heaven (Matthew

6:10). So, if this resonates with you, this book is written for you.

Pause, pray, practise

The aim of this book is not merely to provide information and inspiration, but also to be a means of God imparting His life and wisdom to us. At the end of each chapter, you will be invited to pause, pray and practise as a way of assisting with this impartation. God will give of Himself to you, and of His wisdom and direction in your specific circumstances and mission as you seek Him in this way.

I encourage you to try to find a quiet place, or wherever you find it easiest to be still and gather your senses together on the presence of God. *Pause* to reflect on what you've read, taking time to *pray* those prayers addressed to Father, Jesus and Holy Spirit to show you areas in your life where He wants to minister to you. Sometimes these prayers are mixed with questions for you to consider honestly without fear or embarrassment. Finally, you will be invited to *practise* what God has said by paying attention to what you need to change through consistent practice.

Changing habits takes time. We can rely on the grace of God to help reshape us, as well as the renewing power of the Holy Spirit to affirm and help us let go of old patterns and mindsets, replacing them with new, redeemed ones. It could be that you will need to return to the exercise more than once. Don't feel that you need to rush; let God do what He wants to do before you move on. Journalling is a great way to note what God is saying, your processing, and how you are responding as a result. Start with an open heart towards your loving Father and enjoy the encounters!

1
Why Kingdom Entrepreneurs?

Key points

- The reward for the kingdom entrepreneur is to extend the kingdom of God.

- Redemption is the thread that runs through our enterprises.

We seem to be in an age when anyone who has a bright business idea and attempts to take it to market is called an entrepreneur. There is an increasing number of individuals who want to develop their ideas, USPs or patents. Reports from Companies House (in the UK), as analysed by the Centre for Entrepreneurs[2] (CFE), show that business formations increased from 2015 to reach a record 671,999 in 2019. In a recent report,[3] one in five

---

[2] 'The CFE business startup index', Centre for Entrepreneurs, centreforentrepreneurs.org/cfe-research/business-startup-index/ (accessed 18th February 2021).

[3] 'A fifth of UK adults want to start a business in 2021 – but they need more support', Enterprise Nation, www.enterprisenation.com/learn-something/fifth-of-adults-want-to-start-a-business-in-2021/?mc_cid=6fbc2a3371&mc_eid=40a0c127dd (accessed 18th February 2021).

adults in the UK were found to want to start a business in 2021, with one-third being in the eighteen-to-thirty age group. This is an encouraging trend! Unfortunately, 20 per cent of businesses in the UK fail in their first year, and 60 per cent fail within three years.[4] In the European Union in 2015, enterprises employing fewer than 250 persons represented 99 per cent of all enterprises. Substantial skills need to be applied to setting up and operating a successful business, and it is no different for kingdom entrepreneurs. There is no 'magic wand' that God gives us to make everything work out well.

An important question is what an entrepreneur is, and, in the context of this book, what makes a person a kingdom entrepreneur. I use the phrase 'kingdom entrepreneur' as shorthand and I need to explain what I mean. A kingdom entrepreneur is an entrepreneur whose life is committed to following Jesus Christ, who has entered into the kingdom of God and who lives out the values of this kingdom using their God-given gifts to extend this kingdom in their spheres of influence.

Getting to the heart of the matter

Fundamentally, an entrepreneur is prepared to take risk and to put their physical assets on the line to obtain benefits.

Risk is inherent in the life of an entrepreneur!

---

[4] 'Start–ups across the UK are going bust – they need more careful management for our economy to boom', *Telegraph*, 24th January 2019, telegraph.co.uk/politics/2019/01/24/start-ups-across-uk-going-bust-need-careful-management-economy/ (accessed 18th February 2021).

It is reported that it was the pastor, author and founder of the Vineyard movement, John Wimber, who first coined the phrase 'faith is spelled r-i-s-k'.[5] I have found this to be true. The truth is that life involves risk. When God instructs us to trust Him and not to 'lean … on [our] own understanding' (Proverbs 3:5), He knows there is risk to us in doing so, and we know that too. The key is taking reasonable risk, or faith-filled risk, and not stupid risk. Walking on water (Matthew 14:22-32) may be viewed as stupid risk, but Peter didn't wake up one morning and think, 'I'm going to walk on water today to bless Jesus.' He was responding to the invitation of Jesus to walk with Him on the water. You bet that he learned some lessons that day when he began to sink, but Jesus grabbed him to get him back in the boat! Peter was prepared to take risk in the knowledge that Jesus was there for him anyway. The risk was getting very wet, taking in some water and looking an idiot in front of the other disciples – some of which probably happened. But he trusted Jesus to rescue him. I reckon Peter was an entrepreneur of faith. Sure, he messed up a good few times and needed to be restored, which he was, but Jesus gave to him the keys of the kingdom (Matthew 16:19). Now, that is some benefit!

Kingdom entrepreneurs?

To me there is a significant and tangible difference between someone who is driven by the desire to gain for themselves the benefits from a venture, and a kingdom-

[5] 'Rooted in Risk', Vineyard USA, vineyardusa.org/library/rooted-in-risk/ (accessed 18th February 2021).

minded person who wants to gain benefit for the common good. The big difference is how they go about gaining the benefit, and what the benefit is. The next chapter will look briefly at the kingdom of God, but for now I want to say that, in my opinion, all followers of Jesus are people of the kingdom of God (or kingdom of heaven, if you prefer). They are people who acknowledge the Kingship of Jesus Christ in their lives, their dreams, purposes, actions and priorities. They are those whose focus is firmly fixed on heaven while living their lives on earth.

So I see that a key distinctive in the mindset of the kingdom entrepreneur is what benefit we are expecting, working and praying for in our business, charity, church, etc.

Gaining benefit

I guess you will have heard of people who are ruthless in their quest for profit, fame/celebrity or power because their motivation is to advance themselves. Maybe you've had dealings with someone like this. I have, and I have to say that I have struggled to relate to them. For the kingdom-minded person, the way that they go about gaining benefit must be rooted firmly in the way that Jesus modelled for us to live. As Jesus made clear, for example to the rich man, as the Gospel writer records in Mark 10:17-23, placing our faith, trust or comfort in money or other things where the recipient keeps the benefit exclusively to themselves, or gains an overinflated view of themselves thus affecting their beliefs and behaviours, is not a kingdom motivation. As another Gospel writer,

Luke, demonstrates in his description of a man called Zacchaeus, a supervisor of tax collectors in Jericho, in his encounter with Jesus (Luke 19:1-10), it is about a response to the grace of a lavishly generous God!

What is the benefit?

There could be many ways of thinking about the benefits from entrepreneurship – profit, money, payback on risk, power and purpose are likely to be some of those.

For the kingdom entrepreneur, their vision, motivation and drive are, I contend, 'higher' than these quite narrow, worldly focused intentions. They are concerned with the extending of the kingdom 'on earth as it is heaven' (Matthew 6:10). They are focused clearly on the renewal of creation which God originally declared to be 'very good' (Genesis 1:31), and which will be so again when Jesus returns to earth to judge sin finally, and to establish His rule de facto. Ever since the Fall (Genesis 3), God's plan has been to reinstitute His rule on earth through the work of Christ, and through the Church universal, as those who co-labour with God to achieve His purpose in a world teeming with righteousness, love and justice. Perhaps this can be well summed up in the phrase 'prosperity for all'.

Prosperity in the kingdom?

I find it interesting that many Christians and churches, certainly in the UK, have historically shied away from the concept of prosperity, even becoming uncomfortable because in their thinking there remains the imputed association that prosperity is somewhat sinful and must be resisted. It took me some time to shake off this mindset, and I should say that I'm not sure where I learned this concept. I think that it is based on a premise, false in my opinion, that there is a direct relationship between spirituality and lack. I need to say here that I do not agree with, and I am not advancing, what has been coined the 'prosperity gospel', ie one where people are encouraged, or even told, to give financially to people or causes as the means of God blessing us with more in return than we have given.

In considering the spirituality–lack argument, Douglas Harrison-Mills,[6] in his most helpful thesis, asserts that this demonstrates an incomplete consideration of the scheduling and reason of the varied stages of the cycle of the spiritual and the economic, as scarcity and abundance should be thought of as not the end point but the means of achieving it. In the Old Testament stories, such cycles are designed to drive God's people to prayer and repentance. God then says that He would restore the blessings in His covenants to the people, which in turn leads to a torrent of grain, oil and new wine, leading again to abundance.

---

[6] D Harrison-Mills, 'Hearing About Jesus, but Thinking About Joel: Exploring the Biblical and Historical Relationship Between Spiritual and Economic Transformation', University of Birmingham, December 2011, etheses.bham.ac.uk/id/eprint/3864/1/HarrisonMills12PhD.pdf (accessed 24th January 2021), p84.

Prosperity defined

Biblical prosperity is closely allied with the Old Testament word *shalom*, meaning well-being in its wide sense, and is embodied in Jesus' statement concerning abundant life: 'I have come that they may have life, and have it to the full' (John 10:10) – meaning super-abundantly. It is a full sense of flourishing and lack of scarcity. The truth is that as kingdom-minded people we should flourish and prosper over the long term. It is what we do with our flourishing that is more important to me.

The focus of prosperity is not only on me, but on those around me. Prosperity is to do with appropriately positioned peace, freedom and security, being part of a caring community, good education and training, good healthcare, opportunity to work, to innovate and for recreation, to be truly free and to have space to be. It is about the opportunity and the environment for everyone to discover and fulfil and then to share their potential. It involves both wealth and well-being and destroys the basis for social isolation. Its focus is not only on me but on those around me in my community of friends and colleagues, in my country as a whole and internationally. This reflects the impact and expansion of His kingdom. Old Testament prophecies (Deuteronomy 28:1-14; Jeremiah 31:12-14, 31-34; Ezekiel 36:26-30; Joel 2:18-32) clearly relate to prosperity for the people (community or nation) and not simply for individuals. In his letter to the exiles in Babylon, Jeremiah says that God instructs them to 'seek the peace and prosperity of the city to which I have carried you into exile. Pray to the LORD for it, because if it prospers, you too will prosper' (Jeremiah 29:7).

I believe that kingdom entrepreneurs are well placed, if not uniquely placed, to be the main agents for driving community prosperity. The gathering of wealth in its fullest meaning has as its aim and purpose not principally the aggrandisement of an individual but the prosperity and flourishing of the community.

Shining glory!

A kingdom entrepreneur models the kingdom of God to those around them. Kingdom entrepreneurs are therefore kingdom people whom God has gifted with the ability to create and innovate enterprises, culture, products and services in a way that demonstrates human redemption. They are being prophetic to their world around them, pointing clearly to Jesus, the redeemer of humankind. I see kingdom entrepreneurs as those who are prepared to embrace risk for the return of the advancement of the kingdom. Maybe we can envisage kingdom entrepreneurs as 'true disruptors'– to use the language of those who have pioneered the use of technology and services to disrupt the established markets – except that these true disruptors are disrupting the influences over a largely godless society of the 'the powers of this dark world' (Ephesians 6:12).

A kingdom entrepreneur models the
kingdom of God to those around them.

This modelling of the kingdom of God will be distinctive to kingdom people. It may be in the way that we deliver services, the products that we supply, the culture that we have generated and are 'exporting', the way that we interact with others, in our generosity and grace, in our redemptive actions in the community, that are the fingerprints of our entrepreneurship. Redemption will be the thread that marks out our enterprises from others, signalling that in the words of Jesus, 'The time has come … The kingdom of God has come near. Repent and believe the good news!' (Mark 1:15). So, when we interact with others, we're shining the glory of God and demonstrating that His kingdom has come.

Pause, pray, practise

- Pause: Do I hold the view that it is more spiritual for me, my community and my nation to live in lack or in prosperity?

- Pause: How did I come to hold this viewpoint? Where did I learn it?

- Pray: Father, is my viewpoint fixed by human opinion or by Your truth?

- Practise: What do I need to do if my viewpoint needs to be changed?

2
Citizens of Heaven Resident on Earth

Key points

- We are citizens of heaven with God's mandate to extend His kingdom on earth.

- He places us in positions where we influence people, neighbourhoods, cultures and nations.

The kingdom of God is not a static place that you physically go into … To enter God's kingdom is to benefit from the rule of its King by submitting to the benevolent rule of King Jesus.
(David Devenish)[7]

This, then, is how you should pray:
'Our Father in heaven,
hallowed be your name,
your kingdom come,
your will be done,
on earth as it is in heaven.'
(Matthew 6:9-10)

---

[7] David Devenish, *Fathering Leaders, Motivating Mission* (Milton Keynes: Authentic Media, 2011), p151.

OK, so let's be clear. This is a very succinct summary of the kingdom of God and the entrepreneur's place within it. It's important to present an overview in the context of setting out the calling, mission and character of entrepreneurs in the kingdom. There are theological, inspirational and practical books and texts on the kingdom, and I shall rely on them in presenting this summary. In my humble opinion there are four that I have found excellent, including *How God Became King*[8] by theologian and author Tom Wright.[9]

Apprentices in the kingdom

In our twenties and thirties, my wife and I were part of a church in Farnborough, Hampshire. With other ministries and churches, the church was pioneering in the UK and beyond what it meant and what it looked like in everyday life to live in the kingdom of God. We were journeying through the charismatic renewal and trying to grasp hold of what the Spirit of God was saying about lifestyle and mission in an increasingly secular culture. There were many lessons learned on the journey (not that we ever stop learning), many good and not a few that were painful. More lately we, like so many others, have been further instructed, encouraged and blessed in the lifestyle of the disciple in the kingdom by the ministry of renewal and

---

[8] Tom Wright, *How God Became King* (London: SPCK, 2012), p43.
[9] The other titles are Bill Johnson, *When Heaven Invades Earth* (Shippensburg, PA: Destiny Image, 2003); George Eldon Ladd, *The Presence of the Future* (Grand Rapids, MI: Eerdmans, 1974); David Devenish, *What On Earth is the Church For?* (Milton Keynes: Authentic Media, 2005).

revival centres around the world. So I have had the privilege of living with the understanding of God's mandate to His Church to establish and enlarge His kingdom (eg Mark 4:30-32 for most of my adult life.

There has been a growing understanding in the Church at large over the last few decades of the message of the kingdom of God. This is a momentous understanding by today's Church. It changes our worldview and increasingly causes us to re-evaluate and redefine our identity, purpose and mission. This is really well summed up by Bible teacher and author David Devenish:[10] 'it is important ... that we have a kingdom theology as well as a church theology. Sadly, I believe many Christians have neither, but a "personal salvation" theology.'

The now but not yet

Tom Wright's illuminating comment that the coming of the kingdom of heaven to earth is not just to do with us gaining access to heaven when we die is, I think, most helpful.[11] I believe that all, if not most, proponents would say that the fullness of the kingdom cannot be known in this earthly realm quite simply because heaven is where God dwells and we are struggling with, and somewhat constrained by, the effects of the Fall, even though Jesus paid the full cost to negate these effects. So, while the earth and 'everything in it' is the Lord's (Psalm 24:1), and the earth is His 'footstool' (Matthew 5:35), we do not yet see

---

[10] Devenish, *What On Earth is the Church For?*, p75.
[11] Wright, *How God Became King*, p43.

everything subject to Jesus, or us as His disciples (Hebrews 2:5-8). The time will come when His rule and realm as King of kings (Revelation 11:15) will be full and final. We are living in the age between the coming of the kingdom, when Jesus paid the full and absolute price for our salvation (healed, whole and delivered) and announced that His kingdom had 'come near' (Matthew 4:17) – within touching distance – and the enthronement of Jesus as the King over all creation when everyone and everything will bow before Him (Philippians 2:9-11).

We can be sure that His kingdom is coming, where He will rule, and His reign will be one of righteousness, justice and peace. His kingdom is continually increasing, and it is a kingdom of peace (Isaiah 9:7, NKJV). The apostle Paul too taught about the kingdom of God and looked forward to its eventual triumph:

> Then the end will come, when he hands over the kingdom to God the Father after he has destroyed all dominion, authority and power. For he must reign until he has put all his enemies under his feet. The last enemy to be destroyed is death.
> (1 Corinthians 15:24-26)

Citizens of heaven...

Jesus made it clear that we are to be the agents who extend His rule. He sent us out on mission to makes disciples of the nations and within the nations (Matthew 28:19). This mission is to see God's righteousness, justice and peace extended and established. He sent us with His authority, and we are His 'ambassadors' (2 Corinthians 5:20) and citizens of heaven (Philippians 3:20). Therefore, we represent the country of our citizenship in 'another country' and have the delegated authority and privileges of the Head of State in our country while living in the foreign land. As I often say, we are citizens of heaven resident on earth. We represent a Head of State with absolute, morally perfect and unfettered authority and power. Whereas the delegation to us is entirely effective in heaven's terms, we are imperfect people living by the grace of God in an often-hostile environment, and we mess it up. But God is not fazed by such imperfections. After all, God is an entrepreneur; He took the risk of creating us with free will because of His great love for us so that we could know the intimacy of His love and choose to express and declare His love to everyone. True love can only be expressed in a relationship where both parties are unfettered in the expressions of love. You can express great admiration and commitment to a dictator, but where there is fear, love runs away. 'Perfect love drives out fear' (1 John 4:18).

> True love can only be expressed in a relationship where both parties are unfettered in the expressions of love.

... but resident on earth

The kingdom of God is not a kingdom of physical force.

It's vitally important that we realise that 'our struggle is not against flesh and blood [people], but against the rulers, against the authorities, against the powers of this dark world and against the spiritual forces of evil in the heavenly realms' (Ephesians 6:12).

> The kingdom of God is not a kingdom of
> physical force.

In the context of our lives, it is against mindsets, cultures, authority systems, etc that are acting contrary to, and producing effects that are contrary to, the rule and reign of the kingdom of God and the resulting righteousness, justice and peace. It is not a kingdom of physical force, but a kingdom that demonstrates the power of peace, forgiveness, grace, righteousness and justice (eg Romans 14:17). These are the weapons of our struggle against these principalities and powers. As Bible teacher and minister John Stott said, this kingdom is not brought about by political means or by war.[12]

That is not to neglect the power of prayer. As kingdom people, when we pray rightly, we are not only inviting Jesus' rule into the situation, but we are also binding up or setting free on earth because it will have been bound or set free in heaven (Matthew 18:18). As Bible teacher and revivalist Bill Johnson says, we are only able to bind up or free on earth what has already been bound up or set free in heaven.[13]

Thus, the kingdom has already come, but it will only come in fullness after Jesus returns to earth and so begins the 'age to come' (see, for example, Ephesians 1:19b-21). In the meantime, we are to be bringing into this 'present evil

---

[12] John Stott, *The Message of Acts* (Downers Grove, IL: IVP, 1990), p9.

[13] Johnson, *When Heaven Invades Earth*, p60.

age' (Galatians 1:4) the powers of the 'age to come', the powers of the now-reigning Christ. As David Devenish says:

> In the future there will be no sickness; so as we pray for the sick and they are healed, the presence of the future kingdom comes now. In the future kingdom there is no poverty, for all will have enough to eat and will dwell in security under their own vine and their own fig tree [Zechariah 3:10]; so as we feed the poor, we bring the future kingdom into the 'present evil age'.[14]

The reach of the kingdom

In 1975, Bill Bright, founder of Campus Crusade, and Loren Cunningham, founder of Youth With A Mission, met up in Colorado. God gave both of these men a message to give to the other. During that same timeframe, Francis Schaeffer (theologian and founder of L'Abri) was given a similar message. The message was that if we are to impact any nation for Jesus Christ, then we will have to affect the seven spheres of society.[15] Although there are alternative ways of expressing the seven spheres, they are commonly referred to as: business, government, media, arts and entertainment, education, the family and religion.

---

[14] Devenish, *What On Earth is the Church For?*, p85. All rights reserved. Reproduced with permission of the Licensor through PLSclear.
[15] 'Origin of 7 Mountain Concepts and 7MKI', 8th July 2016, christianinternational.com/blog/2016/7/8/origin-of-7-mountain-concepts-and-7mki (accessed 18th February 2021).

In essence, the message is that these are the seven spheres of influence that need to be scaled by kingdom people if culture is to be changed.

> These are the seven spheres of influence that need to be scaled by kingdom people if culture is to be changed.

While others may argue that there are alternative, or better ways, of describing the culture in which we live in these days, I have found these to be helpful in understanding in a straightforward way the reach of the kingdom of God. God calls and places us in jobs, careers and vocations, with His grace, to be able to influence people in some way that advances His government of peace. These may appear tiny to us, but taken together with all God's 'change agents' across the face of the earth, this is an advancing kingdom!

The reach of the entrepreneur

It follows from the above that God will place His people, including entrepreneurs, into positions of influence in these seven spheres. Some, I guess, are more tangible for the entrepreneur. Classically, entrepreneurs are drawn into the business/commerce realm. However, I have noticed with increasing frequency, perhaps because I've been looking more attentively, that social entrepreneurs are rising up, and also people known as intrapreneurs, ie marketplace people, employed in organisations to lead a new business initiative or stream on behalf of the organisation. And what about pioneering pastors/

ministers in the religious sphere, people who are often also social entrepreneurs?

A good friend of mine has recently retired from being course leader on a Master's programme in the UK concerned with visual communication. He was a kingdom person seeking to demonstrate the kingdom to future leaders in advertising and design. Another person that comes to mind is Simon Ward,[16] who worked for more than thirty years in the fashion industry, most recently as chief operating officer of the British Fashion Council. Both people were God's change agents in the media and art spheres, and they continue to be, albeit perhaps in slightly different ways. There will be other people, both in this industry and others, because God places them into these arenas to influence.

Kingdom entrepreneurs may be mums or dads or guardians at home raising children who are leading their peers in the classroom and, in time, will be key influencers in their generations. These are people who will be influencing people and cultures at the school gate, in the PTA, in community programmes, as governors and so on. They may be pastors/ministers pioneering a work in an area or community, politicians striving to influence regional or national debate or change in their political party for the good of the community, civil servants supporting or influencing those who prepare or make policy decisions. They can be entertainers, artists, filmmakers, critics, school or university teachers, police

---

[16] Simon Ward, *The Character of Fashion* (White Bench Publishing, 2016). Available from www.multitalentedgod.com; see also R Higginson and K Robertshaw, *A Voice to Be Heard* (London: IVP, 2017).

officers... and so the list goes on. God sets into position those who burn with the message and passion to extend the reach of the kingdom, and who innovate, take risks and initiatives to do so.

The reach of the entrepreneur is wherever the kingdom of God needs to be displayed, and this is wherever people are and in whatever field of endeavour they are living and working. Jesus instructs us to 'seek first his kingdom and his righteousness' (Matthew 6:33) and promises that the things we need in our life of mission will be given to us.[17]

Pause, pray, practise

- Pause: What spheres of influence has God placed you in?

- Pray: Father, how are you calling me to extend your kingdom in these spheres?

- Practise: What is the next step that I need to take?

---

[17] Some really useful resources for those interested in reading more about entrepreneurship and/or work in God's kingdom can be found at: www.transformingbusiness.net/; www.fibq.org; http://praxislabs.org/; www.faithdrivenentrepreneur.org; www.theologyofwork.org/about (accessed 25th January 2021).

3
Laying a Good Foundation

Key points

- Keep well connected with Father God.

- Get, and keep, yourself whole.

The loftier the building, the deeper must the foundation be laid.
(Thomas à Kempis)[18]

As for everyone who comes to me and hears my words and puts them into practice, I will show you what they are like. They are like a man building a house, who dug down deep and laid the foundation on rock. When the flood came, the torrent struck that house but could not shake it, because it was well built.
(Luke 6:47-48)

I've done a few reasonable scale DIY jobs over the years as I've moved from house to house, but I wouldn't claim to be an expert in anything related to house building or extensions. I have a good friend who recently completed a

---

[18] Thomas a Kempis Quotes. BrainyQuote.com, BrainyMedia Inc, 2021, www.brainyquote.com/quotes/thomas_a_kempis_383396# (accessed 12th January 2021).

self-build project, constructing a house for him and his wife to move into as a downsizing exercise. It was interesting to watch the project take shape, and it confirmed what I already knew – that this was not for me! I recall him having cleared and dug the land and laid the foundations. It reminded me again of the importance of foundations to whatever we build. As the house grew from the foundations up, the huge cost of the materials in building and fit-out was dependent upon the relatively small cost of getting the foundations right.

In my personal experience of starting, developing and growing a business as an entrepreneur, of being part of the senior management team of a new church, and of watching a few of my friends and colleagues who have done the same, getting the foundations right is hugely important. In the same way as not getting the foundations right when constructing a house is hugely costly, so it is when setting in place the foundations of a business. So often I have seen that the most important foundations to be built are those relating to the character of the entrepreneur. This is not glamorous, and it doesn't make the headlines until it all goes wrong (I'm sure you can think of instances where people's misdemeanours have made the headlines). The cost of having flawed foundations is a grim reward reaped over many years.

Watching and talking to my friend building his house showed me that there are key stages in the process:

- clearing the land;
- digging and laying the foundations;
- building from the bottom up.

This may be obvious, but it may not be so obvious when building a business based around the entrepreneur(s).

> The foundation on which we build is perhaps the most important part in defining the success of the journey.

Entrepreneurs are risk-takers, not foolishly risky I hope, but nevertheless willing to take risk to gain reward. What I have found time and again in my own experience, and by observing those entrepreneurs whom I have engaged with on the course of my journey, is that the foundation on which we build is perhaps the most important part in defining the success of the journey and building a business that adds value and fulfilment to the lives who journey with us, and to society. I am not simply talking about the implementation of our corporate social responsibility. I am talking about the combined effect of our enterprise on the staff whom we engage, their families and loved ones and friends, on those who purchase our products or services or engage in our programmes, on the lives in the locality of where we do our business, and on the economic good of the country/ies with which we interact.

Connecting well

What is our personal foundation built upon, and how will it stand up to the stretching and testing that inevitably come with both difficult times and successes? The primary mission of Jesus was to open the way for me and you to know His Father as our Father. He made the path open to knowing personally Father God as our Papa and invited each one of us to reconnect. This means a radical readjusting of both how we perceive God and ourselves and how we respond to Him.

> The primary mission of Jesus was to open the way for me and you to know His Father as our Father.

When Jesus said that we can speak to Father God as *Abba*, this is equivalent to us saying 'Papa' or 'Daddy'. The word carries the meaning of honour as well as intimacy. In Aramaic or in English it is often one of the first words a child says. Jesus was saying that we can know and trust the omniscient, infinite, majestic Father who unconditionally loves us, just as a pre-toddler knows their loving Papa.

This revelation in our hearts fundamentally addresses who we are, because we know whose we are. This changes our thinking towards obedience to God and His Word to us. As we have read above in Luke 6:47-48, Jesus said that everyone who comes to Him, hears His words and puts them into practice is building on a strong foundation. This does not happen in a moment, but as a result of a fundamental shift in our selves. It's rather like marinating – enough time spent in the presence of Papa causes us to be soaked thoroughly in His nature and character, and that affects every part of our make-up.

My experience did not come overnight, or even in the course of a year. It developed as the result of an ongoing relationship. The more time I spent with Him the more like

Him I became, and the more I got to love who He is even more than what He does!

A really important message in the Bible is that if we fail to be in relationship in a meaningful way with the Father, we are spiritual 'orphans', or, put another way, we are fatherless. The result is that we fail to grasp how much we are loved and cared for, and consequently tend to grasp at causes, movements, people, friends, self-help or self-growth programmes (the list could go on). I'm not saying that these in themselves are not worthy things. What I am saying is that they don't address the fundamental issue of who we are and whose we are.

In this sense, the word 'orphan' would be used to give an equivalent meaning to those who have no father and/or mother, or have absent fathers or mothers, whether through estrangement, divorce, separation, family breakdown, etc. Either we have not known our father or mother or we are distant from them. This is exactly what Jesus was saying: through lack of intimate knowledge of the Father we are orphans, and we adapt our mindset, character and behaviour to cope with the loss. Thus, our foundations get skewed, broken down or damaged.

> You can't prop up a faulty foundation with a quick fix for very long without the building tipping over.

For the kingdom entrepreneur, at least, the problem with this is that we replicate who we are. In our words and actions, we can only live consistently and genuinely as the people we are. I guess many of us have tried to live as those we'd like to be. It's hard work, it's disingenuous and, in my experience, you can't keep it up for more than a few weeks! You can't prop up a faulty foundation with a quick fix for very long without the building tipping over. The story that Jesus told in Matthew 7:24-27 about a house that was built on sand compared with a house that was built on rock was all about the foundations of our lives. The house was the same and built with the same materials; it was only the foundation that was different. And when the rains came, symbolising pressures and difficulties, the sand got washed away and the house fell, while the house built on rock was untouched.

Internal to external

The internal realisation that we are deeply, passionately and intimately loved by God is the most important foundation in our lives. Why? Because this internal reality is played out in our external expression of how we love those with whom we interact. After all, as the Bible puts it, we can only love our neighbour as well as we love ourselves (Mark 12:30-31)! As entrepreneurs we are those who have tremendous potential to demonstrate God's love, grace and mercy to those we employ, partner with or supply to. And I believe that God's calling on the kingdom entrepreneur is to be precisely that; ie through the medium of entrepreneurship to influence those in the arenas in which we operate. For sure, this can be done through the excellence of our products or service, the way we treat our contractors and the way we treat our customers, and so on, but all this comes down to loving our neighbours as ourselves.

There are some clear fingerprints of an orphan mindset. It benefits us to honestly examine whether we show some of these fingerprints:

- jealousy and unreasonable competitiveness;

- fear of lack, rejection, failure, etc;

- arrogance;

- self-sufficiency.

A few years ago, I met with a senior lecturer at one of the UK's leading business management schools. I was interested to know if on their MBA[19] programme they dealt at all with a person's character. The answer was no. The reason given was that people did not want to spend time and a lot of money on a prestigious course examining their character; what they wanted to spend their time on was how to run highly successful businesses. In part I understand that, but if our foundation is flawed, and we hire others with flawed foundations (and probably flawed in different ways to us), two wrongs do not make a right. Granted, if we hire people who complement our flaws and allow them to be complementary in the day-to-day working of the business, then the outcome is likely to be better. But better still is to get our foundations solid. This can only come about by 'foundation surgery', not by programmes that cover them up. The truth will out!

---

[19] Master in Business Administration.

'Wellspring of life'

Shalom is the way things ought to be.

Shalom, usually translated 'peace', is one of the great words for salvation in the Bible.[20] The root meaning is to be whole, sound and safe – the fundamental idea is one of totality. The seamless integration of God, humans and all creation in justice, fulfillment and delight is what the Hebrew prophets call *shalom*. It has been defined as:

> Universal flourishing, wholeness, and delight – a rich state of affairs in which natural needs are satisfied and natural gifts fruitfully employed, a state of affairs that inspires joyful wonder as its Creator and Savior opens doors and welcomes the creatures in whom he delights. *Shalom*, in other words, is the way things ought to be.[21]

God's plan is to bring a universal *shalom* to His creation. This is vastly more than the absence of conflict and immensely more than inner peace or peace of mind – these are shallow reflections of what God means when He uses the word *shalom*. It carries a sense of harmony, right relationship and proper functioning of all elements in the environment. This is how God planted the Garden of Eden

---

[20] 'The Meaning of Shalom in the Bible', NIV, www.thenivbible.com/blog/meaning-shalom-bible/ (accessed 18th February 2021).
[21] Attributed to Cornelius Plantinga Jr in *Not the Way It's Supposed to Be: A Breviary of Sin* (Grand Rapids, MI: Eerdmans, 1996), p10, www.goodreads.com/quotes/711929-in-the-bible-shalom-means-universal-flourishing-wholeness-and-delight--a (accessed 18th February 2021).

and placed humankind within it before our rebellion, and it is the state to which creation will be returned when Jesus presents the Kingdom to His Father at the end of the age. *Shalom* is not simply about being, but a collective well-being. Everything within us and around us is well, fruitful and blessed.

Shalom is the way things ought to be.

What is amazing is that when Jesus said, 'Peace I leave with you; my peace I give you. I do not give to you as the world gives' (John 14:27), He was speaking with *shalom* in mind. The writer of Proverbs had this in mind as well:

> Fill your thoughts with my words
> until they penetrate deep into your spirit.
> Then, as you unwrap my words,
> they will impart true life and radiant health
> into the very core of your being.
> So above all, guard the affections of your heart,
> for they affect all that you are.
> Pay attention to the welfare of your innermost being,
> for from there flows the wellspring of life.
> (Proverbs 4:21-23, TPT)

We fail to understand ourselves and how God made us if we think of ourselves other than as a whole being, and not one that is split into different parts, ie body, soul and spirit. I do not doubt for a moment that we consist of different but complementary 'aspects'. However, if we think of our relationship with God only as spiritual beings, then there is a danger that we underplay or even damage our souls and bodies. We are made as one integrated and whole being and how we treat one aspect of our identify affects the whole. I can speak to my spirit, soul and body. The Psalms contain many instances of the psalmist speaking to his soul (for example, Psalm 42:5). When we declare healing to our bodies, then we are speaking to our body. Our welfare is intimately tied to the wellness of our whole being.

In our busyness we do ourselves no favours if we neglect the affections of our hearts and the welfare of our innermost beings. I've had to work hard at this over many years by constantly finding time in a busy schedule of family, work and church commitments to ensure that I look after my own inner health. Many times I found it while driving to a client, or taking a train or a 'red eye' flight, sometimes taking ten minutes or so before the start of the day in the office, and particularly making sure that I had time at weekends to keep myself in good physical and spiritual health. I imbued a culture in the business that I founded where we worked hard Monday to Friday but tried to keep weekends free for ourselves, our families and our well-being. There were times when we needed to travel on Sunday afternoon/evening to get to a client ready for 9am on Monday, and as the main business grew internationally and we worked more in Middle Eastern countries we had to work their weekends and not those of the West, but we developed a TOIL policy (time off in lieu) to compensate.

I also made space in my demanding lifestyle to ensure that I went to the gym once a week. I found that after dropping my children off at school and before the demands of a day in the office was a good time. I'd be in the gym for 8.45 and after a light breakfast I'd be in the office for 10.15. I tried to do this on the same day each week so that I developed a rhythm. My PA knew this and fielded any calls or enquiries until I got into the office.

In our busyness we do ourselves no favours if we neglect the affections of our hearts and the welfare of our innermost beings.

Jesus called us to be people of peace; peacemakers who are recognised as sons and daughters of God (Matthew 5:9), and those who can promote peace, leave peace in an environment or keep it to ourselves (Luke 10:5-6). But we can only do this when we have developed *shalom* as an internal reality. Thus, our presence can help to create a godly atmosphere in all settings that we live in. As we manage our own being, then we are able to release peace around us – in our own homes and when we enter other homes, workplaces, shops, gyms, restaurants, etc.

Pause, pray, practise

- Pause: Honestly consider if there are fingerprints of an orphan mindset operating in your life.

- Pray: Father, how well established is the foundation of my life? Is it able to support well the structure that is being built?

- Pray: If not, please show me what areas of my life need to be stronger. Will You work with me to strengthen these?

- Practise: How can I better practise being a person of peace?

4
Listening to the Right Voices

Key points

- We need to tune our hearts to listen to what God is saying to us.

- Accountability to trusted people is a gift God has given us to help keep us journeying well on the road.

Listen in silence because if your heart is full of other things you cannot hear the voice of God. But when you have listened to the voice of God in the stillness of your heart, then your heart is filled with God.
(Mother Teresa)[22]

I am the good shepherd; I know my sheep and my sheep know me – just as the Father knows me and I know the Father – and I lay down my life for the sheep. I have other sheep that are not of this sheepfold. I must bring them also. They too will listen to my voice, and there shall be one flock and one shepherd.
(John 10:14-16)

---

[22] Mother Teresa, *In the Heart of the World: Thoughts, Stories & Prayers* (Novato, CA: New World Library, 210), p20.

Francis Barraud was an English painter in the 1890s. When his brother Mark died, he inherited Mark's wind-up gramophone player, some recordings of Mark's voice and his terrier dog called 'Nipper'. When Francis played these recordings, Nipper sat staring at the funnel-shaped loudspeaker of the gramophone listening to Mark's voice. After Nipper's passing, Francis painted this scene and he called it *His Master's Voice*. The Gramophone Company bought the painting and used the scene as the logo of the company and changed its name to 'His Master's Voice' after the title of the painting. The logo was used around the world, and in November 2014 Nipper had his own blue plaque installed at 126 Piccadilly, London. This is the company now known as HMV.

With the proliferation of media providing the means of getting a voice/message/propaganda/ fake news heard, it's very easy to listen to voices. Voices are all around us and seem to be getting louder. Some voices are good, some are evil and are easier to identify; some are helpful and some, perhaps many, are not. With busy lives it takes discipline by us to identify those voices that we want to hear. That raises the question: whose voice is it that you want to give pre-eminence to? Which voice gives you life 'to the full' (John 10:10)? As disciples of Jesus, surely we have to say God's. We need to be like Nipper the terrier, attuned to His voice, and to learn to focus upon it above all the other voices.

Voices and their promotion can be subtle.

The devil does not have the God-given authority to create – but he is an effective and sophisticated liar. The devil's voice most often plays on our past experiences that have harmed us in some way. Many of these come in our childhood (for example, bullying, rejection, lack of love shown by parents/guardians/carers, exploitation by others, being controlled by others… the list could go on), but we can be wounded emotionally at any time in our lives. There are some great tools and courses to expose and help to heal these wounds,[23] but even when they are healed up the devil tries to reopen them. Scripture calls him the 'father of lies' (John 8:44), the most skilful purveyor of believable lies to serve his own ends, with no equal. Jesus said that he seeks to 'steal and kill and destroy' (John 10:10). That's why it's so important in maintaining a healthy relationship with God and with other people that we listen to the right voices, and especially God's voice.

> The devil does not have the God-given authority to create – but he is an effective and sophisticated liar.

Gardening is one of the leisure activities that I enjoy. I live in an area with a heavy clay soil which makes for heavy digging and the need to add organic material to the soil to grow good plants and vegetables. Treating the soil in this way is not a one-off activity but needs to be done every year. The older I get, the harder it becomes! The

---

[23] For example, Bethel Sozo, www.bethelsozo.org.uk; Freedom in Christ, www.ficm.org.uk/the_fic_course; Christian Healing Ministry, www.london.anglican.org/articles/the-christian-healing-mission-launches-free-online-prayer-ministry-training/; Ellel Ministries, https://ellel.org/uk/ (accessed 25th January 2021).

parable of the sower in Matthew 13:1-23 is about the condition of the 'soil' of our hearts. The word that God speaks to us is the seed. His heart is that we become healed up and fruitful. Jesus makes it clear that we need to hear God's word and *understand it* in our hearts so that we are fruitful (Matthew 13:23)

To trust God without fear we need to have learned that He is good, that 'in all things God works for the good of those who love him' (Romans 8:28), that He is entirely trustworthy and that His Word is a faithful representation of His nature. Proverbs 3:5-6 is a favourite scripture of mine.

> Trust in the LORD with all your heart
> and lean not on your own understanding;
> in all your ways submit to him,
> and he will make your paths straight.

Or:

> Trust in the Lord completely,
> and do not rely on your own opinions.
> With all your heart rely on him to guide you,
> and he will lead you in every decision you make.
> Become intimate with him in whatever you do,
> and he will lead you wherever you go.
> (TPT)

Hearing God's word

We need to be able to hear God's voice by tuning our hearts to listen.

I suggest there are at least five ways in which God speaks to us. God created us for relationship with Him and with each other. It should come as no surprise that in relationship with God we talk to Him and He talks to us! There needs to be two-way communication in a relationship for it to be healthy and intimate! So, how does He talk to us?

- through His written Word (the Bible);
- with a 'picture' or vision;
- by an experience;
- in our hearts;
- through other people.

All of these need us to be able to 'hear'. This is not automatic. It takes training of our senses. When someone speaks to us, we can sometimes hear the words spoken but not hear the message. We can be distracted by thoughts or events that compete in our listening self with the message being spoken. I've found it necessary to realise that if I haven't listened to what a person says to me, even though I've heard them speak, then I have to ask them to say it again so that I can focus on what the message is that they want me to hear. We can treat God speaking to us in the same manner. We have to learn to tune our hearts to listen.

> We need to be able to hear God's voice
> by tuning our hearts to listen.

Hearing what God is saying can include receiving a Spirit-filled thought which 'sounds' like a voice. Seeing what God is saying can come in the form of 'pictures', or internal visions, in your mind or in the 'eyes' of your heart. I know of a few people who see in the form of an external vision which is like watching a cinema screen in front of them – this can be known as an 'open vision'. Feeling what God is saying can come through feeling pain or discomfort, or an emotion (commonly to show something about God wanting to heal us or to minister to someone else), or it can be 'feeling' or 'knowing' something in your spirit.

God most frequently speaks to me through my reading or listening to Scripture/preaching and teaching, or through a picture, but I have learned to tune my heart and affections towards Him and then realise how much He speaks to me in my heart. Doing this in a church meeting or conference is one thing; doing it in the workplace I found took more practice.

How God speaks to us

Directional words and prophecies

When someone gives us a directional word or when we receive a picture or vision, and this is not something that God has said to us before, I have found it helpful to:

- seek confirmation from Scripture;

- seek confirmation from one or two others who know me well and whom I trust to speak into my life;

- acknowledge that I will have a witness in my heart, even if it's scary!

I encourage you to do the same.

Prophecy is a gift of the Holy Spirit, given to those whom He chooses. It is a gift to strengthen, encourage and guide the Church and individuals (1 Corinthians 14:3). My experience has been that if or when it gets tough on the journey, then we have the confirmation of God's Word to fall back on and not merely a prophecy or picture that someone gave to us. This is not downplaying prophecy; it is a beautiful gift to His people. However, I have found that the word in partnership with prophecy (after all, they come from the same God) gives us comfort in praying that we can say to God, 'You spoke to me from Your Word, which is eternal; "it stands firm in the heavens" (Psalm 119:89), and does not return to You empty, but will accomplish what You desire and achieve the purpose for which You sent it' (based on Isaiah 55:11). I find that it also gives me the added weight of being able to speak to obstacles in my path that come to hinder me or slow me down, to move out of the way (Mark 11:23).

My wife and I had responded in 1985 to a directional word that the Lord had given us which meant relocating to Northampton, England, and we moved the following year. In 1988, having finished my employment contract, this meant find finding a new job. I was working in a very niche area, and I couldn't find a job, despite making applications in associated fields. We knew God's call and so we were confident that He would supply our needs. When no job offers came along we came to the conclusion that I should become self-employed. I can't say that I felt called to this; it was more of a necessity in order to enable our calling. The first two to three years were difficult financially, but in 1992 the level of activity increased.

In 1993, I was beginning to receive invitations to speak at conferences and professional events. By and large I accepted these. I remember having an invitation to speak at an event which did not seem particularly significant to me, but I thought that the exposure would be helpful. I remember making what I thought to be a good presentation! A couple of weeks after the event I had a phone call from a manager in a major transport operation who had attended the event asking me if we would be able to help them with a programme of work. A few months earlier I had taken a 'leap of faith' and recruited a principal consultant to help me develop the business. In the December of that year, I learned that we had been awarded not just one, but two substantial contracts by this transport operation, and we began to win other contracts on top of that.

I remember a Sunday in October of that year, some eight weeks before we knew we had won the contracts, when I was in a time of worship in church. I had been thinking and praying about whether I should take on other employees. The main debate internally was whether to directly employ consultants or to subcontract the work. At that time, managing subcontractors was something of which we had very little experience, and the value of the contracts would not have made it realistically practicable to employ a contracts manager. On the other hand, employing people carried with it the obvious risks of finding long-term work for them. The situation was compounded by the fact that in the economy at the time, few people were enticed by fixed-term or short-term contracts, instead preferring job security.

God spoke to me very clearly in that time of worship from Isaiah 61:5-6:

> Strangers will shepherd your flocks;
> foreigners will work your fields and vineyards.
> And you will be called priests of the LORD,
> you will be named ministers of our God.
> You will feed on the wealth of nations,
> and in their riches you will boast.

This was wild and crazy! I didn't hear an audible voice, but the internal voice in my spirit was way too loud for me to be imagining it or making it up out of some psychological need. I had been learning over the previous years to discern the way that God speaks – more trial and error than inspiration – but this was inspiring. It was one of those defining moments when God spoke to me so clearly that it became a foundational word for me in running the business from that point forward. I realised that He wanted me to employ people in the business and that it was fine for me to recruit people who were not 'following Jesus'. There was peace in my heart about doing this, and the final confirmation came when we had suitable applicants respond to an advertisement. Within two months I had recruited two relatively young graduates to work on these projects.

Sometimes we become aware of His direction through a growing discernment in our hearts of where He wants us to go. This is then confirmed by circumstances coming together to support it. It's OK to say to God, 'God, I believe that You are saying … therefore, please bring everything together for me that I need to be able to do it.'

Non-directional words and prophecies

Non-directional words are often to do with God's encouragement, building us up and cheering us along on the path. They provide strength and reassurance. They help to build us up, guard the affections of our hearts and keep us in the love of God. Most of the time God speaks to us in this way, whether directly to us or through others. He is a loving God who is constantly wanting to encourage us and bless us. I can count on my two hands the number of times that God has given me a directional word in my forty-five-plus years of following Him. But there have been so many times that God has shown me how much He loves me, encouraged me, challenged me to keep on the path, and blessed me! His presence with me at all times is a constant source of delight as I walk with Him on the route mapped out for me.

> There have been so many times that God has shown me how much He loves me, encouraged me, challenged me to keep on the path, and blessed me!

Safeguards

We need to test everything (1 John 4:1-6) and 'hold on to what is good' (1 Thessalonians 5:21). When God speaks, it is loving, encouraging, edifying and comforting (1

Corinthians 14:3). We should also ask the question, 'Does this word/thought/picture bring "life" or "death"'?

The Holy Spirit will always bring peace, or maintain peace in us, when we receive a word – whether directional or non-directional – if it is from Him. He will not contradict Himself! If you have any sense of unease about a word, then do not receive it but pray about it, seek wise godly counsel, and see what happens to your peace. The unease will either settle or increase. That way we control our own spirits. We are meant to have mastery of our spirit, soul and body, and not to abdicate our God-given rule to others. Make sure you are not someone described by the writer of Proverbs 25:28: 'Like a city whose walls are broken through is a person who lacks self-control.'

Making ourselves accountable

Accountability is a vital gift that God gives us. It is not something to be feared, but something to embrace with joy. He gives us men and women with expertise and wisdom who can mentor, coach and challenge us, and prophesy to us. Accountability isn't handing over the keys to our life, or making ourselves subject to others. It's sharing our heart, our vision, our issues and problems, and letting others speak into our lives and our business to help us be successful. It provides us with another voice that God gives us to listen to, a voice in harmony with His own.

I had two primary people to whom I made myself accountable. One was the senior pastor of the church in which I was an elder, and the other was our accountant, who had journeyed with me from the very beginning of becoming self-employed. To my knowledge this man was not a follower of Jesus, but he certainly spoke into my life. I learned another truth, that God provides professional advisers with godly wisdom (whether they realise it or not)! There are two instances that spring to mind most vividly.

The first instance was in 1995, I was approached by a large insurance company in the US interested in buying the business. I went to meet them in London, and I came back having listened to them, and discussed the approach with my accountant. He clearly laid out the facts in a way that I had not been able to discern. What made my decision easy was realising that the company wanted to buy me and my expertise and contacts, and that the freedom I enjoyed on my faith adventures with Jesus could change markedly if I were to sell to them. I later learned that a main competitor at the time was also approached by the same insurance company and also turned them down.

The second instance was shortly after this. The principal consultant that I had employed decided to move on to a different job. This left a significant hole in the development and management of the business, and put significant time demands on me. I had been considering incorporating the business and bringing in one or two other directors, with me as managing director. I was hesitating because I wasn't sure whether offering to reduce our (my and my wife's) shareholding in an incorporated business was right when considering the scripture that God had spoken to me two years earlier. I discussed this with my accountant (as well as a very few others close to me or the business). I recall vividly his comment, that it was better to own 50 per cent of a business that was worth £300,000 than 100 per cent of a business that was worth nothing. This was the comment that I needed to stop my prevaricating!

Over the next few months, I approached a couple of people known to me about joining, and shortly after I agreed terms with one of them. He was a great help to me personally and also in developing the business. When I retired, he continued as managing director and continues to lead the business today.

I strongly encourage you to seek out one or two people to whom you can make yourself accountable. They may be business people or not. But they need to be people you can trust and to whom you have given permission to speak into your life. I recommend that at least one of them is walking closely to God, and can help you weigh up decisions that you need to make. Someone to ask the right questions of you is a great help!

I strongly encourage you to seek out one or two people to whom you can make yourself accountable.

Pause, pray, practise

- Pause: How well do you hear God speaking to you?

- Pray: Do you have the comfort and strength of a God-given message in your entrepreneurial cause? If not, ask Him for one.

- Practise: Do you have a few trusted people whom you can talk with and to whom you have given permission to speak into your life?

5
Humble-heartedness

Key points

- Humility leads to a healthy self-esteem through understanding our identity before the Father and our position in Christ.

- Knowing our identity enables us to joyfully accept the gifts, positions and influence that God gives us to serve others in our communities.

Pride must die in you, or nothing of heaven can live in you.
(Andrew Murray)[24]

When pride comes, then comes disgrace,
but with humility comes wisdom.
(Proverbs 11:2)

If you ask my friends who know me, or have known me over the years, they will tell you that I've never been someone who by inclination tends towards arrogance. As a young adult I lacked confidence, but I have been changed by experiences in life, in business and through

---

[24] Attributed to Andrew Murray, *The Journey Toward Holiness* (Minneapolis, MN: Bethany House Publishers, 2001).

the ministry of the Holy Spirit. I am able to use accumulated wisdom and insight to be able to make swift decisions when necessary, and I feel comfortable making them. I can recall occasions when an important decision had to be made swiftly in a directors' meeting or on a phone call with a client. I have learned to be confident in such decisions and not to regret them. When my wife and I had to decide whether to sell our shareholding to the other shareholders in the business, we made that decision within a few hours, but then had the luxury of having a few days to let it settle in our hearts before needing to inform the others what we had decided. We didn't change our mind, and we haven't regretted making that decision!

I have come to learn, and to understand, that humble-heartedness is so important in entrepreneurship if we want to do business and lead others well, and to be able to hold our head high and sleep well at night! I have found that humility helps us to walk with integrity.

Through humility I felt that I could maintain good relations with suppliers, clients and staff, and be able to look them in the eye without feeling guilt or shame, or needing to put on a mask to hide my true feelings. I can honestly say that I wanted the best for everyone, for everyone to prosper.

I had to unlearn what I had assumed it meant to be humble-hearted and, by a process of relearning, to grasp hold of what I now see as a much more balanced view of humility. I believe humble-heartedness encompasses:

- having a well-balanced respect for ourselves (self-respect), neither considering ourselves as worthless

nor over-inflating our ego, through receiving the
revelation of who we are through our new life in Jesus
Christ;

- aligning with God's purposes, gifts and capabilities
  that He gives to each one;

- as leaders/pioneers, serving those in our community,
  whatever this community looks like in practice.

A healthy self-respect

I have written about connecting well with God in the
chapter 'Laying a Good Foundation'.

What I want to write here is how this impacts our
humble-heartedness.

How many people understand their position as a son
or daughter of the Father, preferring to believe an
unbiblical narrative concerning our identity in Him?
Believing this narrative is not humility, but as we give it
leverage in our lives it develops its own influence over
us.[25]

We are sons and daughters; we are not worms, failures,
unwanted or unworthy. Neither are we arrogant, proud
or big-headed, nor do we think that we alone are God's
answer to humanity's issues. No, we are the Father's sons
and daughters, passionately and intimately loved by each
person of the Trinity, honoured with His abiding presence
and blessed with gifts that He gives to us in His body (1
Corinthians 12:4). I love the counterbalances that King

---

[25] For further thoughts around this, see Bill Johnson, *The Way of Life*
(Shippensburg, PA: Destiny Image, 2008), p47.

Solomon wrote in Proverbs – surely a man who could claim to be a great success and able to sound off about his own accomplishments! 'Let someone else praise you, and not your own mouth; an outsider, and not your own lips' (Proverbs 27:2), and 'Pride brings a person low, but the lowly in spirit gain honour' (Proverbs 29:23).

Walking in humility with God means that we are strong because we joyfully live in healthy self-image or respect before the Father. And then we can live as the apostle Paul did – doing all things through Christ 'who gives [us] strength' (Philippians 4:13). In wonderful victories and in the valley of difficulties and disappointments – all experiences that we are likely to go through in our journey of entrepreneurship – it is essential to our health and well-being to know Christ's strength within us in these seasons.

> Walking in humility with God means that we are strong because we joyfully live in healthy self-image or respect before the Father.

Aligning with God's purposes

God values His people for themselves rather than focusing on who they are not.[26] How many of us struggle with gifts, graces, capabilities and competencies that God gives us because we'd rather be like someone else that we look up to and honour? We need to stop resenting the person that God has gifted us to be. We can't be the person that we

---

[26] For further thoughts around this, see Johnson, *The Way of Life*, p47.

aspire to be without great stress and toil, and we will be missing the best that God has for us. As God adds gifts and competencies to us as we mature in Him, we often find that God enlarges our borders and promotes us to new positions. Each of us is unique. Let's be authentic and love the life that we lead.

Humility is, I believe, to live joyfully accepting the gifts, positions and influences that God has given to us. We read that God 'opposes the proud but shows favour to the humble' (James 4:6). How we need God's favour – and His grace! Grace empowers us to use the gifts that God has given us. Grace empowers our faith, and God's favour partners His grace. His favour advances us and promotes us. So many times I saw His favour do this for me. It had little to do with my own efforts or endeavours. It had so much more to do with walking closely with God, maintaining humility and walking in obedience. There were times that so many opportunities came to us that they threatened to cause the business to be swamped.

Not all opportunities presented to us come from God.

Here was another important lesson I learned: not all opportunities presented to us come from God, and the devil can attempt to wear us down, and those in our businesses, to make us vulnerable to his schemes and attacks. We need to learn which opportunities are those that God presents to us and which are not. Then we need grace and humility to leave alone those which are not for us. I found that the best place to weigh this was by putting them on the scales of His Word and promises, checking my heart to see if the opportunity disrupted my peace, and whether it flowed with the prophecies that had been spoken over me.

At a point in our development, we began to be approached by government departments and agencies, as well as corporations, with requests for quotations, or invitations to tender. Those who have completed these will know that they require a lot of preparation. The joy of winning them was that they provided medium- to long-term financial stability, but the downside could be how best to resource them. When we were not appointed there was a natural disappointment, but realising that I trusted God to provide for us meant that it was easier to let these go by, as they were not for us.

I remember a specific occasion in August 2010 when God clearly spoke to me and promised me opportunities that would come my way and would be for me. A month earlier my wife and I had sold our shares in our previous business and I had left it. I had decided to continue as a sole trader for a period of time as we needed the income. Although I had brought some accounts with me as part of the sale agreement, they would not have been enough, and I needed to find other clients. I had been praying about this and asking God to provide me with additional work and income.

Early in the month I was taking the opportunity to have a workout in the gym. I was on the treadmill and I was playing worship music on my iPhone. Suddenly I heard the Holy Spirit say to me, 'Watch what I do!' Although there were other transitional moves that we were praying about at the time, and to which I needed to respond, I knew that this message to me was primarily for business. I also sensed that this was a 'very soon' word. Exactly one week later I took a call from someone, asking me to work with them on a project that they had won in a tender bid. Within another week we had agreed the contract and I had begun the work. This gave us a fantastic footing for the first three months of trading in my new company. This is the favour of God!

Serving our community

My experience has been that favour is contagious! As we receive God's favour, then those around us come into His favour with us. We see this in Joseph's life. Joseph was the second youngest of Jacob's twelve sons, but God gave him a dream, the story made famous in the stage musical. Here was a man upon whom rested God's favour. He was tested in the fire of rejection, disappointment and isolation. Yet I believe that he kept hold of the promises of God and never lost hope. Despite being imprisoned for something that he didn't do, in an act of favour God promoted him from the prison to the palace in a single day! We read his story in Genesis 37, 39-50.

In Genesis 46:31-34, when Joseph was second-in-command in Egypt, reporting only to the pharaoh, he spoke to his brothers and his father's household, all now resident in Egypt:

> I will go up and speak to Pharaoh and will say to him, 'My brothers and my father's household, who were living in the land of Canaan, have come to me. The men are shepherds; they tend

> livestock, and they have brought along their flocks and herds and everything they own.' When Pharaoh calls you in and asks, 'What is your occupation?' you should answer, 'Your servants have tended livestock from our boyhood on, just as our fathers did.' Then you will be allowed to settle in the region of Goshen, for all shepherds are detestable to the Egyptians.

Jacob and Joseph's brothers were shepherds, and had been all of their lives. They had brought their flocks with them to Egypt – some undertaking, I would imagine. This was an occupation that was detested in Egypt. Not a vocation that would be suggested at a careers forum! And despite this, because of Joseph's standing in the nation, all of his family and flocks were allowed to settle in Goshen, which was the best part of the land. Sharing God's favour is a great way for people around us to encounter God's goodness.

We see that leadership is about serving others and caring for their needs. As the current Archbishop of Canterbury, Justin Welby, says, leadership should flow out of love and service, as in the three persons of the triune God, not in any way seeking to outdo the other.[27] And as the writer of Proverbs 22:4 says, 'Laying your life down in tender surrender before the Lord will bring life, prosperity, and honor as your reward' (TPT).

---

[27] Justin Welby, *Dethroning Mammon* (London: Bloomsbury Continuum, 2016), pp95-96.

Sharing God's favour is a great way for people around us to encounter God's goodness.

Humility and favour are some solid anchors in our entrepreneurship. They help to keep us in a healthy place of reliance on God's goodness and grace.

Humility does not mean that we become doormats for people to walk over and wipe their dirt on. It does not demean us or belittle us; it promotes us. Neither does humility mean that we empty ourselves of power; it means that we know how to use power and favour righteously for the blessing of others as well as ourselves.

Pause, pray, practise

- Pause: Is your self-respect rooted in how the Father sees you and esteems you?

- Pray: Ask the Father how He sees you.

- Practise: Ask a few good friends who know you well to comment on your level of humility. How do their comments make you feel? Ask the Father why you feel these emotions.

- Practise: Do you consistently find God's grace at work in your life, at home and in business? If not, ask Him why not.

6
Integrity

Key points

- Integrity reveals our value system;

- Fear losing the closeness of His presence more than you fear missing out, or the displeasure of those living with a secular value system.

Integrity without knowledge is weak and useless, and knowledge without integrity is dangerous and dreadful.
(Samuel Johnson)[28]

Honest scales and balances belong to the LORD;
all the weights in the bag are of his making.
Kings detest wrongdoing,
for a throne is established through righteousness.
Kings take pleasure in honest lips;
they value the one who speaks what is right.
(Proverbs 16:11-13)

---

[28] Samuel Johnson Quotes. BrainyQuote.com, BrainyMedia Inc, 2021, www.brainyquote.com/quotes/samuel_johnson_121576 (accessed 15th February 2021).

In an enlightening report authored by Edentree Investment Management Ltd,[29] it was reported that at the time of the publication in 2015, the amount of money wasted through corporate misconduct was estimated to amount to $150bn over the previous five years. This equates to just over 1 per cent of the gross domestic product of the UK each year for five years. It is chilling to realise that this loss is down to a failure of corporate business ethics. The report lists many fundamental behaviours and issues that constitute unethical practices. Practices such as payment protection insurance (PPI) in the UK, where such insurance had been applied to loans and credit card borrowing without the borrower's express permission, are more obvious, but other types of mis-selling and unethical practices have been the cause of substantial fines and repayment orders made in favour of customers. Unfortunately, I'm sure we can remember high-profile leaders in many walks of life who have been exposed for their lack of integrity. In some instances, these have caused a business or corporation, or a church or charity, to suffer great harm, and for some to fail completely.

Higginson and Robertshaw[30] note that entrepreneurs can go astray given their personal drive, willingness to innovate and generally to embrace risk. However, they

[29] 'Corporate Misconduct: When Business Ethics Fail and Shareholder Value is Destroyed', Edentree Investment Management, strgcmstrustnetukeuwprod.blob.core.windows.net/media/Default/Docs/amity-insight-corporate-misconduct.pdf (accessed 19th February 2021).
[30] Higginson and Robertshaw, *A Voice to Be Heard*, p141.

need integrity if they are to contribute to the benefit of society.

When the apostle Paul wrote to the church in Corinth and the province of Achaia, he set out his integrity as an apostle:

> Now this is our boast: our conscience testifies that we have conducted ourselves in the world, and especially in our relations with you, with integrity and godly sincerity. We have done so, relying not on worldly wisdom but on God's grace.
> (2 Corinthians 1:12)

Paul boasted that he acted with integrity in the world and in the Church. There was no 'secular/sacred divide' in his dealings, and no hidden agenda. He had the joy of keeping a clear conscience.

In my own experience, acting with integrity at all times in business practices requires wisdom and courage. Recognising the more obvious unethical practices is relatively easy if we're walking closely with Jesus and being filled with the Holy Spirit. Sometimes the ethical/unethical balance is less obvious, and it is easier to persuade ourselves, and argue in the organisation, that 'this is simply the way that business has to be done in this sector, or in this country'. We must at all times act within the law(s) of the country, state or domain in which we operate. At the very least, if we act illegally, we are not displaying integrity, and we must, with a humble heart before God, re-examine our value system.

There have been recent examples of corporate enterprises paying 'bungs' to key personnel or agents in other corporations, or percentages of contract values being agreed to win approval for contracts, either for personal use or to advance the corporation. I have talked with country leads in missionary organisations concerning the issue of getting goods through customs in some countries where the commonly accepted practice is to pay a bribe to 'ease its passage through the system'. Their practice was to refuse to pay but to choose to pray and have faith that our supernatural God would overcome human practices designed to benefit others through evil intent – surely a great example of praying for heaven's will to be done on earth (Matthew 6:10). However, we must recognise that in certain contexts, the issue is more one of extortion rather than bribery for commercial or personal gain. In such cases we must not condemn the one who suffers extortion, which is a form of oppression of the poor, or of those defenceless in the particular context. I have talked with an experienced teacher on cross-cultural issues who has seen examples of this.

> Acting with integrity at all times in business practices requires wisdom and courage.

Higginson and Robertshaw comment that bribery is condemned in the Bible because it champions personal gain over personal and community ethical standards. It acts to corrupt justice.[31]

---

[31] Higginson and Robertshaw, *A Voice to Be Heard*, p147.

This is a telling observation that speaks to the heart of the issue and brings us back to the matter of judgement and trust. I believe that the kingdom entrepreneur needs to form and keep a well-developed conscience as well as the ability to step back to examine what's actually at stake.

Why integrity?

We might wonder why integrity is such a foundational issue for the follower of Jesus. In a helpful insight, Robert Solomon, former professor of philosophy at the University of Texas at Austin,[32] says that integrity isn't a quality in its own right, but it is a set of qualities that combine to form an upright and reliable personality. Further, he says, integrity suggests a person living in an integrated way.

So, integrity, it seems, reveals a value system that forms a coherent character. It is not a single value in itself. Integrity encompasses everything that we do and say, no matter in what environment we are placed. Whether it's personal integrity before God, with the nearest and dearest people to us, in our wider community of friends and associates, or as we lead our enterprise, the same standard of integrity is to be applied. We cannot have different standards of integrity for different environments. That reveals a personal value system that lacks authenticity.

---

[32] Robert Solomon, Ethics and Excellence: Cooperation and Integrity in Business (NY; Oxford University Press, 1992).

What the Bible says about the need for and benefit of walking in integrity is a great starting point, and Proverbs hits pretty hard! For example, 'The integrity of the upright guides them, but the unfaithful are destroyed by their duplicity' (Proverbs 11:3); 'Honest scales and balances belong to the LORD; all the weights in the bag are of his making' (Proverbs 16:11); 'Good leadership is built on love and truth, for kindness and integrity are what keep leaders in their position of trust' (Proverbs 20:28, TPT); and 'One who loves a pure heart and who speaks with grace will have the king for a friend' (Proverbs 22:11).

These promise that integrity will lead to success; protecting purity protects your life, and kindness and integrity are what keep leaders in positions of trust. Developing and keeping integrity helps to keep us safe, walking closely with God, and in good and healthy relations with others. People will know that we live by a godly value system and will follow us and put their confidence in us. We will be held in good regard as being followers of Jesus, and our lives will glorify Him. It's when conditions become tough or when we lose sight of God in the midst of a flurry of pressure and activity that temptation to compromise creeps in to make the edges of our integrity 'fuzzy'. 'Creative accounting' and unrighteous inventive sales techniques are two that can creep in if the kingdom entrepreneur fails to keep a grip on the culture and practices or fails to keep themselves in close union with Christ.

Keeping integrity

In keeping integrity I've found that a helpful practice has been to ask myself, 'Would I do this if X was here with me now?' 'X' can be your business partner, spouse, children, or Jesus! Fill in the 'X' and then make that judgement. If you find that you are uncomfortable or have a feeling of loss of peace in your spirit or conscience, you have your answer. Then apply courage and 'do not grieve the Holy Spirit' (Ephesians 4:30). Integrity is foundational. It has to be fought for and can put you at odds with others in the enterprise.

Being in a hotel room alone in the evening with nothing to immediately engage your attention and focus can be difficult. 'Adult' movies on the TV in the room can be purchased with the click of a button, a welcoming bar to ease your loneliness or homesickness, possibly with a 'companion' available, and a casino ready to swallow up your cash to fund a gambling habit are all in place to assuage the boredom and grab your attention. These temptations are to be resisted. I found it helpful to purposefully keep myself engaged by making the most of my time to work in the evenings, to listen to a podcast or watch a previously downloaded film or programme, or to meet up with a friend or colleague to have dinner together and spend some time in conversation.

> Integrity is foundational. It has to be fought for.

Fortunately, there were very few such temptations that came my way. There were the occasional attempts by a contractor (often a very small business) to suggest that we could keep the work that we had given to them off the account book by paying cash, so avoiding them the need to declare the income. There were very occasional requests to us not to charge VAT (equivalent to sales tax) by them paying cash and thus benefiting our cashflow. These fraudulent acts (which is what they would have been) were easy to identify and turn away. We had one interesting occurrence which actually caused us no issue but caught us by surprise.

Another director and I ran a training course for managers and executives in the Middle East. The course went well and at the end of the five days our host paid our invoice, which was a great help to our cashflow. As we were getting into the cab to take us back to the airport to fly to the UK, he gave us a large envelope containing the cash in £UK for payment! We looked at each other with a knowing glance, thanked our host for his hospitality and payment and were on our way.

When we arrived at the airport, we had a dilemma. First, how would we deal with customs carrying a wad of cash, and second, how could we guarantee safety of the cash on the flight? The issue for us was not that we had been paid in cash and that we could benefit ourselves or defraud the UK tax authorities, but that we had been taken by surprise, not knowing that this was the custom in this company, and that we were totally unprepared to have to carry the cash through two large airports and on a busy international flight. Anyway, all went well, and the cash was swiftly paid into our UK business bank account!

I remember, with some amusement, an occasion when I was travelling in Europe with my host from a global clothing brand. I was conducting a programme of facility audits and we were staying at a standard business-brand hotel. One evening, when we returned from the factory, we agreed to meet in the hotel bar for a drink before dinner. Having done this, we returned to our rooms to get ready. In the lift my host turned to me and asked whether I was aware of the lady who had travelled down with us in the lift and who had sat next to me at the bar. I honestly hadn't. I had been concentrating on our discussion. He made it clear that the lady's services were to be procured and that this was common in such business-brand hotels in this country. We laughed about this when we met up on other occasions. I was simply thankful that I hadn't noticed the lady, and that her services were of no interest to me!

For the kingdom entrepreneur, we would do well to remember that possessing qualities such as enthusiasm, energy, creativity, innovation and a willingness to take risks are all very well, but they can be harnessed to evil ends. Walking in integrity needs to be ingrained in us and in our enterprises. We need to be sure that this is followed in all aspects of our endeavours and not just the more obvious ones. For example:

- honesty in sales and marketing practices and materials – perhaps particularly where staff are paid by commission;

- consistency in practice – having set out our stall, in our operational procedures, policies, our delivery standards, etc – making sure that we keep them and lead by example;

- transparency with clients and business partners.

Fear losing the closeness of His presence

We have to choose not to be mastered or enslaved by anything, and in this case by anything that promotes me or the business in an unethical way (1 Corinthians 6:9-14 is a helpful text). Run from temptation when it comes; have those whom you trust pray for you; have a couple of intercessors whom you keep honestly informed with the struggles, joys, issues and opportunities, and listen to what they feed back to you. Trust God's protection and keeping power.

We have to choose not to be mastered or enslaved by anything.

Fear God. Hold Him in the highest esteem. Fear losing the closeness of His presence more than the displeasure or embarrassment of your client host or business partner, or of your friends who live according to the prevalent secular culture and value system. God meets all our needs without us needing to be snared (Philippians 4:19)!

Pause, pray, practise

- Pause: Are you satisfied that your organisation's ethics match those set out in Scripture?

- Pray: Holy Spirit, are You highlighting to me a personal character trait that You want to realign or change? What is it?

- Practise: How do you know if integrity is operating in all of your organisation's practices? If not, what do you need to do?

7
Creating Culture

Key points

- We model the culture that we create in our organisation.

- As kingdom people, it's heaven's culture that we want to be demonstrated and experienced.

As believers engage with the world, they take the rule of Christ with them. In the workplace, for example, a believer's integrity, honesty and working for the Lord are all to be expressions of the rule of Jesus.
(David Devenish)[33]

Stop imitating the ideals and opinions of the culture around you, but be inwardly transformed by the Holy Spirit through a total reformation of how you think.
(Romans 12:2, TPT)

I don't know if you've ever been in a country with a markedly different culture from your own. I found that those in the Middle East required me to adapt the most,

---

[33] David Devenish, *Fathering Leaders, Motivating Mission* (Milton Keynes: Authentic Media, 2011), p152. All rights reserved.

but then I think that the English culture must be strange to many as well! One of the aspects of my work that I enjoyed was observing and working in a wide range of corporations and businesses in many industrial and commercial sectors. We found that sectors have their own cultures, and corporations in these sectors also have their own cultures overlaying the sector culture. We had to learn to adapt to these cultures very quickly. We could be working in the financial sector one day and with a smaller business in the manufacturing sector the next. Sometimes all we could do was complete the assignment and move on. On other occasions, as we were more integrated into the business we were able to work with others to help to shift the value system and culture. Challenging but hugely enjoyable! Trading internationally further stretched us.

As kingdom entrepreneurs, the culture that we create in our enterprises is an essential component in demonstrating the kingdom to those with whom we interact. In considering the culture that we set, I believe it is appropriate to consider:

- our internal (personal) culture;
- contemporary secular culture;
- kingdom culture.

Internal culture

Our internal culture is made up of personal values and virtues. This is what people pick up about us. I've heard people talk about atmospheres that people create, and

I've certainly experienced these around others, both positive and negative. With a sensitivity of spirit, we can discern what's in other people. It's an interesting exercise to ask those who really know us to state values and virtues that they see in us – both good and not so good – and to see how they match up with our own assessment of our internal culture. A good test of how brave your assessor is, and how close a friend they are to you, is measured by them feeling able to point out the not-so-good traits in your culture!

We can shift our internal culture. The apostle Paul said as much in Romans 12:2. We need to undergo an inward transformation of our mindset as we mature in our relationship with Father, Jesus and Holy Spirit, fuelled by the power of the Holy Spirit. A spiritual reformation. I have seen, on many occasions, people being radically changed through the power of God's love and grace by being able to untangle themselves from experiences that have influenced or harmed them. In this way, we can be 'restored to the manufacturer's default setting', that is, our God-given self, with the result that we shift the atmosphere that we create. Doing so requires humility and integrity, as well as determination.

> Be 'restored to the manufacturer's default setting'.

Since our internal culture affects how we are perceived by others, this in turn affects how they respond to us. You know the sort of situations yourself. That person in the office whom you must treat with care so as not to get a bad reaction, the workplace 'gossip' with whom you are circumspect about what information to share in case everyone knows by the time you get into the office tomorrow, or the person who is only too quick to tell you what is wrong with you, leaving you humiliated and deflated. Who we are, how we are perceived by others and the response that we receive back from them can easily affect us. So can our social contact group – whether physical or virtual. Such groups can develop their own worldview and culture.

Who we are in our internal culture drives the way we act and respond towards others. These triggers and signals are quickly picked up by our staff and, unless they are particularly resistant people, they are moulded into recreating the culture that we set. This can be both frightening and a delight to us; frightening because we are far from perfect, but a delight because something of heaven's culture is being displayed.

I'm not suggesting that we replicate clones of ourselves in the organisation. What I am suggesting is that, whether unknowingly or deliberately, we dictate how we want and expect people to act and behave towards us, towards our customers and stakeholders, towards each other and, of course, towards God Himself.

Setting culture

So, what culture do you want to set in your organisation? The chances are that who you are as the entrepreneur/business-shaper – your internal culture – will mould the organisation's culture. However, if we abstain from setting culture in our organisation, then someone else in our organisation will do it for us. At least we can consider carefully what we want, rather than default to someone who perhaps has a particular 'axe to grind' or is setting culture biased by their own life experiences.

What culture do you want to set in your organisation?

I have already referred to the amazingly powerful scripture penned by the Holy Spirit through the apostle Paul in writing to the church in Rome: 'Stop imitating the ideals and opinions of the culture around you, but be inwardly transformed by the Holy Spirit through a total reformation of how you think' (Romans 12:2, TPT).

I'm told that the Roman culture at the time was perverse, violent and often governed by unstable individuals, such as Emperor Nero. What the apostles were having to address, particularly those planting churches in Gentile nations (without the history and experience of God in Jewish culture), was that the culture of the Roman system and Empire was not one to be copied and adopted by followers of Jesus. Instead, they were taught not to entertain those values and 'ill' virtues, but to be inwardly transformed by the renewing power of the indwelling Spirit in their thinking about themselves and others. While this required discipline, it was empowered by the renewing power of the Holy Spirit within. This verse, and the process that Paul exhorted the Roman Christians to experience, remains vital today. Our inner transformation needs to change our mindset and to drive the culture that we set within our organisations.

> Our inner transformation needs to change our mindset, and to drive the culture that we set within our organisations.

By nature, I have been one who shies away from confrontation. This is partly my personality and partly my life experience. My dad was similar. Life experiences reinforced this by me internalising what others said or how they acted towards me and confirming the feeling of rejection that I was struggling to overcome. My personal encounters with God made me realise in myself that He truly and deeply loves me. In turn, this had the effect of cutting off the flow of fuel to the rejection that I felt and enabled me to become bolder in my interactions with others. Rather than squirm in a confrontation, I felt that I could explain myself, listen to what the other person was saying and work through what needed to be done to address the issue.

It's interesting that Jesus was described as 'meek' (2 Corinthians 10:1, NKJV). It took me many years to find out that an appropriate meaning of meekness is 'power under control'.[34] This helped my internal transformation by enabling me to throw out the mindset that it meant weak and powerless, making it easy for someone to walk over

---

[34] For example, as in Vine's Expository Dictionary of Old and New Testament Words, www.studylight.org/dictionaries/eng/ved/m/meek-meekness.html (accessed 7th February 2021).

you. Jesus' supernatural power was under supernatural control!

Contemporary culture v kingdom culture

The phrase 'kingdom culture' needs a little explanation. The kingdom of God is expressed in different ways in different cultures. That's not to imply that any one culture is preferable to or better than another. So when I refer to 'kingdom culture' I mean the values of the kingdom of God expressed in a particular culture. There is much that can be said about this hot topic, and much has been written about it. I commend you to explore and read.

I have found one of the most insightful commentators on the clash of contemporary culture and kingdom culture to be Mark Sayers. In his excellent pair of books, *Disappearing Church* and *Reappearing Church*, he takes us on a journey of navigation through the secular culture in which we live. He succinctly summarises secularism as humanity's effort to devise a structure for prosperity without the need for God.[35] On the contrary, we are those who have the immense joy of knowing God's presence, or, as Sayers says, for those who long for and seek His presence, it is accepted as surges of love, whereas for those who are wrapped in the culture of progressive secularism, he describes these as identified as surges of God's judgement.[36]

---

[35] Mark Sayers, *Reappearing Church* (Chicago, IL: Moody Publishers, 2019), p83. *Disappearing Church* was published by Moody Publishers in 2016.

[36] Sayers, *Reappearing Church*, p51.

As kingdom people, marked by His presence, we should not be surprised by the clash of cultures exposed by those whom we employ and otherwise interact with. This is important. We need to understand that as we carry God's presence, and as we make room for those who are wrapped up in the secular to encounter God, it could be, or perhaps it is inevitable, that they will first experience His presence as judgement – that is, conviction of sin, rebellion and the exposure of their lifestyles. This, as we know, can be disturbing and disruptive. At this point we need to lead with grace, first and foremost, not our own strength, leading people from exhaustion to God's presence, which opens the doorway to their hearts. As Paul writes to the church in Corinth:

> For we are to God the pleasing aroma of Christ among those who are being saved and those who are perishing. To the one we are an aroma that brings death; to the other, an aroma that brings life.
>
> (2 Corinthians 2:15-16)

Kingdom culture: Developing a culture of honour

> Good leadership is built on love and truth,
> for kindness and integrity
> are what keep leaders in their position of trust.
> (Proverbs 20:28, TPT)

This raises the question, how much can we expect a kingdom culture to be the prevailing one in our organisation when we employ people who are of a different faith, or of no faith? I believe that we can, and should, create a business culture around the values and practices of a kingdom culture, which includes a culture of honour. This takes courage, and it takes effort over the long term. Staff, suppliers, contractors, and others experiencing a kingdom culture opens the opportunity for them to experience God's presence; it could be the motivator for them having that experience.

> One of our principal roles as kingdom entrepreneurs is to help people find their God-given identities.

Working with other people is not straightforward! Jesus found it difficult to develop a godly, heavenly culture with twelve men of contrasting personalities! It's interesting that with Peter, He changed his name from Simon to Cephas (John 1:42), meaning 'the rock'. It was, I suggest, His way of helping to transform Cephas' (Peter's) thinking, by treating him according to his God-given identity (the rock on which Jesus built His Church, Matthew 16:18), rather than the name given to him by his parents. It was part of Jesus' discipling of His followers to Himself. In the culture that we develop and the way that we treat and lead staff, we are doing the same thing, discipling them to Jesus. As a pastor friend of mine says, 'We disciple people to Jesus, not merely in Jesus.' Surely, developing a heavenly community culture is a key to discipling nations (Matthew 28:19). We have the God-given opportunity of doing so among those within our organisation or enterprise. One of our principal roles as kingdom entrepreneurs is to help people find their God-given identities.

Kingdom culture: A safe place

A kingdom culture creates a safe place for people. A safe place is included in the biblical understanding of *shalom*. A safe place means people are likely to feel more able to let down their walls of self-built protection from the consequences of guilt and shame and open up to the presence of God engendered in an authentic and caring culture. Such a culture does not mean that sales targets, personal development plans, reviews and disciplinary procedures should be abandoned. In fact, the opposite should apply. We should build our kingdom cultural expectations of our staff into these. Remember, people follow where we lead. We can't expect them to follow us if we're not demonstrating the culture in our life by the way we treat them.

> A kingdom culture creates a safe place for people.

I remember an important lesson that I learned as our business was in a growth stage. The directors were exceptionally busy travelling all over the country, and fully engaged every day. The result was that when I or the other main director were in the office (and, incidentally, not located in the same office), the chances were that other consultants were not – or at least most of them were not. This made effective communication difficult. Email and Skype were great, and these days apps and software can be used in a team environment very effectively if the boundaries are correctly set (culture again), but having quality time with the team was difficult.

One day when I was travelling I received a call from this other director, leaving me a message to call him when I was free. I returned his call while seated in my car in a hotel car park on the outskirts of Leicester. He had heard from a member of staff that they felt that they were not receiving effective feedback on how they were getting on, and they were feeling discouraged and unsure about how they were doing.

We came up with a plan to address this, but first we had to recognise their concern and realise that it was a fair criticism. Better to have the feedback than have valuable staff members hand in their notice!

Encouragement is vital.

This lesson has stayed with me since: encouragement is vital. We have an innate need to be encouraged, no matter how strong we may be. It's my theory that giving encouragement leads to people being courageous. It's certainly what I've observed and experienced. And let's never dismiss the need for courage in entrepreneurship.

We had built a culture where it was OK to raise a hand and say, 'This isn't working and here's why.' What we had failed to realise was that staff were not feeling sufficiently supported. Time to admit that we had got it wrong, even though staff knew that we were really busy. The culture that we set enabled us to do that without diminishing ourselves and looking foolish to the staff. We didn't have an attitude that said, 'We're right, you're wrong, get on with it or leave.' We valued our staff and wanted them to advance in the business. Having the ability to challenge where things were not working was evidence of an open culture that showed that they too valued being a part of the business and valued the directors. And that takes us back to being humble-hearted...

A different situation arose much later in the business. An important member of our staff, whom I will call Sam,[37] came into the office late one day. He was really upset and he was wet through, having left home in a hurry without a coat, even though it was raining. He told me that he had been in a relationship for some time that had become intolerable. I spent some time with him, and then a colleague joined me so that we were able to devote time and attention to him. I was able to contact a good friend of mine with professional experience of these issues, and they offered me some excellent advice which I passed on to Sam. He decided that he needed to move away as a means of permanently breaking the relationship. This was disruptive to the business, but his welfare was more important.

What we tried to give him, and model for him, was the grace and compassion of Jesus. Kingdom culture was, I trust, demonstrated to him. I lost contact with him but hopefully that has remained with him.

Kingdom culture: Banish fear and shame

My advice is always back your team up. If we have any issue with someone, we should speak about it in private.

---

[37] Details have been changed to protect identity.

That honours the person. Keep trust and honour your team. Communication is such an important skill in keeping team together and on focus. We mustn't let busyness rob us and others of effective communication. They need to know that we are for them. Even when correction is necessary, that needs to be done in love and in a way that honours the person. Fear of the boss is like creeping ivy climbing up a wall – it sucks the life out of everything. Such fear drives out respect, honour and love, and all that remains is duty and being worried about getting it wrong. Creativity and innovation thrive on security and dry up in fear. What we desperately need in a team is life and vibrancy for it to grow and prosper, and a vibrant, responsive and strong team means a vibrant, responsive and strong business or enterprise.

> My advice is always back your team up
> ... They need to know that we are for
> them.

By wisdom a house is built,
and through understanding it is established;
through knowledge its rooms are filled
with rare and beautiful treasures.
(Proverbs 24:3-4)

Pause, pray, practise

- Pause: Who has set the culture in your organisation? Does this culture reflect heaven's culture?

- Pray: Are there steps to take to redress the culture in terms of values, principles and practices? Ask the Holy Spirit to give you wisdom in how to do this.

- Practise: What measures are you going to take?

8
Discipling a Scarcity Mindset

Key points

- Scarcity thinking attacks us at the deepest level of our identity, value and purpose.

- Our old nature's desire to consume is itself consumed in His presence and purpose.

Poverty smothers while mammon inflames. The two work like a team to trap you in a pointless condition of unrest over money. One laments, "There is never enough," while the other insists, "You deserve it all." This dichotomy between the two is no accident; this strategy is the enemy's way of preventing people from escaping his bilateral influence.
(Stephen K De Silva)[38]

But remember the LORD your God, for it is he who gives you the ability to produce wealth, and so confirms his covenant, which he swore to your ancestors, as it is today.
(Deuteronomy 8:18)

---

[38] Stephen K De Silva, *Prosperous Soul: Advanced,* Volume 2. Published March 2021. Available from: stephenkdesilva.com/store (accessed 19th February 2021).

Wealth, riches and the kingdom

It is often said that Jesus in his earthly ministry addressed the topic of money more than any other. I don't consider money to be inherently good or evil; it is how we view money and how we use it to act out what resides in our hearts that turns money into a force in our world that has great power for good or evil. As my friend Stephen De Silva says, 'money exaggerates what is in the heart'.

A significant question for us to consider is, how are kingdom entrepreneurs distinctive in their approach to money, power and influence? Surely God is not opposed to money and wealth. After all, you could say that God is infinitely wealthy, since 'The earth is the LORD's, and everything in it' (Psalm 24:1). For a fun idea, how much wealth does God 'own' when the global gross domestic product in 2019 amounted to $87.5tr?[39] And that's just the human output of one planet! He is the owner; we are the stewards of His wealth. The Bible is clear that wealth comes from Him. It is a result of God's grace and favour (Deuteronomy 8:18).

I consider it necessary to view this over the long term. There are cycles in national and global economies caused by various factors. In my lifetime I have seen these caused by long-term industrial relations issues, geopolitical strife, financial crashes and pandemics. We are affected by these, but God is not. His ability to produce wealth remains. Many of us have experienced financial setbacks in various

---

[39] 'Global gross domestic product (GDP) at current prices from 1985 to 2025', Statista, www.statista.com/statistics/268750/global-gross-domestic-product-gdp/ (accessed 19th February 2021).

forms, but that does not mean that His favour is not on us. It may mean that we have to be patient in our enterprise for economies to rise again. It is also apparent that some people choose to live a life that can be considered to be disadvantaged by the standard of common culture because of their devotion to Christ. His favour is on them also. It is not money that is the 'root of all kinds of evil' but the love of it (1 Timothy 6:10). It is money in the hands of a sick heart that leads to evil.

The Bible says that it is God's intent that the 'riches of the nations' should come to his people (see, for example, Isaiah 60:5-7) – the wealth of unrighteous and righteous people, communities and nations coming to His people for us to administer. A great example of this is seen in Joseph's administration of Egypt under the pharaoh, as we explored earlier, in the book of Genesis. We have seen this in small measure, but nothing like to the extent that I believe Scripture makes clear. I believe that a reason for this is because His kingdom people have not mastered either scarcity mentality or Mammon. This means that we either run away from money because we do not trust ourselves with it (scarcity mentality), or we run after it but do not have it because God cannot entrust it to us because of the way that we misuse it (Mammon).

Perhaps you, like me, have seen wealth inappropriately used by individuals, corporations, even the Church, and have been disenchanted by the spectacle? I suggest to you that wealth is not meant to be placed into the hands of a few to build up their privileged status, but to benefit a community and the wider society at large. This was also the case for the nation of Israel, and this did happen under certain leaders and kings who brought revival to the nation.[40]

We are disciples of Jesus before being consumers.

One of the actions that the Holy Spirit is doing in His people in these days is redressing the place of wealth in His kingdom by impacting our hearts and minds and enabling us to take on the transforming of our minds and refusing to be conformed to the world's mindset (Romans 12:2). There feels like a Holy Spirit impetus in this as we grasp what it means for His kingdom (and therefore His will) to come to earth as in heaven (Matthew 6:10). Not that this is easy. We are continually bombarded by the world's mindset. I expect you, like me, face it every day in your workplace, with some colleagues and friends, and perhaps in your family. It is pretty unrelenting, and we have to be purposeful in holding on to a godly mindset. We are disciples of Jesus before being consumers. Our old nature's desire for being soothed in our orphan mentality by consuming (buying unnecessarily to comfort us) is itself consumed in His presence and purpose, and we bless others as we follow Jesus. We need to learn how scarcity thinking and Mammon master us, and how we dethrone and displace them. After all, kingdom entrepreneurs are well suited to being entrusted to handle responsibly the

---

[40] Harrison-Mills, 'Hearing About Jesus, but Thinking About Joel: Exploring the Biblical and Historical Relationship Between Spiritual and Economic Transformation', December 2011.

'riches of the nations' and to distribute them with wisdom and equity.

Orphan thinking

Lucifer was the original orphan spirit. His rebellion meant that God separated Lucifer from Himself and he was banished from heaven (Isaiah 14:12-15). When humanity 'fell' in the Garden of Eden from the place of honour that we were created to hold, and we became isolated from our heavenly Father, we became strongly influenced by a fatherless, or orphan, spirit. This way of thinking creates a mindset that is prone to two strong roots that can take hold in our lives – scarcity mindset and Mammon. Both limit us or repress us. Neither is life affirming. Both attack our experience of the fullness of life that Jesus came to give us through His death, resurrection and ascension to the Father. Both work to hold us in that place of being sinners. Neither belongs to the kingdom mindset, what the apostle Paul called the 'mind of Christ' (1 Corinthians 2:16). As Welby so eloquently puts it, our worth comes from God, not our monetary yield.[41]

Both the scarcity mindset and Mammon are lies. They emanate from Satan, who is the 'father of lies' (John 8:44). He has no creative abilities, but he is skilled at getting us to believe lies that are a twisted version of the truth. They are the antithesis of God's truth.

Do we run away from wealth because we fear having to manage it well, not trusting ourselves? I do not consider that the scarcity mindset and Mammon are strictly

---

[41] Welby, *Dethroning Mammon*, p92.

opposites but are best considered as guards that protect the orphan spirit – our old unregenerate ways of thinking – and comfort our fears. It takes courage to defeat these guards, and it takes time and determination (and sometimes gritted teeth) to throw off these mindsets and establish godly ones in their place. When we demolish them, we do not find ourselves subservient to another tyrant, but to God, who is 'rich in mercy' and unconditionally loving (Ephesians 2:4). We need to navigate the narrow path between them, a journey that is not often travelled. I am convinced that a scarcity mindset and Mammon are both based on a spirit of fear: fear of having resource and having to be accountable for it (scarcity mindset), or greed based on fear and insecurity (Mammon).

> Do we run away from wealth because we fear having to manage it well, not trusting ourselves?

Fear has its root in an orphan spirit. This results in a scarcity mindset being 'I am the beggar' and the Mammon mindset being 'beggar your neighbour'. Neither is a virtue of the kingdom.

Scarcity thinking

It is really helpful to understand that a scarcity mindset is possessive because it is based in and held by fear. As Mullainathan and Shafir state, scarcity ensnares us by arresting our minds.[42] So even though we may believe that poverty in a general sense is an injustice, and we campaign against it, we can ourselves be entrapped by a scarcity mindset. A scarcity mindset is not dependent upon our financial status; it is a heart attitude.

There are those who take lower-paid jobs to bless and serve others, and those who give up successful careers in order to be obedient to God's call on their life, meaning they take a significant cut in pay and benefits. This does not mean that they are subject to scarcity thinking; it shows that they are willing to accept lower remuneration in order to fulfil their God-given purpose. God created us to be His image bearers (Genesis 1:27).

> A scarcity mindset is not dependent upon our financial status.

The great danger of being exposed to the orphan spirit is that we distort this image-bearing and succumb to worshipping false images; those tools that God meant for our good we make tools that the devil uses to master us. Thus, what God meant to bless us becomes something that cause us to be troubled, or even afflicted. The possessive nature of the scarcity mindset despises success and attacks the dreams and redeemed imaginations of success. Joseph went through great struggles and disappointments, but he was faithful to God and he held on to his dream.

In the face of opposition from those who, in their scarcity mindset, attack our dreams, we are tempted to

---

[42] S Mullainathan and E Shafir, *Scarcity* (London: Penguin, 2014), pp5, 14.

hide our dreams for fear that people or circumstances will turn against us. People touched by a scarcity mindset oppose success, believing it to be in some way ungodly. They find it difficult to celebrate the flourishing of others because of jealousy. They want to hold people back from achieving their God-given purpose. It was Joseph's dreams that gave him courage to achieve what God had called him to do.

The basic message of scarcity thinking is this: there is never enough. When people live long enough under the influence of this message, it takes on a personal tone: there is never enough for me because I'm not worthy. Lack in any area of our lives – whether our basic needs like food, clothing and shelter, or our psychological needs such as opportunities, friendship, affection and intimacy – shapes our soul and spirit.[43] It becomes personal. Because a scarcity mindset is rooted in beliefs about ourselves and the world, it has a very powerful hold. It attacks us at the deepest level of our identity, value and purpose. The verse, 'For as he thinks within himself, so he is' (Proverbs 23:7, NASB), is a succinct way of expressing this. The mindset that guides our thinking is reinforcing our beliefs (actually lies about our God-given identity) and perpetuates our reality. Our habits of mind define our habits of life, or our internal reality becomes our external reality. And as creatures of habit, one of the most difficult

[43] A helpful introduction to our human needs was first expounded by Abraham Maslow in 1943. It has since been modified but remains an important element of the understanding of human psychological behavior (see, for example, 'Abraham Maslow and the pyramid that beguiled business', BBC News, www.bbc.co.uk/news/magazine-23902918 (accessed 19th February 2021)).

things for us to do is to question the reality in which these habits work.

Breaking the scarcity mindset

We will never overcome the influence of scarcity thinking until we learn to become stewards of what we listen to. This is why Jesus instructed us to be vigilant about our 'hearing':

> 'Consider carefully what you hear,' he continued. 'With the measure you use, it will be measured to you – and even more.'
> (Mark 4:24)

We need to 'retune' our hearts to what God says is the truth, so that our internal reality is readjusted. His reality having authority over our mindset gives permission for our hearts to be healed and brought into line with God's plan and purpose for us to be 'fruitful and increase' (Genesis 1:22).

The apostle Paul, writing to the church in Corinth, specifically mentions the generosity of those in the Macedonian churches:

> In the midst of a very severe trial, their overflowing joy and their extreme poverty welled up in rich generosity. For I testify that they gave as much as they were able, and even beyond their ability. Entirely on their own, they urgently pleaded with us for the privilege of sharing in this service to the Lord's people.

And they exceeded our expectations: they gave themselves first of all to the Lord, and then by the will of God also to us.
(2 Corinthians 8:2-5)

Paul uses their example of radical generosity, despite their economic circumstances, to encourage the church in Corinth to 'excel in this grace of giving' (v7). He asks them to remember that 'whoever sows sparingly will also reap sparingly, and whoever sows generously will also reap generously' (2 Corinthians 9:6), for 'he who supplies seed to the sower and bread for food will also supply and increase your store of seed and will enlarge the harvest of your righteousness' (v10). Here we see God's people unhindered by poverty thinking despite their economic status.

In a similar way, Jesus comments on radical generosity:

Jesus sat down opposite the place where the offerings were put and watched the crowd putting their money into the temple treasury. Many rich people threw in large amounts. But a poor widow came and put in two very small copper coins, worth only a few pence.

Calling his disciples to him, Jesus said, 'Truly I tell you, this poor widow has put more into the treasury than all the others. They all gave out of their wealth; but she, out of her poverty, put in everything – all she had to live on.'
(Mark 12:41-44)

She gave out of a generous heart, out of her poverty. I don't encourage anyone to give their money or themselves to anything or anyone that will result in financial debt or in illness. We give in faith to bless others, knowing that God will supply what we need (Philippians 4:19). We are created to flourish, not merely survive.

Taking on an attitude of generosity displaces a scarcity mindset. It is giving to such an extent that it is contrary to what is expected in the prevailing culture in which we live. In this way we break the power of our entrenched way of thinking, and of the culture's influence over us. It is exerting the kingdom culture despite the hold that is exerted by the popular culture. This doesn't happen overnight; it takes a determined fight to break clear of it. It is a process of displacement.

> We are created to flourish, not merely survive.

It took me some time to break this way of thinking. It took a few dear friends, and of course the Holy Spirit, to help me.

I remember the time when it suddenly came to me what was the root of this thinking. I was born in post-Second World War Britain. My parents grew up as children experiencing the effects of the Great Depression, and as young adults the Second World War and the huge economic impact that this had on the UK. It led to severe rationing of what today we consider to be everyday necessities – many foods such as butter and meat, and clothing and fuel. Health suffered. The Beveridge Report published in 1942 identified five giants impacting the population: want, lack of education, squalor, lack of work, and disease.[44] (Most of these are basic human needs as classified by Maslow.) The Holy Spirit showed me that my parents, through no fault of their own but because they had been shaped in their mindset by their experiences, brought me up to survive above all else. Flourishing and achieving was not the primary message, not that it wasn't talked about. I learned that my primary role was to survive, and that this had fed my feeling of isolation from my heavenly Father (I came to Christ when I was eighteen, just before I left my parents' home).

I commend my parents' thrift in trying circumstances. By careful financial management and wise living, they were able in time to move away from scarcity thinking. Thrift is not the same as scarcity thinking. Thrift is the exercise of constraint to spend what is necessary rather than what we wish to consume. Unnecessary consuming can lead to debt, although I do not suggest that personal debt is necessarily a result of the desire to consume.

It took me many years to break free from the mastery of this mentality. Mostly this was simply through God's grace. First, being led to start a business in a niche area of consultancy; second, being blessed in my business; and then, and most importantly, by learning God's intention for us in Christ and who I am as a son of my heavenly

---

[44] For a short description of the economic effect of the Second World War on Britain, see 'Social Impact of WWII in Britain' BBC Bitesize, www.bbc.com/bitesize/guides/z6ctyrd/revision/1 (accessed 19th February 2021). Information about The Beveridge Report is available at '1942 Beveridge Report', UK Parliament, https://www.parliament.uk/about/living-heritage/transformingsociety/livinglearning/coll-9-health1/coll-9-health/ (accessed 15th March 2021).

Father. I have to remind myself occasionally of who am I in Christ and not revert back to an old mindset. But I am not mastered by it! I am 'the head, not the tail' (Deuteronomy 28:13). My prayer is that you would know that too.

Pause, pray, practise

- Pause: How am I distinctive from those not following Jesus in my approach towards, and use of, money, influence and power?

- Pray: Honestly, before the Father, ask Him to work graciously in your life to free you from being trapped by a scarcity mindset and to help you to reimagine the possibilities of your life in Christ.

- Practise: On a scale of 1 to 5, put a number (whole number only) on how much scarcity thinking affects your belief system. Then ask two others very close to you to rate you in the same way. What do these three assessments tell you? How do you feel about this? Does fear rise in you? Forgive those who taught or demonstrated to you that scarcity thinking is godly. Renounce this lie and receive the grace of Jesus.

9
Displacing Mammon

Key points

- We do not serve money; money serves us as we serve God.

- Mammon causes us to surrender our liberty in Christ.

It is as necessary for a poor man to give away, as for a rich man. Many poor men are more devoted worshipers of Mammon than some rich men.
(George MacDonald)[45]

So if you have not been trustworthy in handling worldly wealth, who will trust you with true riches? And if you have not been trustworthy with someone else's property, who will give you property of your own?
(Luke 16:11-12)

There I was looking at a roller cage filled with shrink-wrapped bundles of £20 notes in a secure storage room. This was a serious amount of cash – by far the largest amount I had ever seen. There must have been hundreds of thousands of pounds in this cage and, as I looked

---

[45] George MacDonald, *Adela Cathcart* (Johannesen Printing & Publishing, first published 1875).

around, I saw many more cages filled with finished notes of various denominations. It was an amazing sight, and yet I remember feeling absolutely nothing about what I was seeing! It wasn't mine, and I had no right to it. I was being paid to do some work for this company, and this was their output.

In the same way that the Father was providing the company with His provision through this consultancy work, so the Father provides for us according to our needs. What we receive we have authority over to use wisely and righteously. Money is His gift to us. As Stephen De Silva says, 'I am not mastered by money, riches or wealth. They serve God through my hands.'[46]

As I have said, God has no lack of resource and provision! What I was seeing was nothing compared to God's 'wealth'! It is striking how many parables that Jesus taught about the kingdom of heaven are to do with economic trade, merchandising or power, and frequently centred on return on investment, profitable trades and so on.[47] The irony is that He was speaking to people mastered to a greater or lesser extent by Mammon, yet He was teaching about heaven! The contrast is clear. We 'cannot serve both God and Money' (Matthew 6:24).

What is Mammon?

The word translated in most Bible versions as 'money', 'riches' or 'wealth'[48] is 'Mammon'. The translators were

---

[46] Stephen K De Silva, *Prosperous Soul: Advanced*, 2020, Volume 2.

[47] An example is the parable of the talents in Matthew 25:14-30.

[48] NIV, NCV, NASB.

attempting to capture the meaning of a word that is unfamiliar to our Western minds. Mammon is very different from simply riches, money or wealth. It means to put your trust or confidence in wealth in a way that personifies it as a god. It is spelt with a capital 'M', like a person's name is spelt with a capital first letter. Mammon is a controlling spirit, one that displaces God in our sight and is in opposition to the kingdom of God. Consequently, Jesus strongly opposes it.

We must learn to master unrighteous Mammon, while recognising that it seeks to master us. Like a scarcity mindset, Mammon leaves clues like fingerprints. For example, it:

- thrives on secrecy and untruth;

- encourages unhealthy comparisons and factions between individuals and groups;

- hungers for immoral and sensuous living;

- promotes greed and envy of others' success.

The 'love of money' (1 Timothy 6:10) deceives us into thinking that we can buy comfort, power and celebrity, which in turn fools us into thinking that we are in control of our destinies.

Welby says the trick of money is to have us believe not that we need to grasp what is ours, but that what we have is ours to spend as we want.[49] When the apostle Paul wrote his letter to Timothy he said that people who want to

---

[49] Welby, *Dethroning Mammon*, p59.

become rich 'fall into temptation and a trap and into many foolish and harmful desires that plunge people into ruin and destruction' (1 Timothy 6:9). We see that Mammon also traps us and subverts the truth. Jesus modelled true humility. He came from His place of ultimate power and glory to become nothing, and of no value in the world system of those He created (Philippians 2:6-8). Taking on this mindset changes our worldview, misshapen and warped by the lure of Mammon, and frees us to take on the kingdom worldview.

Displacing old mindsets

How do we counteract Mammon? Welby suggests that both the worship of God and exaggerated generosity are what is necessary to dethrone Mammon.[50]

We can see this as we look at one of Jesus' parables and His encounter with the rich young ruler.

1. The unjust steward (Luke 16:1-15)

The steward faces the destructive result of worshipping Mammon. His position is lost, his career is ruined, and he faces having to gain favour with his employer's creditors or else begging as a means to fend off starvation. He begins to make deals with his master's creditors to try to rebuild some reputation so that when he loses his job he will still be welcomed into people's houses, perhaps to find employment once again. This information gets back to the master, who praises the steward for his shrewdness. Remember that the steward was not reinstated; he was

---

[50] Welby, *Dethroning Mammon*, p78.

still disqualified and faced a destroyed career and the strong possibility of having to beg for his needs.

One of the fascinating comments that Jesus makes is in verses 8 and 9: 'The sons of darkness are more shrewd than the sons of light in their interactions with others. It is important that you use the wealth of this world to demonstrate your friendship with God by winning friends and blessing others ... your generosity will provide you with an eternal reward' (TPT). Are we 'more shrewd' with money than these sons of darkness are without Christ as Lord of their lives? Where we deposit our treasure is where our heart is.

2. The rich young ruler (Luke 18:18-30)
In this encounter Jesus told the ruler that he lacked one thing and to combat this he had to: 'Sell everything you have and give to the poor, and you will have treasure in heaven. Then come, follow me.' He was held in the grip of Mammon. Radical and appropriate generosity was needed to dethrone Mammon in his life. Here was a man who was storing up treasure on earth as his source of comfort, power and perhaps notoriety; Jesus instructed him to realign himself to storing treasures in heaven by forsaking Mammon and by giving his life to Him.

The line 'where your treasure is, there your heart will be also' (Matthew 6:21) is a great plumb line for us to honestly and humbly measure ourselves against.

Proverbs 11:24 is instructive: 'One person gives freely, yet gains even more; another withholds unduly, but comes to poverty.' Proverbs 21:25-26 is telling:

Taking the easy way out is the habit of a lazy
man,
and it will be his downfall.
All day long he thinks about all the things that
he craves,
for he hasn't learned the secret that the generous
man has learned:
extravagant giving never leads to poverty.
(TPT)

1 Samuel 2:7 says, 'The LORD sends poverty and wealth; he humbles and he exalts.' We are not immune from God humbling us and bringing poverty to us if we maintain a heart attitude of pride in our wealth accumulation. As Proverbs says (13:18), 'Whoever disregards discipline comes to poverty and shame, but whoever heeds correction is honoured.' Better for us to be confronted with the enthroned Christ and turn around to display the fruits of repentance than to refuse Him and be humbled by Him.

As Welby says, do we use money and power in serving God and ministering to others, or do we use it to isolate ourselves from those with whom we would rather not associate?[51] In the context of the kingdom of heaven, if we seek power through worldly ways then we are living in an old age. Now worldly power and status exist only for the sake of service. And this causes a great joy within us. Stephen De Silva says that Jesus wants to romance us so that we find such pleasure in His presence that Mammon's pull is neutralised. The lie that Mammon sells us as an idol is scarcity, and this compels us to hold on to what we have.

---

[51] Welby, *Dethroning Mammon*, p97.

It is born out of fear. We can be wealthy but still be controlled by scarcity thinking. We need to replace this thinking with generosity and abundance, taking on the grace of Jesus, who lavished his love on us beyond what we can imagine.

Cheerful generosity

So, defeating the spirit of Mammon can be easy when our hearts are won over to Christ's love. Just as poverty thinking is displaced by radical generosity, so is Mammon dethroned. It is a spiritual reformation by looking through a different lens. This kind of giving is spiritual violence against strongholds of Mammon and scarcity. When Mammon is overcome, we do not have idolatry, injustice and abuse of power, but the demonstration of God's love and grace.

Radical generosity doesn't need to be limited to money. It can be the giving of time or letting go of power that has been used in an abusive way to control other people – anything that has mastery over us. Cheerful givers (2 Corinthians 9:7) understand what they are giving away; they know what they are sacrificing, and they do it anyway. This is the grace to give with understanding!

What we have is not truly ours but on loan from God. Holding our possessions, power and influence lightly is a really useful practical means of counteracting Mammon's hold in our lives. In this way, when the Holy Spirit challenges us to give of our resources, we are less likely to have conflict about giving generously.

How do we defeat Mammon and keep it in check? By emulating the radically generous God who has freely given us all things. What did Jesus say? 'Freely you have received; freely give' (Matthew 10:8).

Money is meant to be used but not used to abuse. Get the priority wrong and it wraps us up in its tentacles. My advice is to steer well clear of letting the 'love of money' and its acquisition master you. Rather, use it for the benefit of others.

Summary of a scarcity mindset and Mammon

- They both cut us off from the work of the cross of Christ; a scarcity mindset by crushing us with condemnation and shame, Mammon by stuffing us with things and drowning out our hunger for forgiveness and restoration.

- They both cut us off from recognising our adoption as sons or daughters (Ephesians 1:5). A scarcity mindset keeps us as a nobody; Mammon tries to keep us being somebody through accumulation and achievement.

- They both keep us from looking up and looking out. A scarcity mindset promotes a negative focus on self; Mammon promotes an overinflated focus on self, but they both prevent us from seeing what is greater than ourselves, and from embracing the race that is set before us.

- They are both broken, or displaced, by a God-worshipping lifestyle and by extravagant generosity.

Pause, pray, practise

- Pause: Are you able to demonstrate your friendship with God in the way that you use worldly wealth? How do you do that?

- Pause: Where do you store your treasure: on earth or in heaven?

- Pray: Does the Father want you to act differently?

- Pray: Does radical generosity fill you with joy or fear? If fear, honestly and humbly ask God to help you displace this fear and begin a journey of increasing generosity.

- Practise: How can you extend your generosity further?

10
Redeeming Power

Key points

- The abuse of power leads to the diminishing of others, preventing them from fulfilling their God-given purpose.

- As disciples of Jesus, restored to our original, created, image-bearing capability, we are empowered for flourishing.

Most people can bear adversity; but if you wish to know what a man really is give him power.
(Robert Green Ingersoll)[52]

I have hidden your word in my heart
that I might not sin against you.
Praise be to you, LORD;
teach me your decrees.
(Psalm 119:11-12)

I must have been fifteen or sixteen, and my best friend had bought, or had had bought for him, a motorised scooter.

---

[52] Robert Green Ingersoll Quotes. BrainyQuote.com, BrainyMedia Inc, 2021, www.brainyquote.com/quotes/robert_green_ingersoll_101343 (accessed 11th February 2021).

This was no 50cc scooter but a more powerful version altogether. In his joy of showing it to me when I first saw it in his back garden, he asked me if I would like to have a go on the driveway, but not on the road. In the exuberance of youth, of course I enthusiastically said, 'Yes, why not!' He showed me how to rev it up, how to put it in gear and, importantly, how to operate the brakes!

So, carefully I sat astride the seat, pulled in the clutch and revved up the engine to make a gentle pull away and around the corner onto the driveway. Unfortunately I hadn't tested the bite point of the clutch. Well, I exceeded it on the first attempt! I shot forward, straight into the neighbour's fence, and the scooter and I ended up on our sides. I was a bit shaken and bruised, the neighbour's fence stood up to the impact, and my friend's dad suitably, and correctly, told us off, with the instruction that this was a machine not to be messed with. It was a painful introduction to failing to correctly bridle power! Needless to say, there have been many other occasions when this message has been reinforced to me.

Power, the 'love of money' and other 'power-loving cousins', such as celebrity, seek to buy us influence and help connect us to people higher up the ladder of influence. Power-loving lures us to control and master others in order to hide the effects of our own inadequacies and lack of power by minimising the effects of our God-given gift of power. This is confused thinking. Surely this is not how it is meant to be. Why are we drawn to such behaviour? We need to go back to the beginning.

God the Trinity is an amazing creator. And yet there are truths wrapped up in God's creation of us as humankind that can be overlooked or unrealised, and these are really important to us in the way that we understand our own creativity and use of power. Imagine for a moment that you are God (crazy I know, but bear with me). You are all powerful and all knowing. Imagine that you want to create. What would it be? Don't think small scale here. Take a moment and think what that would be. Why do you want to create that? Is it for your own good or for the common good? Is it so monumental that it's crazy? Is it created out of your own desires? Now consider whether it is intrinsically very good, mediocre or just poor. How do you judge that?

The point I am exploring here is that God's creation is authentically good because it was made by an entirely good God. He could have created what was nearly all good but then that would not be an accurate expression of who He is. How would our 'creation' be judged on the scales of 'goodness'?

> We are unique in creation in being
> invested with power over it.

When we were made, we were not made with God saying, 'Let there be ...' but with, 'Let us make ... in our image' (Genesis 1:26). Thus, God as Trinity decides to make us, and to make us as His image-bearers. As a communal act we were made from perfect unity and community, not out of some mere exertion of power, but out of a deep longing for intimacy and communion. And our mandate as image-bearers was to exert dominion, and to be 'fruitful and increase' (Genesis 1:28). We are unique in creation in being invested with power over it. We became the people who could themselves say, 'Let there be ...' and, 'Let us make ...' in fulfilling our directive.

Fractured power

We know that the beauty of this creation was messed up by our fall from this amazingly balanced order. Indeed, all of creation is now 'groaning' with the burden of carrying the imbalance that humankind brought about by disobedience (Romans 8:22). Now we have the capability not only to be imagers of God, but also to be imagers of sin. Our humanity has become twisted. Unfortunately, now what comes to mind when we think of the use of power can be what is often portrayed by the media as human failure, ie abuse. We can think of many examples of the seemingly strong imposing their will upon the weak through violence and abuse in its variety of means – physical, psychological, sexual, etc. And unfortunately we can think of many examples of this expressed in the Church of Jesus Christ. None of these is life-affirming or leads to personal or relational flourishing. They all produce the opposite. You will see that the abuse of power is the antithesis of God's power, the fruit of a broken humanity twisting our God-given ability to be creative. It leads to the diminishing and controlling of others, keeping them 'under the thumb' and preventing them from fulfilling their purpose through the fruitful use of their gifts.

My friend Stephen De Silva has a great parable to illustrate why we as Christians have abdicated our power-bearing purpose given us by God. He says that we are like food blenders without lids. We pack it with all sorts of good nutritious stuff that will do us good, such as gifts and fruits of the Spirit (Galatians 5:22-23). We also place into the blender the ungodly lies that we learn, alongside the fruits of Spirit. We collect these things through life – by acts of betrayal, pain, mistrust and distrust, and so on. We put the blender power on low and the processing begins. As we grow in our career, in our relationships, in our positions in which we lead others, etc, the power of the blender gets turned up. All of a sudden, with the power on high, the contents of the blender splash out onto the walls and floor of the kitchen! Now what we have is one big mess that needs clearing up. So in a moment of panic we turn the power down and quickly put a lid on our blender. As good followers of Jesus we don't want to embarrass Him through our poor use of power. What started out as a joyful opportunity for wholesomeness and community flourishing turns into a mess where we isolate ourselves, turn down the power and spend our energies clearing up the mess.

> We don't want to embarrass Him
> through our poor use of power.

It was not meant to be like this. We should not be limiting God's power delegated to us. To have power, we think, is ungodly. This is an error. The *abuse* of power is ungodly. We recoil when our old sinful nature pops up with such force to surprise us. God's imagers on the planet are then disengaged, and this creates a vacuum that the worldly system moves in to fill. This is not what we were made for.

Remember, as disciples of Jesus, restored to our original created image-bearing capability, we were empowered for flourishing; for teeming, fruitful, multiplying abundance, to bring the whole creation to its fulfilment. What God wants is that when we grow more powerful, we are able to hold our capacity and manage it well.

Power, influence and success cause suspicion for many, and the Church has questioned historically the integrity of those who are successful. It's time to demolish this stronghold in ourselves, our business, Church and national culture. Father God wants a people who can be trusted with power, influence, money and success. It is a lie to believe that there is anything inherently wrong or evil with any of these. Our thinking has developed this way because those who have failed and have been powerful and influential have hit the headlines and been the subject of gossip and scandal. We need to be bigger than this. The Bible showcases godly men and women who were entrusted with His resources and huge responsibility, and who acted with integrity and faithfulness to bring flourishing to the community. Think of Abraham, Joseph, Moses, Joshua and Daniel in the Old Testament, and Lydia in the New Testament. The issue is the preparation of the person to ensure that the expression is of good fruit. Would you or I rather be around a successful and just person, or a person who fails to take responsibility for what God has given them to carry to extend His kingdom?

Father God made us in His image (Genesis 1:27). As a result, we love, we love being loved and we try to build community in His love. His love for us is fearless and furious. He loves us with such an intense love that with our invitation He simply burns up what is not of love. Our internal drivers are to keep finding community with our heavenly Father and with each other.

People seek to manipulate and control others by causing offence in order to keep them down. I believe that people do this because it validates their fears, insecurities, etc, and gives purpose to their broken lives. Father God did not make us that way. Exercising control and manipulation of others does not honour them. It fails to consciously acknowledge their competencies and gifts and what they bring to a situation or an organisation. Honouring others means that I work positively to bring out the best in them. I'm not making myself look good by holding others down. The real power in these relationships is demonstrated by the person who has been offended forgiving the offence. The abuse of power over someone which led to the offence is cancelled by the power of the offended person to forgive.

> Honouring others means that I work
> positively to bring out the best in them.

Taking on true power

Jesus, in His human form, lacked no power, and yet there is no way we could claim that He was on some 'power trip'. The apostle Paul describes Jesus as being meek (2 Corinthians 10:1, NKJV). Matthew 5:5 states that the meek 'will inherit the earth'. Psalm 37:11 says that 'the meek will inherit the land and enjoy peace and prosperity'. The meekness manifested by Jesus, and commended to followers of Jesus, is the fruit of humility and power. He was meek because He had the infinite resources of God at His command, but He was fully submitted to His Father. He did not exert His power in any way that could be described as abusive.

What a beautiful picture of how it's meant to be – full of godly, supernatural power and yet having a mature character and understanding of how this power is meant to be used and displayed. This riled the religious leaders of the day, who seemed to govern mainly by controlling others. Jesus failed to act according to the social norms of the culture of His day. Think how He respected and treated all people equitably: men, women, children, other ethnicities, sick and disabled, the demon-possessed. But when He saw injustice, abuse of power and other acts of the devil, He strongly brought to bear the power of God to confront and deal with the situation. If we are followers of Jesus, then we should also be described as meek.

Godly servanthood does not disempower us.

I believe that there is another balancing truth to be learned here. Servanthood has had a very bad press. That's because historically, in many nations' consciousness, it's been all about the abuse of power rather than the proper use of power. Godly servanthood does not disempower us. Jesus' example of washing feet (John 13:5) demonstrates that true humility is to honour and raise up others. He didn't lose His power when He washed the disciples' feet – He demonstrated how to use power effectively and in love. And that is a truth that underpins so much of what I believe lies at the heart of a kingdom entrepreneur.

How do we run a business, a church or an organisation according to its vision without the abuse of power and the resultant idolatry and injustice? How do I do this myself, and what about other principals and senior managers? It follows that first and foremost we need to examine ourselves and to honestly come before God and ask Him if we are faithfully and accurately exercising power according to His created order. As we restore ourselves by the grace of God to how we were meant to be, then we can set culture in the organisation according to the truth of the kingdom. We need to learn to step away from our preconceived mindsets and learn to think differently; to take on the 'mind of Christ' (1 Corinthians 2:16) and to reckon ourselves dead to sin and its effects, taking off our old coat that no longer fits us (the literal meaning of Ephesians 4:22 – the phrase 'putting off' means not wearing the old coat of sinful actions over the new self underneath). It's about learning to live as the new being that Christ made us in His death and resurrection.

God intends to add more and more to our lives because He trusts us. Stewardship, and everything else to which God calls us, is all about partnership. God wants partners to be like Him. He doesn't call us to do something without showing us how to do it Himself. He doesn't simply ask me to trust Him – He trusts me! Many times, God has to dismantle lies that we believe about Him and ourselves, which have shaped our thoughts, beliefs and attitudes, so that He can develop the pure gold that He has placed in our lives.

> God intends to add more and more to our lives because He trusts us.

Pause, pray, practise

- Pause: Do I properly recognise the power God has given me? What is this power to be used for?

- Pray: Father, please show me where I have abused the power that You have invested in me.

- Pray: If Father God shows you where you did this, then ask for His forgiveness, and ask the Holy Spirit to fill you and help you change your behaviour. Apologise to the person/people involved and ask for their forgiveness.

- Practise: How can I put safeguards in place, and what are they, to ensure that I don't misuse power?

- Practise: Remember that servant-hearted leadership doesn't disempower or embarrass us. It's doing what Jesus did. Is there something that I can do today that blesses others with no expectation of reward or return for myself?

11
Contending

Key points

- Success and flourishing are not handed to us on a plate – contending for them is often necessary.

- Faith properly positioned when persevering helps us to stand well when we've done everything.

Start by doing what's necessary; then do what's possible; and suddenly you are doing the impossible.
(St Francis of Assisi)[53]

The crucible for silver and the furnace for gold,
but the LORD tests the heart.
(Proverbs 17:3)

Life is not an equation. Perhaps one day some mathematician will work one out, but I'm sure it would have many variables! Life is a journey. It has a definite start, and in purely physical terms it has a definite end.

We don't set out on a journey without knowing the destination. We either know the route or we will have set our satnav to get us there. Perhaps you, like a lot of

---

[53] www.azquotes.com/quote/11880 (accessed 28th January 2021).

people, me included, have dutifully followed the satnav directions to find yourself directed to a farm gate with a route across a field, or down a single-track country lane with no passing points. What's the moral of this story? There are occasions when we get into a situation on our journey which we find uncomfortable and perhaps really stressful. It seems like we're in unknown or unplanned territory which isn't on our grid of expectations or experience. How we navigate these situations is really important to make sure we come through them with a good heart.

In our entrepreneurship, as in life, we suffer trials. James writes:

> Consider it pure joy, my brothers and sisters, whenever you face trials of many kinds, because you know that the testing of your faith produces perseverance. Let perseverance finish its work so that you may be mature and complete, not lacking anything.
> (James 1:2-4)

And Peter writes:

> In all this you greatly rejoice, though now for a little while you may have had to suffer grief in all kinds of trials. These have come so that the proven genuineness of your faith – of greater worth than gold, which perishes even though refined by fire – may result in praise, glory and honour when Jesus Christ is revealed.
> (1 Peter 1:6-7)

God is good, kind and loving; He is for us and not against us! He's also committed to us persevering in faith so that we may be mature disciples, being fruitful in our ministry and witness, and as a result bringing glory and honour to Jesus. There is no conflict between the two. Any loving and devoted father or mother teaches and corrects their children so that they may grow up well balanced and become great members of society. Suffering and trials should be viewed through this lens.

> God disciplines us for our good, in order that we may share in his holiness. No discipline seems pleasant at the time, but painful. Later on, however, it produces a harvest of righteousness and peace for those who have been trained by it. (Hebrews 12:10-11)

Faith properly positioned

Living in faith is not a recipe for an easy lifestyle. Barriers, obstacles and opposition in the earthly and heavenly realms need to be brought down by the authority given to us in Jesus Christ. They don't move without us exercising our authority in faith.

As entrepreneurs we are called to lead in the market realm, to demonstrate redemptiveness, compassion and love while running an enterprise. Doing this undoubtedly requires – yes, even demands – that we live in faith, exercising our God-given authority. I used to get frustrated when people I talked with who were 'living by faith' thought being an entrepreneur was different! The work that our clients commissioned paid our staff and suppliers, and we made profit, all by faith! The idea that we were not living by faith showed a lack of understanding of the challenges faced by the kingdom entrepreneur.

Here's what I have learned so far about faith and its application. Much of this is based on what the writer to the Hebrews sets out in chapter 11.

- Faith has 'confidence' and 'assurance' – it is not ephemeral;

- it provides the legal right to possess those things that 'we hope for' (the definition of 'hope' is the expectation of good);

- it is the evidence of those things that we hope for but do not yet see with our physical eyes; it is peering ahead in our spirits into heavenly places to see what is yet to come;

- it is not a formula but a relationship with the Trinity;

- it is supported and nourished in a believing community of faith-filled people.

Remember that 'faith comes from hearing the message, and the message is heard through the word about Christ' (Romans 10:17). Faith hears the promise and grasps the hope planted in our spirits. Presumption is based on wishful thinking. Being certain that we have received faith and are not living in presumption will save us much discouragement and possible rejection.

And what of the place of prophecy in navigating to
our destination? God speaks to encourage us, to cheer
us on and to assure us of His love, grace and favour.
Prophecy is given to express God's heart and intent. I had
to learn that because God speaks it does not necessarily
mean that 'it will come to pass'. We pray and bring it into
our world. It is partnering with God to hear, pray, act and
possess while staying positioned in the place of rest and
not toil. We can and should contend from the place of
peace and rest. All authority has been given to Jesus Christ
(Matthew 28:18). That is done and nothing can undo it. We
are to reinforce that authority on earth.

Faith in perspective

The truth is that faith is always fruitful, but it may not
always produce the fruit that we expect. Sometimes we are
forging the way for others to inherit and follow. For
example:

- Abraham waited twenty-five years for his son
  (Genesis 12:4; 21:5);

- Moses journeyed for forty years and didn't reach the
  promised land, but Joshua did – the person he
  mentored (Joshua 5:6; Deuteronomy 3:28);

- David didn't build the temple, but his son Solomon
  did (1 Chronicles 22:6-10);

134

- Many prophets didn't see the Messiah come, but they saw Him from afar (eg Isaiah 9:6-7).

You may recall people in similar situations that you know or have heard of. Whatever happens, faith sees and receives what is ours to come. Mentoring others and passing on our legacy is such an important part of our journey. We pass on, encourage and lead those following us to stand on our shoulders. Pioneers of faith are well placed to equip the next generation to produce greater fruit.

We only see in part and not with the full picture as God sees. We should keep pursuing God, brush ourselves down, freshen our relationship with the Father, Jesus and the Holy Spirit and be renewed in faith again. We're in the good company of pioneers who were commended by God. Note what the writer to the Hebrews says:

> Therefore, since we are surrounded by such a great cloud of witnesses, let us throw off everything that hinders and the sin that so easily entangles. And let us run with perseverance the race marked out for us, fixing our eyes on Jesus, the pioneer and perfecter of faith.
> (Hebrews 12:1-2)

Perseverance

So, we know God's calling, we have His Word planted in our hearts, our enterprise is flourishing, we have the assurance of God's encouragement, and the order book is full. Great! But cash flow begins to cripple investment and staff development. I often heard it said that cash flow is king. I dispute that because Jesus is King! However, cash flow is very important and needs to be treated seriously. There are companies who have had full order books but have had to declare bankruptcy because the business ran out of cash and the creditors would offer no further support to them.

I've been at the place where cash-flow problems had a serious impact on the business, more than once. In fact, for periods of time we were in a position where we were operating at full capacity but as much as 25-30 per cent of our debtor value was unpaid within credit terms. This seriously hampered us. Our clients were mainly global enterprises and large corporations, and we were very small in comparison. Many agreed reasonable payment cycles, but then some flagrantly ignored them! We had one large organisation write to us to advise us without warning or discussion that they were unilaterally prolonging their terms from sixty days (which was already a difficulty to us) to ninety days. This was crippling! We had to consider carefully whether to advise them that in those circumstances we could no longer work with them.

We were fortunate, and favoured, to have many clients, and we were able to ride cash-flow problems in this way. I still had to make some difficult calls to our bank when we had to pay our employees and payments had not come in. I thank God that we had a supportive bank manager who saw our value and what we were achieving. By God's grace they agreed to temporarily extend our overdraft facility every time to get us over the problem. We also had an accounts manager who worked hard to address cash-flow issues, with some success. I had a few trustworthy friends who prayed with us to see this situation turned around, and I developed a prayer style to address the situation. To be honest, sometimes the prayer had more desperation than faith, but I never doubted God's goodness. It went along the lines of, 'Father, this is Your provision for me/us; it belongs to me and not my debtor/s. I release any and all obstructions and blockages. Please work in and through computer systems and software and internal arrangements, and please deal with people holding up payment. I ask that You send angels to bring in the overdue money. I receive this is the name of Jesus.'

Contending is a part of the life of an entrepreneur. We can't ignore obstacles that we have to face through fear, self-doubt, wounds or passivity inherited from our unregenerate nature. They won't just go away if we close our eyes and pretend they don't exist. They are raised up to oppose what God is doing. Our position is to enforce the victory of Jesus using the authority that He delegated to us. There were occasions when I felt that I had done everything that I could and I was simply holding my ground and refusing to let go.

> Contending is a part of the life of an entrepreneur.

In such times, Paul's instruction to the church in Ephesus is so helpful:

> Be strong in the Lord and in his mighty power.
> Put on the full armour of God, so that you can

take your stand against the devil's schemes. For our struggle is not against flesh and blood, but against the rulers, against the authorities, against the powers of this dark world and against the spiritual forces of evil in the heavenly realms. Therefore put on the full armour of God, so that when the day of evil comes, you may be able to stand your ground, and after you have done everything, to stand … And pray in the Spirit on all occasions with all kinds of prayers and requests.

(Ephesians 6:10-13, 18)

Having done everything we can, we stand. We are thrown wholly onto the mercy and grace of God to see us through. We can do nothing else except stand to hold our ground and watch to see God's salvation. It can be so frustrating for the personality type who is a 'doer', but we'll have done everything. We are surrendered entrepreneurs. We don't earn our salvation; we receive it purely by God's grace. As Dallas Willard says, and I paraphrase, God's grace does not excuse us from endeavour, but it is against us working to try to earn salvation.[54]

Prayer partners

I found it very helpful to have a small band of people praying for me and the enterprise. They were mature followers of Jesus whom I respected, and I valued their input. I gave them permission to speak into my life, and I

[54] Dallas Willard, *The Great Omission* (Oxford: Monarch Books, 2014), p61.

prayerfully weighed up what they brought to me. I strongly encourage you to do the same, and I believe you will be blessed.

Pause, pray, practise

- Pause: Are there obstacles standing resolutely in the way on the path of what God has called you to?

- Pray: Ask the Holy Spirit to empower you, encourage you and support you. Is He saying anything to you, or showing you anything? Receive His grace and favour!

- Practise: Are you prepared to contend, pray and stand for God's kingdom to come and be done[55] so that these obstacles are moved out of the way? Are there others who can join you or support you?

---

[55] See Matthew 6:10.

12
Success and Failure

Key points

- We need to set our grid for success and failure according to a kingdom mindset.

- Should we have better terms than 'success' and 'failure', ones that encapsulate the journey as well as the outcome?

I have not failed. I've just found 10,000 ways that won't work.
(Thomas Edison)[56]

Counsel and sound judgment are mine;
I have insight, I have power.
(Proverbs 8:14)

In Helsingborg in Sweden, there is, originally, a Museum of Failure.[57] Ironically, it proved to be popular! There is now an exhibit in Los Angeles and in Paris housing more

---

[56] www.goodreads.com/author/show/3091287.Thomas_A_Edison (accessed 27th January 2021).

[57] The collection can be seen at: collection.museumoffailure.com (accessed 22nd February 2021).

than seventy failed products from around the world. The full collection can be seen on its website. The purpose of the museum is actually to highlight the role of failure in the risky business of product innovation.[58]

In a kingdom worldview, what is entrepreneurial success and failure?

Failure is an interesting event. It can be traumatic, evoking a range of emotions – frustration, anger, repentance, etc – but its real usefulness is as a way of learning. These emotions place us beyond the limit of our own resourcefulness and cause us to re-evaluate what we are doing. These are places we wouldn't choose to be, but they can be places we *need* to get to.

Success teaches us what we are good at, and contributes to us understanding our God-given gifts, capabilities and skills. It builds confidence. However, failure is also an excellent teacher. As Nick Tatchell says, our impulse when we fail is to retreat and lick our wounds, but we need to resist this; rather, we present our failure to God, who is both full of grace and faithful.[59]

Failure can be defined as not meeting the results that we expect or want. It disempowers the thinking that failure is to do with personal failing. I'm not talking here about what we could call 'moral failure', but about entrepreneurial failure. It helps us to disassociate

---

[58] For further information see the TEDxCluj presentation 'Failure is an Excellent Teacher' by Rebecca Ribbing,
www.youtube.com/embed/RI9FjqBwqEc (accessed 14th January 2021).

[59] 'Failing, to Grow', LICC, licc.org.uk/resources/failing-grow/ (accessed 22nd February 2021).

ourselves from the supposed correlation between an outcome not being fully achieved and being a failure, that you're not good enough and that you should give up.

Henry Ford famously said, 'Failure is simply the opportunity to begin again, this time more intelligently.'[60]

Proverbs 16:1-3 says:

> To humans belong the plans of the heart,
> but from the LORD comes the proper answer of
> the tongue.
> All a person's ways seem pure to them,
> but motives are weighed by the LORD.
> Commit to the LORD whatever you do,
> and he will establish your plans.

Or as The Passion Translation says:

> Before you do anything,
> put your trust totally in God and not in
> yourself.
> Then every plan you make will succeed.

As entrepreneurs we need to have our goals firmly set on achieving the desired result, which is the calling that God has placed on our lives. Nobody sets out as an entrepreneur to fail. You don't want to bring a novel service or a niche product to the market, put so much of yourself into it with the intention of failing! US statistics show that of new businesses started in 2011, just under

---

[60] Henry Ford Quotes. BrainyQuote.com, BrainyMedia Inc, 2021, www.brainyquote.com/quotes/henry_ford_121339 (accessed 27th January 2021).

one-third of new businesses failed after three years and about 50 per cent after five years, with just over one-third still active in 2020.[61] UK data shows that about 13 per cent of business failed every year between 2014 to 2019.[62] That means that success requires persistence, learning from mistakes, putting them right, brushing ourselves down and moving forward again.

> Nobody sets out as an entrepreneur to
> fail.

Businesses and organisations need to make profit. That's true whether you run a for-profit or not-for-profit. That's a given. There needs to be profit for investment, for research and development and so on and, depending on your business type, a return to investors and shareholders. So when I talk about success and failure, profitability is always a key indicator. Businesses and enterprises fail if they are not profitable. How quickly they fail depends on financial reserves and the willingness of investors, shareholders and lenders to keep the business trading. Another key factor is cash flow, which I wrote about earlier.

---

[61] 'Table 7. Survival of private sector establishments by opening year', US Bureau of Labor Statistics,
www.bls.gov/bdm/us_age_naics_00_table7.txt (accessed 22nd February 2021).
[62] 'Business demography, UK: 2019', Office for National Statistics, www.ons.gov.uk/businessindustryandtrade/business/activitysizeandl ocation/bulletins/businessdemography/2019 (accessed 22nd February 2021).

Metrics and key performance indicators are vital for any type of business. How else will we know whether the business is profitable, how profitable, whether the business is cash solvent, where new orders are coming from and what's in the sales pipeline? These are tools to help us to target success and prevent failure.

Reflections on success and failure

Was Jesus a failure, or did He succeed? It seems a blasphemous, or at least strange, question, but take a look at the end of His earthly ministry:

- He was crucified as a blaspheming villain.

- All His closest followers left Him, or at best, all but a few did.

- His 'movement' appeared to have died out.

If you had viewed this on the day of the crucifixion, the answer would most probably have been, 'He failed.' But of course, we know differently. Now we can look and say that He was extraordinarily successful! We can look at how we're doing one day and things might seem pretty desperate, but when we look back some years later that seeming failure has been turned to great success.

Was the apostle Paul a failure, or did he succeed? He, with a few other helpers, spread the message of Jesus throughout much of the Roman Empire, established churches in centres of commercial influence, and replicated himself wherever he went. Great success! But at what cost?

> Five times I received from the Jews the forty lashes minus one. Three times I was beaten with rods, once I was pelted with stones, three times I was shipwrecked, I spent a night and a day in the open sea, I have been constantly on the move. I have been in danger from rivers, in danger from bandits, in danger from my fellow Jews, in danger from Gentiles; in danger in the city, in danger in the country, in danger at sea; and in danger from false believers. I have laboured and toiled and have often gone without sleep; I have known hunger and thirst and have often gone without food; I have been cold and naked. Besides everything else, I face daily the pressure of my concern for all the churches.
> (2 Corinthians 11:24-28)

In many places he had to work as a tentmaker to support his ministry (Acts 18:3). He didn't have a strong ministry support base. Is this success, or would we view these results of our ministry in terms of our personal distress to be a mark of failure?

Is persecution a sign of success in the kingdom?

> Blessed are those who are persecuted because of righteousness,

for theirs is the kingdom of heaven.

Blessed are you when people insult you, persecute you and falsely say all kinds of evil against you because of me. Rejoice and be glad, because great is your reward in heaven.

(Matthew 5:10-12)

Or in The Passion Translation:

How enriched you are when you bear the wounds of being persecuted for doing what is right! For that is when you experience the realm of heaven's kingdom. How ecstatic you can be when people insult and persecute you and speak all kinds of cruel lies about you because of your love for me! So, leap for joy – since your heavenly reward is great.

In Aramaic, the language that Jesus spoke when He said these words, 'blessed' means 'enriched, happy, fortunate, delighted, blissful, content, blessed' (TPT).[63] It means to have the capacity to enjoy union and communion with God. Surely this is success in the kingdom of God! Accolades from our peers and contemporaries are great, and welcome, but an accolade from our heavenly Father is so much better! 'Well done, good and faithful servant' (Matthew 25:21) is surely the best accolade we can receive.

---

[63] Footnote to Matthew 5:3.

What's God's return on investment in us?

The parable of the talents can be summarised as managing well what has been entrusted to us by God – providing God with a good return in terms of fruitfulness.

> His master replied, 'Well done, good and faithful servant! You have been faithful with a few things; I will put you in charge of many things. Come and share your master's happiness!'
> (Matthew 25:21)

The one who gave to God a good return on investment was praised, and the bigger the return the better! God loves us to use effort to produce fruitfulness. That has been the case since we were first positioned in the Garden of Eden.

Is success, then, living life well, flourishing in life?

> Let love and faithfulness never leave you;
> bind them round your neck,
> write them on the tablet of your heart.
> Then you will win favour and a good name
> in the sight of God and man.
> (Proverbs 3:3-4)

Would it be better to have new terms instead of 'success' and 'failure'? Perhaps fruitfulness?

There can be fruitfulness metrics in terms of providing a good return to our heavenly Father. What about 'prospering', as in 3 John 2: 'Beloved friend, I pray that you are prospering in every way and that you continually enjoy good health, just as your soul is prospering' (TPT), or perhaps, 'flourishing'?

Flourishing anticipates fruitfulness.

I favour flourishing because it encapsulates Jesus' phrase about abundant life (John 10:10) but acknowledges that life includes trials, which are endured, and perseverance, which some seasons of life require. Flourishing doesn't deny that life can at times be tough, and can include failure, but it does suggest that all of life can be lived by the grace and favour of God, and with the reality at all times that God is good – 'in all things God works for the good of those who love him, who have been called according to his purpose' (Romans 8:28) – and that we live in union with Christ, a son or daughter of our heavenly Father, unconditionally loved. In this truth we live in a heavenly environment where we grow and live in a healthy and vigorous way. I think that flourishing anticipates fruitfulness. God's blessing over us was to 'be fruitful and increase in number' (Genesis 1:28). He repeated it to Noah (Genesis 8:17), Isaac repeated it to Jacob (Genesis 28:3), and God repeated it to Jacob (Genesis 35:11). Jesus expects fruitfulness as we 'remain' in him (John 15:5), and so we will show ourselves be His disciples (John 15:8). As the apostle Paul wrote:

> But the fruit of the Spirit is love, joy, peace, forbearance, kindness, goodness, faithfulness, gentleness and self-control. Against such things there is no law.
> (Galatians 5:22-23)

Or as expressed in The Passion Translation:

> But the fruit produced by the Holy Spirit
> within you is divine love in all its varied
> expressions:
> joy *that overflows,*
> peace *that subdues,*
> patience *that endures,*
> kindness *in action,*
> a life full of virtue,
> faith *that prevails,*
> gentleness *of heart,* and
> strength *of spirit.*
> Never set the law above these qualities, for
> they are meant to be limitless.

How do we measure success, and learn from failure?

Success and failure are generally not binary, while accepting that ultimately failure is the business going into administration or bankruptcy. My conviction is that, above all, a successful kingdom entrepreneur is one who creates an environment for those with whom we personally associate to encounter God for themselves, for the kingdom to come to them. But then there are many other expressions of the kingdom that can be considered as success:

- providing products or services that bless your customers, making life easier for them;

- providing employment for people who have found it difficult to hold down jobs;

- committing to give a percentage of your profit to charity/good causes;

- training young people, or those of mature age, in new skills for their improved employability;

- being an influencer in a specific market sector;

- bringing to market a new product or service that provides a countercultural (ie kingdom culture) viewpoint or influence, for example, setting new standards in code of conduct in terms of employment, pay and employee well-being;

- fashion brands that do not sexualise the wearer, etc;

- promoting a novel approach that motivates people to take action on environmental protection, or health and medical care;

- being cultural ambassadors, social policymakers or representatives of the people in the 'corridors of power';

- and so on!

My experience

In my own experience of founding and running a vibrant consultancy, there were times in growing the business I could see from analysing our growth in clients that recruiting key personnel at a very senior level was becoming very important. Otherwise we would quickly reach a point where we were saturated with the client work we had and would be unable to continue to grow. I sensed God prompting me to act and I set out to implement this growth strategy.

The first phase was to bring in another director, or very senior associate, who would grow the business with me and add value. My first attempt partially succeeded but ultimately failed. We found out that the model we were trying to adopt for the growth was not sustainable in the long term. As a result, I talked with someone I had known for some years and, following detailed discussion and negotiation, he became a director, allowing us to open an office in the south of England, and this became very successful.

Together we then sought to add an office in Scotland, staffed by a principal consultant. We'd been successful in winning a number of contracts there and as a result staff, including the principals, were finding it necessary to commute to Scotland. This was OK in the short term but was not the right long-term model. On the third attempt to recruit we found a person with the right skills base. Within a couple of years, we had three consultants working mainly with clients in Scotland and the north of England.

We needed to see the long-term goal and not be put off by the short-term failure to implement the strategy. Finding the right people was the key for growth. It would have been wasted effort to have tried to grow without these individuals in place.

Keeping a healthy perspective

So, my experience is that success and failure are not single events and should never be viewed over the short term. In cultures that anticipate swift returns on investment, I suggest that there can be conflicts between what God releases to us and what our investors anticipate or expect.

What timescale do we set to achieve success? Is it solely in terms of return on investment, meeting sales targets and so on? These are important, particularly where the business is funded by investors who are looking for their return. I was fortunate in that the businesses had grown organically, and we didn't need to approach 'business angels'[64] or investors. But taking steps that seem to fail is all part of learning how to succeed. My approach in running the businesses was that I was CEO, but God was Chair of the Board! His Lordship had to be relevant to the businesses as much as it was in my personal life. It wasn't right to segregate different aspects of life; either I was following Jesus or I wasn't!

> What timescale do we set to achieve success?

What we see as failure may well not be how God sees it. He is more interested in the process to build our character. As the famous US basketball coach John Wooden says, it is our character that we need to

---

[64] A person who provides capital for the development of a business, typically a small or medium-sized enterprise, in exchange for shares in the business.

concentrate on and not our status in life. The former is who we are while the latter is how others perceive us.[65]

On that day when we give an account of our lives to God (Romans 14:12), what will we say? Will it be, 'I earned lots of money for You, I supported this ministry and that mission, and this church and that work'? That's commendable, and laudable, and it is an expression of the kingdom of God that we have entered. But the challenge is, did we also create an environment in us and around us, in our spheres of influence, for people to encounter God for themselves and for the kingdom of God to be demonstrated by us 'on earth as it is in heaven' (Matthew 6:10)? That surely is true fruitfulness and success.

Pause, pray, practise

- Pause: How do you define success and failure in a kingdom worldview?

- Pray: Ask the Holy Spirit to lead you 'into all the truth' (John 16:13), and honestly consider whether you need to realign yourself to God's call and purposes for your life.

- Practise: What do you feel about personal and corporate success and failure in the context of discipleship? Is your thinking linked to your identity? If so, consider asking for relevant ministry.

---

[65] John Wooden with Jack Tobin, *They Call Me Coach* (NY: McGraw-Hill Education, 2003).

13
Beacons in a Broken World

Key points

- God's love shining through us must have the highest priority in our lives.

- Through our transformative and redemptive actions we can bring more godly justice, order and beauty to a broken world.

Darkness cannot drive out darkness; only light can do that. Hate cannot drive out hate; only love can do that.[66]

Arise, shine, for your light has come,
and the glory of the LORD rises upon you.
(Isaiah 60:1)

God's love is the most important thing, the pinnacle of the expression of Himself, the most compelling of all. As the Gospel writer John says, 'For God so loved the world that he gave his one and only Son, that whoever believes in him shall not perish but have eternal life' (John 3:16). This is

---

[66] Used in a BBC online teaching article on Martin Luther King, www.bbc.co.uk/programmes/articles/hwpZlYldr75hclw0bYL0Xb/martin-luther-king (accessed 27th January 2021).

His only Son, the Son whom He loved perfectly, to restore you and me to full communion with the Father, and humankind to the fullness of the beautiful order and symmetry of life 'in the Garden'. John put it a different way in his first letter: 'This is love: not that we loved God, but that he loved us and sent his Son as an atoning sacrifice for our sins' (1 John 4:10). He initiated love and we love because He loves us.

God's love in us and shining out of us must have the highest priority in our lives and be the motivation, even the compulsion, for our purpose as a kingdom entrepreneur. 'Wait,' you say, 'that sounds like legalism.' I disagree. It must be love that compels us, His love pulsing in our lives and bursting out through our expression of entrepreneurship. It is a natural consequence of King Jesus living in us and through us and of being filled with the Holy Spirit.

Jesus reiterated that love is the first and foremost commandment: 'Love the Lord your God with every passion of your heart, with all the energy of your being, and with every thought that is within you', with the second commandment following close behind: 'love your friend in the same way you love yourself' (Matthew 22:37, 39, TPT). Love is the great and 'beautiful prize for which you run' (1 Corinthians 13:13, TPT).

I could go on with similar Bible verses, but I hope the point is clear. Loving God with all of our being means that all of His being shines through, as He delights to display Himself to a broken world.

The Spanish reformer and mystic Teresa of Ávila said:

Christ has no body now but yours. No hands, no feet on earth but yours. Yours are the eyes through which he looks compassion on this world. Yours are the feet with which he walks to do good. Yours are the hands through which he blesses all the world. Yours are the hands, yours are the feet, yours are the eyes, you are his body. Christ has no body now on earth but yours.[67]

We who know the power of Christ's redemption and the restoration of what was lost are the very people that God has called to 'the ministry of reconciliation' (2 Corinthians 5:18) by being His hands, His feet, His eyes, a community who express the love of God through redemptive acts.

What does redemptive action look like? I suggest that it can take many forms, but it is the embodiment of God's love to a broken and hurting humanity, and caring for the world in a way that does not subdue it to the point of destroying its capacity for future abundance. We are those who collaborate with His vision of wise order and glorious beauty and justice. It starts by loving the one in front of us. We need only to look at the fledgling Church in the New Testament to realise that the first social action undertaken by them was to take care of the poor and to create resources to do so (Acts 6:1-3; 2 Corinthians 8:1-7).

The kingdom entrepreneur embraces a holistic mindset in considering the totality of the witness of the enterprise by working redemptively. Such a mindset includes both personal and corporate conduct. All the wisdom of God is

---

[67] www.goodreads.com/quotes/66880-christ-has-no-body-now-but-yours-no-hands-no (accessed 28th January 2021).

available to us. Wisdom shows us how we can be a people of love in everything that we do in and through our enterprises. Through our creativity we can bring more godly justice, order and beauty to broken places, even though ultimately it will be only when Jesus returns to this earth that all of creation will be fully restored (Revelation 21:1-5).

> We can bring more godly justice, order and beauty to broken places.

We may think that this understanding is new to us, but we would be mistaken. We can see this demonstrated in the Bible. For example, God instructed His people in the agrarian economy in which they lived not to reap as they harvested to the very edges of their field or to 'gather the gleanings' of their harvest, but to 'leave them for the poor and for the foreigner' living among them (Leviticus 23:22). This is equivalent to not maximising our profit but distributing a percentage of it to the poor.

A brief social history shows that redemptive entrepreneurism is not new.

The Quaker entrepreneurs

In the eighteenth and nineteenth centuries, the British Quakers (Society of Friends) strongly influenced the blending of entrepreneurship and redemptive action. For them, the spirit of a business was not in the balance sheet, but in the different decisions taken by those heading up the enterprises. As Deborah Cadbury, the author and descendant of the famous Cadbury dynasty, comments, it was not the amassing of belongings and assets that was their primary focus in their business vision, but rather their spiritual riches.[68] Their entrepreneurship is to be viewed through the lens of the Victorian age, when business failure and bankruptcy could lead to the debtor's prison or the workhouse. Despite these awful consequences for personal bankruptcy, in the early nineteenth century, around 4,000 Quaker families in Great Britain ran seventy-four banks and more than 200 companies.

Although Quakers comprised only 0.2 per cent of the population, men (as it was in those days) such as Richard Cadbury and his grandsons Richard and George, Joseph Rowntree, Francis and Joseph Fry (all chocolate businesses), Sirius and James Clark (footwear), Jesse Boot (pharmacies) and Titus Salt (textile milling), a Congressionalist rather than a Quaker, established very profitable enterprises that devoted large proportions of their profit to substantially bettering working conditions for their employees, including building housing developments and providing free healthcare, education and libraries, works outings to the coast, a pension fund, and food and entertainment in deprived areas around their communities. Boot's concern for the poor led him to develop affordable medicines. These men gave away much of their wealth in their lifetimes, or gave endowments to foundations, such as the Joseph Rowntree Foundation, which remains active today in Britain.

For these Quakers and many others who followed, their love for God and for their fellow humans brought a

---

[68] Deborah Cadbury, *Chocolate Wars* (London: HarperPress, 2010), p5.

transformational element into their entrepreneurship, which created a true alternative based on kingdom values to the prevailing business culture.

Later entrepreneurs

While the Quakers were great role models, there are many others who followed in their footsteps. Catherine Booth, the co-founder of the Salvation Army, is one. Raised with a strict evangelical upbringing by her mother, and then inspired by the works of John Wesley and Charles Finney, she raised her eight children while supporting her husband, William. She gave many speeches, and eventually persuaded William that she should preach, an unusual act at the time. It is reported that she won many converts.[69]

It was while working with the poor in London that she found out about 'sweated labour' – women and children working in terrible conditions for long hours with pay just a little more than one-fifth of their male counterparts. She and a colleague led a campaign against the use of noxious yellow phosphorus for women making matches and working sixteen hours a day. In 1890, the Salvation Army opened its own match-making factory using harmless red phosphorus and paid their workers twice that paid by the dominant matchmaker of the day.[70]

---

[69] www.salvationarmy.org.uk/catherine-booth (accessed 14th December 2020).

[70] https://spartacus-educational.com/Wbooth.htm (accessed 14th December 2020).

John Laing took over his father's regional house-building business and over the years transformed it into a national construction company. He committed his life to Christ at the age of seven, went to university and then entered and later took over the family business. He was known to be extremely generous and gave large sums to many Christian causes, often anonymously. He was one of the first employers in the construction industry to introduce paid holidays, and although he could be tough in reprimanding poor behaviour, he granted time off for employees in difficult circumstances, or provided them with financial support. He provided funding for the London Bible College (now the London School of Theology).

There were other entrepreneurs in the twentieth century who adopted similar redemptive actions, but these serve to illustrate that embracing such actions in entrepreneurship is not new. There are many fine exemplars in the here and now of kingdom entrepreneurs who through their enterprises are witnesses to the kingdom come now in the measure that it has while pointing to the fullness of the kingdom that is to come. We are not perfect in these actions, but we are faithfully witnessing to what will come, and the way that it will be when Jesus returns to earth and God again will say everything is 'very good' (Genesis 1:31).

Current exemplars of kingdom entrepreneurship

The difficulty with highlighting current examples is that I will be missing many entrepreneurs who are following the same path. Please forgive me for these omissions. While I am aware of these enterprises, I do not know the entrepreneurs personally. I have researched them to be able to give the reader practical examples of what seem to me to be expressions of God's transformative and redemptive love through kingdom people operating kingdom-focused enterprises.

In the US, the Hignell Group of Companies[71] provides property development services and management. It sets out on its website its principles and beliefs, which include valuing relationship with God, 'Honoring and Encouraging One Another', 'Unwavering Integrity' and 'Uncommon Generosity'. It states that the company is both 'Spirit Led and Empowered', and says that those who run the company seek to live transformed lives in their internal and external spheres of influence.

Jetta Company Ltd,[72] a major Hong Kong-based toy manufacturer with production facilities in mainland China, says that its employees are its most valuable assets. Further, it says that the company regards its customers as partners while aiming to be their best supplier. It claims that it is committed to being a responsible employer and

---

[71] www.hignell.com/why-hignell/mission-values-vision (accessed 15th December 2020).

[72] www.jetta.com.hk/index.php/company/our-philosophy (accessed 15th December 2020).

corporation; its objective is to create 'prosperity and opportunity for others', and to contribute to the well-being of its stakeholders.

The Equal Justice Initiative,[73] an Alabama-based free, non-profit law practice founded by the multi-award-winning lawyer Bryan Stevenson, works to end mass incarceration, excessive punishment and racial inequality in the US, and to protect basic human rights for the most vulnerable people in American society. For an inspiring presentation of their work see his TEDx talk.[74]

The Entertainer[75] is the UK's fastest-growing family-owned high street toy retailer operating 163 stores, an e-commerce business and a growing international business. Founded by Gary Grant, the group's executive chair, and branded 'the Christian toyshop entrepreneur', he is well known for not opening its stores on Sundays, knowing that in so doing the company loses revenue and profit. It states on its website that it is committed to acting ethically and with integrity in its business relationships, and that neither the business nor its supply chain is involved in

---

[73] christiansforsocialaction.org/resource/connecting-with-the-struggle/ (accessed 16th January 2021).

[74] 'We need to talk about an injustice', www.ted.com/talks/bryan_stevenson_we_need_to_talk_about_an_injustice?language=en#t-43407 (accessed 16th January 2021).

[75] 'An open and shut case: Meet the top–shop entrepreneur who puts Christian values before profit', *Independent*, www.independent.co.uk/news/business/news/open-and-shut-case-meet-toy-shop-entrepreneur-who-puts-christian-values-profit-9020224.html. 'Modern Slavery Statement 2018/19', tinyurl.com/v3uah5wt (accessed 15th March 2021).

slavery or human trafficking. It donates 10 per cent of its profits every year to charity.

Julian Richer,[76] previously the sole owner of the UK chain of stores Richer Sounds, decided to turn his enterprise into an employee-owned business by gifting 60 per cent of his shares to his employees as a thank-you bonus. The company was already known for donating 15 per cent of its profits to a number of charities and says it is founded on decency, truthfulness and honesty in its activities. In 2013 it was reported that he had written into his will the plan to hand shares to his employees after his death.

Cook[77] is a UK retail brand providing 'remarkable food for your freezer' with eighty shops, half-franchised, half-owned, and with a rapidly growing online delivery business. It says that it makes a point of investing in its people and its communities, and has a commitment not to use processed food. The business was founded in 1997 with the belief that there was a better way than pursuing profits above all else, and this remains its principle. It says that from its foundation its objective was to create a company that was good for shareholders and for everyone who comes into contact with it.[78]

---

[76] 'Richer Sounds staff to get windfall as founder hands over shares', BBC News, www.bbc.co.uk/news/business-48269171 (accessed 16th January 2021).

[77] www.cookfood.net/info/Nourishing-Relationships/ (accessed 16th January 2021).

[78] For details of the wide range of benefits to employees see: https://cook.blob.core.windows.net/downloads/benefits_of_Cook_201 6_printable_atoffice[1].pdf (accessed 16th January 2021).

Interstate Batteries,[79] a leading US brand with more than 150,000 dealer locations and 1,400 team members, states that the company's purpose is to bring glory to God and to enhance people's lives, while providing 'the most trustworthy source of power'. It goes on to say that it fulfils its purpose by doing business based on biblical principles in a way that is welcoming and expresses love to everyone.

IMGroup[80] is a family owned importer and distributor of vehicles in the UK and Europe. It states that its purpose is to build a group of successful businesses that is profitable and sustainable. It is clear that its success and resources are used for good in the world, in accordance with its Christian faith and values. It funds two charities – the Grace Foundation, whose mission it states is to transform young people's lives through 'holistic education', and Christian Vision, with more than 350 staff working on initiatives to share the Christian message, and which supports in-country mission-worker programmes.

Timpson Group,[81] with more than 1,600 stores in the UK and Ireland specialising in shoe care, signage, engraving, cleaning and photographic services, has a policy of recruiting 10 per cent of its workforce from ex-

[79] www.interstatebatteries.com/about/our-culture (accessed 16th January 2021).
[80] www.imgroup.co.uk/about-us/values/ (accessed 16th January 2021).
[81] www.timpson.co.uk/about/careers-at-timpson (accessed 16th January 2021).

offenders.[82] It states that it aims to 'act with integrity and transparency in all tax matters', and to pay its fair share of taxes on time. It reports that the company was one of the first businesses in the UK to adopt the National Living Wage, although it states that most of its employees earn a lot more than that because of its unlimited bonus scheme. Its employee benefits include a branch bonus scheme, free use of holiday homes, wedding gift, financial incentive to stop smoking, match funding of charitable gifts, provision of a mental health counsellor, a hardship fund and interest-free crisis loans in emergencies, gifts towards maternity wear and a day off for a child's first-ever day at school, and colleague discounts of up to 90 per cent.

Be generous, but be realistic

There are many inspiring stories here. Whether you already have a business, whatever model this takes, or are considering starting one, then you are probably thinking, 'What can I do?' Above all, love the one in front of you! Consider what agency you have at your disposal. This was a question that we regularly had to ask ourselves. What could we reasonably do? It's important that we are realistic in what we can do in and through our enterprises to benefit our communities. We were not running a business that was generating huge amounts of profit. We couldn't compete with large corporations that had grand Corporate Social Responsibility programmes, and we

---

[82] 'Timpson discusses the benefits of employing reformed offenders', www.youtube.com/watch?v=7zf7Bk2RSfs&feature=emb_rel_end (accessed 16th January 2021).

didn't try to. The focus of our attention was on personal and corporate conduct, carefully supporting our staff and their family lives while grappling with work type and locations that seemed to be contradictory. I realise that these need to be relevant to the culture in which you live and work while expressing the values of the kingdom of God. I include in the Appendix a range of ideas and suggestions to help you prayerfully consider what you can reasonably do.

We each need to operate fiscal wisdom by not depleting our enterprise's reserves, whether financial or human. A major event like the recent Covid-19 pandemic has reminded us of the prudence in doing this. Making sure that we are able to support our staff through times of financial hardship in their personal lives, and in the global economy, demonstrates love for them and they are, in themselves, redemptive acts. We should not feel guilty about the extent to which we can devote our enterprises' resources. 'Loving the one in front of you' is a helpful maxim. We can all do that.

Our kingdom entrepreneurship is meant to play a part, maybe even only a tiny part, in being a beacon in a broken world, but collectively these beacons link across the globe to be a system of lights set on a hill that are not being hidden (Matthew 5:14). As entrepreneurs we are pointing to a redemptive King through whom there is healing for a broken world – a world in which there is hurt, pain, abuse, injustice, separation and harm. Redemptive actions can be costly, both personally and to the enterprise, but we are prophesying of what is to come and what is at hand, as well as displaying the mercy of God. As entrepreneurs we can and should be those who demonstrate to a broken world the beauty of our redemptive God by our redemptive actions. In this way we disrupt the prevailing business culture. Through us people can peer into the future to that time when all things will be under the feet of Jesus, catching a glimpse of the King upon His throne.

> Through us people can peer into the future to that time when all things will be under the feet of Jesus.

Pause, pray, practise

- Pause: How do you show love in the way your enterprise operates? How is it different from your competitors, or others against whom you can benchmark?

- Pray: Ask God to show you how He wants you and your enterprise to show redemptive love. Do you need to make any adjustments to your mission or values as a result? If so, what practical steps do you need to make, and by when?

- Practise: Do you need to compose business values for your venture, or re-examine them in any way if you have been trading for some time? Do you need to determine ways in which you can realistically show God's redemptive love?

- Practise: Make a list of the practical ways in which the values of the enterprise are put into practice. Be honest! How do you know that customers, suppliers and staff see love expressed in these actions?

Appendix

Ideas and suggestions on restorative actions

Your team

- Personal integrity.

- Consistent behaviour.

- Believing in and facilitating each member of staff to achieve their full potential.

- Supporting staff in their home lives – not encouraging or placing an expectation on them to overwork and put a strain on their family life.

- Respecting and honouring suppliers – for example, being reasonable in our expectations of them in our payment terms, assisting them as we are able to help their business.

- Cultivating a value of celebration in what the enterprise is doing, and valuing each individual's part in it.

- Relating to everyone in our team – clients, suppliers and contractors – as people loved by God. Do we unconditionally accept them?

- Providing financial awareness and management programmes for our staff.

Environmental impact

- Systematically reducing our environmental impact.

- Focusing on products and services that are good for the customer and the world. Considering whole-life cycle (raw materials, manufacture, packaging, distribution, disposal) and adding value in a kingdom worldview to the buyer.

- Considering our operations – do they exploit the earth's resources, or are they at least resource neutral? Better still, can we invest in these resources to preserve natural resources?

Tax and legal affairs

- Paying rightful and appropriate taxes due, recognising that we do so for the common good and by way of modelling generosity.

- Refusing to pay bribes or other forms of improper payments in order to win business deals.

- Being honest in our advertising and promotion by not exaggerating our capabilities and expertise, product performance and usefulness, etc, or seeking to create an ungodly need, but promoting where there is genuine merit and life-enhancement in our offer or product.

Charitable acts

- Showing love and compassion to the poor and homeless in our communities.

- Encouraging volunteering to causes that support the well-being of our community.

- Engaging a chaplain for our workforce.
- Funding, or helping to fund, or partnering in another way, with a foundation or charity (for example, engagement in social justice, education, food provision for the poor).

Ethical matters

- Do we squeeze the profit margins through our supply chain to such an extent that the suppliers are unable to pay employees at least a living wage in their own country, or cannot afford to uphold sustainable and relevant health, safety and environmental standards?
- Which standards do we apply in our supply chain – those of our home country, or those of the country of our supplier?
- Do we check that our supplier is fulfilling the requirements that we set out in terms of labour and health, safety and environment and code of conduct, for example?

Examples of benefits that can be offered to employees

- Occupational health provision, to include mental health.
- Shopping discounts.
- Employee assistance programmes.
- Paying enhanced maternity and paternity pay.
- Flexible, agile, family-friendly and remote-working capability.
- Providing more holiday than statutory holidays.

- Ability to buy additional days' holiday.

- An income protection scheme in case of illness.

- In-service death benefit.

- A contributory pension scheme.

- Profit-share scheme.

- Childcare vouchers.

- Gifts on significant life occasions.

- Loans for specific and identified purposes at below-market interest rates, or zero interest.

Acknowledgements

Although I am the author of this book, it couldn't have been written without many people contributing to the process in so many different ways. Some people may not even know the importance of their contribution. Inevitably I will miss some because my memory of events and of people's contributions is lost in that mysterious world of recall. Please forgive me for my omission.

Mum and Dad; thank you for the stability and love that I knew in my upbringing, and for supporting me through university.

Thank you, Derek, Mike, Phil and Dave, and to those in Antioch Ministries, for pouring yourselves into me in the formative years of my Christian life. To friends in King's Church, Aldershot. We shared some of the best and worst of times together. Thank you for modelling Christ's love.

Thank you, Brian, Allison, Marcus, Rich, Martin and Brian for the years we spent together learning about the kingdom of God and growing church. What special times. Thank you also to my friends in Kingdom Life Church, Northampton.

Thank you, all those who worked with me in the businesses. We learned so much together and did a lot of good. Thank you to my valued advisors, always on hand with wisdom when your help was needed.

Thank you, Clive, for your constant encouragement to write about kingdom entrepreneurship, and to you, Grace, Paul, Marianne and Paris. We spent many hours poring over this topic and your contributions have helped to shape this book.

Stephen De Silva, thanks so much for your friendship and encouragement and for helping me to understand how to live as a prosperous soul (3 John 2). Inevitably, the heart of my message on scarcity thinking and Mammon is influenced by your teaching. Thank you to Stephen's wonderful Ministry Core Team. I'm enjoying pioneering alongside you to release financial freedom to people.

Thank you, Jonathan, Clive, Stephen, David and Humberto for your brilliant help in reviewing and helping to refine the early texts. Your assistance has been invaluable.

The team at Instant Apostle. Your support from the beginning has been undaunted. I wouldn't have got to this point without you. Thank you for leading me through the publication process. You've saved more grey hairs!

And, of course, a massive thank you to my ultimate 'team', Helen, Lucy, Kate, Tom and Ashleigh, Elsie and Ada, and those yet to join us. You are the best, and I love you dearly.

LEADING BETTER BEHAVIOUR

LEADING BETTER BEHAVIOUR

A GUIDE FOR SCHOOL LEADERS

JARLATH O'BRIEN

CORWIN

CORWIN
A SAGE company
2455 Teller Road
Thousand Oaks, California 91320
(0800)233-9936
www.corwin.com

SAGE Publications Ltd
1 Oliver's Yard
55 City Road
London EC1Y 1SP

SAGE Publications India Pvt Ltd
B 1/I 1 Mohan Cooperative Industrial Area
Mathura Road
New Delhi 110 044

SAGE Publications Asia-Pacific Pte Ltd
3 Church Street
#10-04 Samsung Hub
Singapore 049483

Editor: James Clark
Assistant editor: Diana Alves
Production editor: Nicola Carrier
Copyeditor: Gemma Marren
Proofreader: Salia Nessa
Indexer: Silvia Benvenuto
Marketing manager: Dilhara Attygalle
Cover design: Naomi Robinson
Typeset by: C&M Digitals (P) Ltd, Chennai, India
Printed in the UK

Library of Congress Control Number: 2019947878

British Library Cataloguing in Publication data

A catalogue record for this book is available from the British Library

ISBN 978-1-5264-8922-7
ISBN 978-1-5264-8921-0 (pbk)

At SAGE we take sustainability seriously. Most of our products are printed in the UK using responsibly sourced papers and boards. When we print overseas we ensure sustainable papers are used as measured by the PREPS grading system. We undertake an annual audit to monitor our sustainability.

Dedicated to the memory of Len Clark (1937–2019)

Much-loved teacher and dear friend

I have found it of enormous value when I can permit myself to understand another person. The way in which I have worded this statement may seem strange to you. Is it necessary to *permit* oneself to understand another? I think that it is. Our first reaction to most of the statements which we hear from other people is an immediate evaluation, or judgment, rather than an understanding of it. When someone expresses some feeling or attitude or belief, our tendency is, almost immediately, to feel 'That's right'; or 'That's stupid'; 'That's abnormal'; 'That's unreasonable'; 'That's incorrect'; 'That's not nice'. Very rarely do we permit ourselves to understand precisely what the meaning of his statement is to him. I believe this is because understanding is risky. If I let myself really *understand* another person, I might be changed by that understanding. And we all fear change. So as I say, it is not an easy thing to permit oneself to understand an individual, to enter thoroughly and completely and empathically into his frame of reference. It is also a rare thing.

Carl Rogers, *On Becoming a Person*

CONTENTS

ABOUT THE AUTHOR

Jarlath O'Brien has been a teacher for two decades. He has worked in comprehensive, independent, selective and special schools, including in schools for children with social, emotional and behavioural difficulties. Jarlath is also a Trustee in a multi-academy trust of mainstream primary and secondary schools. For the last nine years, Jarlath has been a Headteacher and Executive Headteacher. Early on in his teaching life Jarlath was also a volunteer Special Constable with Thames Valley Police.

Jarlath is a behaviour columnist for the *Times Educational Supplement*, has written for *The Guardian* and for several other education publications.

Also by Jarlath O'Brien

Better Behaviour: A Guide for Teachers (SAGE, 2018)

Don't Send Him in Tomorrow (Independent Thinking Press, 2016)

ACKNOWLEDGEMENTS

Emma for continuing to put up with the guy who wrote in the acknowl-
edgements in *Better Behaviour* that he was writing when he should have
been spending time with her.

Hannah and Aidan for their love and support, and for the games.

Diana Alves and James Clark at SAGE for the encouragement and the
professional support that turned this into a book.

Jon Severs at the *Times Educational Supplement* for allowing me to
write regularly on the topic of behaviour, and for his sound advice and
clever editing.

Joel Smith and Kate Allely for their advice on certain parts of this book.
I owe you both a drink!

INTRODUCTION

'Behaviour in this school is good.'

'No, it's not. It's way better than that. It's outstanding.'

The first comment in the exchange above was uttered by an Ofsted inspector to me as Headteacher at the end of an inspection in January 2014.

The retort was delivered almost instantaneously by me with such conviction and certainty that I surprised myself by how bold I was considering the circumstances.

'So what?' you might say. There will be little mention of Ofsted, England's school inspectorate, in this book (government inspectors are not unimportant, but nothing in this book should be done *for* them), but this moment in time was critical for our school and for all involved in it because it officially marked the end of a period of 15 months where our school was judged by Ofsted to require improvement (an official grade on a four-point scale of performance at that time ranging from *outstanding* down to *good*, *requires improvement* and, lastly, *inadequate*) on the basis of the behaviour of our students. Further, any organisation that is judged by an inspectorate of standards to be performing below a minimum level of acceptability has, by definition, leadership that has not been good enough. In this particular case, the leadership that wasn't good enough came from me. What the *requires improvement* judgement for our school really meant was that the *leadership of the school* required improvement as it could not guarantee an acceptable level of good behaviour from the students. And, as painful as it is for me to admit that my leadership was for a period of time not good enough, it is undoubtedly true.

I became a Headteacher for the first time on 1 September 2011. Despite years of leadership experience before then, I now realise that this is the precise moment that my education in the leadership of behaviour really began. Up to that point I considered myself a skilled teacher and I had a reputation as someone who could build relationships with children who violently rejected schools and the adults in them. 'You're good with the unteachable naughty boys', as I was once memorably told. I had a track record of helping them improve their behaviour and, as a result, carried a certain level of confidence within myself when dealing with behaviour, however intense or violent, in schools. This confidence was bolstered by my part-time occupation, alongside full-time teaching, as a Special Constable with Thames Valley Police. I was a good communicator, a decent judge of body language and mood, I could convey a sense of authority and control and made, for the most part, sensible decisions under pressure. All useful qualities in the heat of the moment, but not the complete skillset needed to lead a school and foster good behaviour beyond the walls of one's own classroom. I got by largely on feel and instinct, but this only got me so far.

The vignette at the start of this introduction captures a point along the journey that I took as a teacher and Headteacher of that school, and that my team took with me, where we learned the hard way how to improve behaviour in a school. When I took up the headship in 2011, the school had a relatively fresh Ofsted grading of *outstanding*, but behaviour in the school quickly deteriorated for a number of reasons, all of which I was responsible for as that is part of the deal and the pay packet when you become the boss. The relatively swift decline in behavioural standards in the school and the subsequent improvement was a painful, messy process for all concerned and I made many mistakes, largely because I was learning by trial and error to begin with. I don't recommend this, either for your own well-being as a leader, or for that of your colleagues, the children and their parents and that is the main motivation for writing this book. I sometimes joke that you can't buy that kind of professional development, but the joke isn't funny at all. I'd rather you learned from my bigger mistakes, so that any mistakes that you do make later on are much smaller than they otherwise might have been.

I realised later that there were large gaps in my knowledge of both behaviour and the leadership of behaviour. To compound these problems, much of the advice I could find or was given was superficial, such as introducing Saturday detentions to heighten the stakes for the children; counter-productive, such as publicly increasing the use and severity of fixed-term exclusions to set an example to other children; or simply baseless, such as the advice that I introduce blazers and ties as a smarter uniform would encourage children to behave better. For the record, I ignored all those pieces of advice.

The Behaviour Guy

Leadership of behaviour is categorically not about being the Behaviour Guy. This is the caricature teacher, inevitably an alpha male, with a fierce reputation who can instantly silence a hall full of raucous Year 10s simply by clearing his throat with a stage cough, and to whom problem children are sent in order to sort them out. There was a significant weight of expectation on me to be the Behaviour Guy in my early days as a Headteacher, and I had known a few Headteachers who had revelled in that role, but it was an expectation I singularly failed to live up to. Two comments from a particularly difficult staff meeting during the early part of my first headship stay with me to this day:

> The children in my class need to know at all times that you're wondering if their work and behaviour is good enough and, if it isn't, that you're going to turn up and deal with them.

> We need you in the corridors all the time during lessons.

I have no criticism for the teachers that made those demands on me. They were well intentioned and indicated an understandable desire for support. They were used to this and had come to expect that Headteachers were to be omnipresent enforcers. Instinctively, I rejected this approach, feeling nervous that it could create a dependency amongst the adults and a climate of fear amongst the students. I was and always will be keen on getting around the school regularly during the school day, being on the gate at the start and end of the day, and being with the children at break times, but this expectation was different. I didn't want children to be worried if I walked into their classroom, I wanted them to crack on with their lesson and, when appropriate, let me know what they were learning. This concern about a dependency culture deepened when a member of the support staff told me that the Deputy Headteacher used to park her car in the Headteacher's spot if he was out for the day so that the children would think he was in school. 'If the Headteacher wasn't in, we knew we'd be in for a tough day', she said.

I was also sure that behaviour needed to be everyone's business – indeed, this had largely been my experience up until then – and to deny that meant that I rendered the rest of the adults in the school powerless. It did mean, though, that I had to reassure colleagues who felt that this approach meant that I was uninterested in dealing with behaviour issues or supporting others and that I would leave it all to them.

It has been said to me on more than one occasion that children should feel at least a little bit scared of the Headteacher. I reject this out of hand. If the only reason a child or class is behaving well is because they are petrified of the adult or adults, as per the Behaviour Guy, then we have gone badly astray in our approach to working with children.

> It is possible to lead behaviour in a school without being the scariest person in the building.
>
> It is possible to lead behaviour in a school without being the person to whom children are always sent when there are problems.
>
> It is possible to lead behaviour in a school without being the Headteacher.
>
> It is not possible, in my view, to lead behaviour in a school without first having got to grips with behaviour in your own class as a teacher.

I had experienced this gendered expectation before in another school. When I was a Deputy Headteacher, I led a review of how we'd handled a particularly difficult Friday afternoon that involved a child ending up on the roof of the Headteacher's flat after smashing a window and setting off the fire alarm. The activation of the fire alarm resulted in two fire engines and about a dozen firefighters arriving on site complete with blue lights and sirens. This happened at the end of the school day so, as is the case with many special schools, we had a fair number of taxis and minibuses on site, all of whom were keen to round up their children and head off for the weekend. Managing the child and the fire brigade as well as trying to work out who was left on site turned out to be more than I could manage. I handled it badly, delegated ineffectively and a review was a good way for us all to learn something. 'We need some burly men round here', opened Leanne, a member of the support staff who'd been involved in the incident. Leanne was entitled to her opinion and I was pleased that she voiced it (apart from the sadly accurate bit about my implied lack of burliness), but I tried to explain as best as I could why I thought that neither a different gender ratio nor people of greater physical size would have improved the situation we'd been through. What was required from the adults in such a fraught situation was composure, a solid understanding of the needs of the child that informed how they dealt with the situation, and the ability to communicate that understanding to both the child and to each other as they supported each other and the child. We disagreed, but it remains an interesting episode for me to reflect upon as the gender stereotype was a solution that immediately offered itself to colleagues. It chimes with the oft-heard call for former soldiers to become teachers to instil some much-needed discipline into today's generation of slack teenagers. I am sure that former service personnel, both men and women, can and do become excellent teachers but it is certainly not because they strike fear into platoons of children by barking orders at them (O'Brien, 2018).

Good behaviour. Poor policy

I met recently with some colleagues with whom I used to work when I first started teaching in a comprehensive and we were discussing changes in behaviour that we had seen over time. With the benefit of both hindsight and of my later behaviour leadership experiences, I could now see things that were invisible and unknown to me at that time, which encompassed the first five years of my teaching life in that comprehensive. Behaviour was solidly good at that school throughout that period. We had our fair share of difficulties and I remain very proud of the fact that we were often asked to take students that had left other schools under a cloud and generally did well with them.

I can see now that we fostered good behaviour and dealt with incidents of poor behaviour relatively well almost solely because of the skill and confidence of a critical mass of teachers, not because we had an effective policy – we didn't. There were enough of us, and I want to believe that I became one of these people, who were really confident when it came to behaviour and were able to ensure that almost all children behaved well in our lessons and that most incidents never got beyond minor disruption. Occasionally, we leant on the school's behaviour policy, which when translated into real life, essentially amounted to someone from the school's leadership team arriving to remove a child from our lessons at our request when we ran out of our own homemade strategies. This meant that most children, most of the time, experienced orderly lessons, safe corridors and playgrounds, skilled form tutors and Heads of Year, lots of extra-curricular activity and a healthy sense of belonging. This collective institutional confidence and skill was vital, but the absence of an effective policy to support us meant three things for the school:

1. Behaviour across the whole school was never going to be exceptional.
2. The children who had the most deep-seated behavioural difficulties were less well supported and stood less of a chance of improving, as we had no commonly agreed way of approaching such issues so they relied on teachers' different and potentially contradictory approaches.
3. Behaviour standards in the school were highly susceptible to staffing changes. It was this last point which resulted in the school being unable to maintain that behaviour standard over time.

This tale highlights the importance of getting the systems and processes right that underpin and support the adults working in your school and of getting the adults to buy into what you're trying to do. Their individual expertise may well be impressive but institutional confidence and proficiency is hard won and easily lost. One of the schools I currently work at had nine teachers, half the teaching workforce, leave at the end of the last academic year. This is obviously a large proportion of the team, and was largely due to overseas teachers returning home as their visas had expired. It meant, though, that the school's leadership team had to effectively start again to get the culture right. Luckily, the school has a good policy that supports teachers and visible, supportive senior leaders so it stands a decent chance of getting back up to top speed without too much drama.

Credibility

Leading behaviour effectively in a school is not the same as being effective in the promotion and maintenance of good behaviour as a teacher in one's own classroom, but they are interlinked. You are likely to struggle, in my view, to be good at the former without being good at the latter. But it does not automatically follow that good teachers make good leaders in any or all aspects of school leadership.

You could also contend that it is not possible to write a credible book about improving behaviour in schools without first having done it yourself, and I would obviously agree, although it must be stressed that all school improvement is a team game – no one does it on their own. Credibility is very important to teachers and we, rightly, test people when they lead us or stand in front of a hall full of us on a training day. That is why the end of the conversation from the opening of this introduction is important.

'You're right. Behaviour is outstanding', the lead inspector admitted after I had reminded him of the overwhelming mass of evidence proving as much, cross-referencing against the Ofsted inspection handbook for good measure.

I reiterate that Ofsted inspections and their judgements are not the be all and end all. I include it here to establish with you right from the outset that this book is written from a credible position of lived experience and builds on all the learning that I have been fortunate to assimilate throughout my teaching life and especially the school-wide process of successfully improving behaviour.

The chapters are designed to exist as stand-alone pieces so that the book can be used to dip in and out of as the need arises. However, there is a semblance of order to the chapters too, as some aspects of the leadership of behaviour such as sanctions *should* be informed by the culture and values of a school. I stress *should* as one of the most common errors I have seen in the leadership of behaviour, indeed one I made myself, is to develop a behaviour policy and all of its fine details without setting it into the context of the ethos of the entire school or aligning it with other policies such as those for special educational needs. Behaviour policies written in this way, sometimes in situations of some urgency like my own, are likely to be less effective.

Chapter 1 discusses what kind of school you want to be, and how the actions we take to foster good behaviour and in response to poor behaviour should be informed by our values. This feeds into Chapter 2 and the various policies you have such as behaviour, anti-bullying and e-safety. We then go on in Chapter 3 to consider what staff need to know, and in Chapter 4 to suggest how you and your colleagues can support staff without creating that aforementioned culture of dependency.

In Chapter 5 we look at how you gauge how good behaviour actually is in your school – this is more sophisticated than relying on totting up how many more good days than bad there have been lately. We consider what kind of information is useful information when assessing school-wide behaviour standards.

Later on, we examine strategies and tactics for individuals with the effective use of behaviour plans and behaviour reports in Chapter 6. We look critically in Chapter 7 at the endemic rewards and incentives, and extend that to look more deeply at the underlying motivations children have and the power of recognition as opposed to reward.

Chapter 8 will grapple with the thorny issue of sanctions and, as with rewards, will run a critical eye over the effectiveness, or otherwise, of much of what is out there.

Given its seriousness, bullying gets Chapter 9 all to itself where we look at the evidence that's out there for schools to reduce, and hopefully eradicate, this highly damaging act.

Support staff make a sizeable proportion of the school workforce these days so they appear in Chapter 10, where we look at how to ensure we get the best out of them, how to help them to feel well supported in their role and admit that they can be some of the most effective professionals out there when working to improve behaviour. Many of our colleagues in the support staff team spend much of their working weeks with children with special educational needs and disabilities (SEND) so this cohort of children need a focus in Chapter 11. The gross over-representation of children with SEND in the statistics for fixed-term and permanent exclusion means that we need to lay out the potential contributory factors for this and what schools and their leaders can do to address this. Our duties under the Equality Act (2010) will appear in this chapter too.

There are also laws to follow when excluding children either for a fixed-term or permanently and these will be made clear in Chapter 12 alongside the evidence for the effectiveness of this response to poor behaviour.

No book on any aspect of school leadership would be complete without including governance, including for groups of schools (multi-academy trusts (MATs) in England), so Chapter 13 addresses this.

I have a great deal of respect for anyone that takes on any of the demanding jobs in school leadership. Few, though, can sometimes feel as thankless as leading on behaviour especially if things seem like they are not going well out there in the classrooms and corridors. I hope that this book offers support to those of you undertaking this vital task, encourages you to share learning and new ideas with colleagues and, above all, helps you feel more confident about your work.

Good luck and let me know how you get on!

Reference

O'Brien, J. (2018) 'Four things schools can learn from the military', *Times Educational Supplement*, 9 October. www.tes.com/news/four-things-schools-can-learn-military (accessed 17 September 2019).

1

VALUES AND CULTURE

When children become a liability for their school's performance education has come to an end.

Professor Gert Biesta (n.d.)

THE HEADLINES

- There is an established culture in your school. If the culture is not of your deliberate making then it will have crept into the vacuum you've left and grown unchecked all by itself.

- An agreed set of values that permeate throughout the school is one of the foundations of good behaviour as these values influence and inform your policies and your decision-making.

- A school vision will lead naturally from a strong set of shared values and will communicate your collective ambition for your children. It will be a tangible thing to visitors to your school, evident in every aspect of school life.

- This vision and these values are susceptible to professional pressures on school leaders such as those that arise from inspection, external exam results and government floor targets. A collective strength and commitment to standing by your values can help leadership teams from compromising their values when faced with difficult decisions and situations. Being open about what those pressures are, discussing them honestly with each other and with governors or the leaders of a multi-academy trust can protect against succumbing to the pressure.

- A positive behaviour culture amongst the staff is sustained by ensuring negativity is systematically and routinely challenged, and that colleagues receive the support they need to deal with the potential sources of the negativity.

- Deciding on what kind of school you want to be can help when trying to translate a school's vision and values into a behaviour policy. Completing the following sentence openers can be useful:

    o   We are a school for ...
    o   We are a school where ...
    o   We are a school with ...
    o   We are a school that ...

Professor Gert Biesta's superb paper 'Why "what works" still won't work: From evidence-based education to value-based education' (2010) should be mandatory reading for all school leaders. In it, Biesta persuasively highlights the deficits in knowledge,[1] effectiveness[2] and application[3] that exist as limitations in an evidence-informed or evidence-based approach to decision-making in educational leadership. Do not make the mistake of interpreting this as a view that evidence is unimportant – he doesn't say that – rather it should be used as a helpful reminder of what can be omitted or lost when we fail to take into account the *role* evidence should play in our decision-making.

Biesta summarises this neatly by contending that, 'If evidence were the only base for educational practice, educational practice would be entirely without direction'. And that 'Questions about "what works" – that is questions about the effectiveness of educational actions – are always secondary to questions of purpose' (Biesta, 2010: 500).

It is a call to ensure that an examination of how school leaders use the significant power available to them and their school's values is given sufficient weight when they formulate policy and make decisions that affect the hundreds of children and adults in their care.

Nowhere is this more important than in the leadership of behaviour. Why?

There is an ever-present risk of school leaders making up policy on the matter of behaviour in isolation or as they go along, or by simply lifting an idea from another school because, from a distance, it seemed to work for them or has superficial appeal. I've done this myself on more than one occasion. The regularly reported immediate increase in stringency of uniform standards when a new Headteacher takes on a school which had previously poor standards of behaviour suggests itself as one such example.

The behaviour of children, and school leaders' responses to it, are two of the most emotive and controversial topics in the teaching profession. Listen in on any staffroom conversation or social media bunfight and you won't have to wait too long for it to surface. The acceleration in emotion that these topics can bring about can make cool, measured discussion and decision-making difficult. I've been in precisely this position numerous times, both as a teacher exasperated with my own inadequacy or with what I perceived as poor support from my leaders, and as a Headteacher when I knew colleagues felt exactly the same way about me. As a school leader it provoked an overpowering urge to do something, anything right that second to help my colleagues and to show them that I was a tough, uncompromising Headteacher who wouldn't take any messing from the children. Of course, what I was really doing was suppressing my own insecurity and hiding the fact that I didn't really know what to do. It was inaction masquerading as action, procrastination dressed up as decisiveness.

This urgency, and its accompanying stress response, can cause leaders to make those knee-jerk decisions to satisfy demands that can come in the form of:

> 'Everyone says you've got to do something about Luke Hadley/Year 8/ break times/haircuts/phones!' [Delete or amend as appropriate.]

Colleagues look to us as leaders for solutions and we are keen, sometimes desperate, to provide them with those solutions without delay. However, decisions made in the heat of the moment whilst coping with the glare of expectant onlookers are more likely to be taken in order to meet the immediate needs of the decision maker rather than the needs of the children and adults involved. It is one thing to know this. It is quite another to hold your nerve and tell everyone that the road ahead may feel long and bumpy, that there are things we can do straight away to help, but that lasting improvement will take time in the way that losing weight takes time. The worst part of this inevitably temporary respite is that the problem remains essentially unsolved and must be confronted sooner or later, perhaps once it has deteriorated.

Improving behaviour is neither swift nor simple and we know this for sure because we would have cracked it by now if it was. Without a reasoned and careful consideration of the values – the principles that should guide and influence the behaviour of the adults – that are important to a school community, and the culture that the community wants to foster, leaders run the risk of developing policies seeking to improve behaviour that are desiccated, transactional documents that do not coexist well with the other policies and practices that all schools have. What's worse is that they then fail to reflect what happens out there in the real world of the classrooms, corridors and playgrounds where teachers will fill in the gaps for themselves.

One such example of a practice entirely at odds with a school's stated values sticks in the memory from my first day as a Headteacher. I was in my office well before school started when a colleague came in and handed me a sheet of A4 paper, saying, 'This is the rota for Year 10 to clean the staffroom'.

Without a moment's hesitation I responded with, 'If the staffroom is dirty, we'll clean it or it will stay dirty. I'm not having children cleaning up after adults'.

I regret the way that I made that decision. I should have thanked the member of staff, explained to her what my thoughts were and then explained to the whole staff team why this was incompatible with what we were trying to do as a school and that the practice had now ceased. The swiftness with which I did it stemmed from the glaring dissonance between that particular practice and the school's stated values. We quite clearly gave no regard to the dignity of the children by doing this, and I could find no justification to rob them of some of their learning time so that the staffroom could be clean.

That example and a host of others led me to take a good look at our values as an organisation and how, or if, they manifested themselves in the day-to-day life of the school. If they didn't, and I worry that schools' values sometimes get decided in a senior leadership team (SLT) or staff meeting but only exist in a pristine display in the entrance hall, then we needed to make some changes to ensure that they did.

REFLECTION POINTS

- Can you think of a time or times when you have felt under pressure to solve a behaviour issue quickly?

- What was it about the situation(s) the made you feel pressurised?

- How did you cope with the pressure and expectation?

- What did you say to the people around you?

- How did the situation turn out?

- Were the solution and the actions you took consistent with your values?

- What would you have done differently?

When children leave our school they should be ...

For most of my teaching life I thought that the idea of a school vision was an empty gesture. I listened with some interest when the subject was brought up on leadership courses such as the National Professional

Qualification for Headship (NPQH), but I'd seen enough inane management speak in my time and thought that much of what I saw was more of the same. ('An outstanding school where outstanding teaching leads to outstanding learning' remains my all-time favourite.)

I changed my mind on that, as with many other things, when I became a Headteacher, but this time quite by accident. One of the things that I did manage to get right when I first took up the post was to talk to all the staff and governors and as many of the parents as I could about their hopes for the children of the school. I, of course, asked the same of all the students too. I framed all of the discussions around the question:

What should our children be able to do when they leave here?

I decided on this approach as I wanted to force us to think of the end point (as far as our involvement was largely concerned). That is what I understood a vision to be – an almost literal look forward to the hopes and aspirations of the future.

The results were illuminating. The parents' responses centred around enabling their children to live and work independently; the students' answers were remarkably similar to each other's – they wanted school to equip them with the skills and knowledge to realise their ambitions of getting a job, a flat, a car, a boyfriend or girlfriend and to earn their own money. Not too much to ask, you might think, but the life outcomes for people with learning difficulties in the UK at the present time are all gut-wrenchingly poor (O'Brien, 2016) so this should give a very sharp focus to anyone working in schools with children with special educational needs.

I dreaded trying to assimilate all of this information into something coherent, yet it quickly became apparent that some key characteristics emerged. From this we ended up with our school vision. We had decided on the things that we valued and that we would explicitly aim to develop in our students in order to give them the best possible chances in adult life once they left our secondary special school.

When students leave [this school] they should be ambitious, articulate, caring, confident, determined, independent, resilient, respectful, responsible and successful.

I wanted it to be free from teacher jargon and easily understood. I was also determined that we would centre the positive side of our behaviour policy on recognising these things when we saw them. I came to see via this process that it was possible to have a meaningful and tangible school vision that laid out what we valued and that was visible in the day-to-day life of the school. However, in order for it to become tangible we had to ensure that our curriculum was aligned with our vision. If we weren't providing our students with the opportunities to develop confidence or to become more articulate, to take just two examples, then we were back to the vision simply being a slogan on a glossy prospectus that no one in the school could recite.

It was also important for this school vision to be a positive influence on our behaviour policy. We chose to reinforce the school values by recognising them whenever we observed our students doing well. Everyone had told us that these things were crucial, so we had to do whatever we could to provide our students with the opportunities to get better at these things. I remember Kieran in Year 11 getting to the top of a challenging pitch at a climbing wall as part of his Duke of Edinburgh Award Scheme programme and shouting down to me, 'Look, Mr O'Brien! I've been successful!' We used bonus points as a device for recognition (not reward; see Chapter 7 for the difference) and it became commonplace for children to come up to me in the playground at break or lunchtime to tell me that their teacher had made a point of letting them know that they had made good progress with their independence or that they had been particularly determined that day.

The penny really dropped for me that a school vision could be a truly real thing when I toured prospective parents around the school – one of the most important parts of my week. I always shared feedback from parents with the staff and governors and I remember doing a little jig down the corridor of our main block the first time a parent told me that she was struck by how confident and articulate our students were. This observation was made time and time again by visitors, teachers and parents alike, and each time it was a further affirmation of what we were trying to do.

There is one major point I want to stress about how our values informed our behaviour policy – that equity was built into it. Too often I see policies that are by their very nature inequitable. I don't mean a confetti of rewards for all here. I mean how, for example, higher attainers are more likely to be beneficiaries of a behaviour reward system that purports to recognise effort and application but instead recognises poor proxies for effort and application, such as attainment. Too many schools and too many policies effectively reward some children for finding school easier than others.

> We need to acknowledge that some children find schools easier places to feel and be successful than other children.

It amazes me that we don't make a bigger deal of this fact, and I strongly urge you to keep this at the front of your mind when we look into policy in more detail in Chapter 2. If we don't, we run the risk of inadvertently valuing the pure attainment of children, inevitably those who attain most highly, over the progress that all children make from the position in life in which they currently find themselves.

REFLECTION POINTS

- What is your school vision?
- What are the values upon which your school is built?
- Does your behaviour policy encourage you to recognise those values when you see them displayed by children?

'Culture exists in every organisation, but is yours by design or by default?'

This provocation by Mark Finnis (2018) should make all leaders feel at least slightly uncomfortable because, despite a strong set of values and our best efforts to maintain them, practices and habits from individuals or teams can creep in over time, which inhibit our progress towards our behaviour goals and contaminate our culture. The quote certainly forces me to think about problems that have arisen under my leadership and how I could have prevented them by being clearer about the culture that I wanted in the teams that I led, instead of weakly allowing issues to fester when they were minor.

Too often when discussing behaviour we dive straight into trying to answer, 'What shall we do?' when we should spend time first on answering the far more important question 'Why are we doing this?'. This prioritisation of doing (sometimes mistakenly called 'strategy' if it isn't consistent with everything else the school is doing) over ensuring our actions are consistent with our values is likely to result in an incoherent set of policies and limited, if any, progress. Any new ideas, whether that be across the whole school, in a department or for an individual teacher, need to pass the values test before they are let loose on children.

Two, 'What shall we do?' examples spring immediately to mind. My first few years of teaching were in a comprehensive and one thing that came around fairly regularly was a crackdown (their word, not mine) on uniform. In briefings, we would be instructed to 'go zero tolerance on uniform this week'. It was done in response to a feeling that behaviour in the school had slipped – the top button being undone on students' shirts being a surefire sign that the insurrection was about to begin – and this would be a good way to send a strong message to the students. I'm not against uniform, but I know that any behaviour problems we experienced had nothing to do with how the students dressed, and weren't solved or improved one iota by an isolated tightening up of our policing of all children's clothing.

The other example is the creation of reward systems that monetise good behaviour by offering enticements such as Vivo points or iTunes vouchers in an attempt to improve behaviour. These systems are easy to implement and seemingly straightforward for everyone to understand, however, because they are all about material gain and nothing to do with valuing work or behaviour for their own sake, they can run counter to schools' claims that they aim to inculcate in their students a love of learning and a habit of life-long self-improvement. ('Shouldn't children be rewarded for doing the right thing, Jarlath?' – see Chapter 7 for more on this, and the answer is a firm 'no', by the way.)

A key part of developing culture for me has always been about reinforcing positive habits and routines in adults that typify 'how we do things round here' and, more importantly, eliminating poor practice that undermines or destroys a healthy culture. When I first took on leadership responsibilities there were times when I avoided confronting poor practice because I feared confrontation with a certain colleague. I can see now that there was a culture in my department and that it was created by me. But it wasn't by design, it was due to my wilful negligence. I would have had a hard time answering the oft-posed leadership question, 'What's it like round here when no one's looking?' This ate away at me and I remember sitting in the staffroom giving myself a talking to when it became too much. I felt nauseous at the thought of the task ahead but reminded myself that if I was serious about being a leader I should deal with things that I knew weren't right or get out of the way so someone else could lead. Only years later did I come across this aphorism from General David Hurley, former Chief of the Australian Defence Force:

The standard you walk past is the standard you accept.

With behaviour this is not just true of leaders. This must become true for all adults working in schools. As I stated in the introduction to this book, behaviour is everyone's business and this helps us all support each other. This shared responsibility also helps guard against the rise of the Behaviour Guy that we encountered in the introduction. The dark, but fortunately rare, side of shared responsibility is where genuinely poor practice exists, which leaders need to deal with. If we are afraid to inform leaders of potential maltreatment of children because we fear the consequences from our colleagues then, as General Hurley says, we condone it and this can ultimately lead to further bad things happening to children. In the worst situations we become complicit, and let us not forget that failing to prevent harm to a child or children is in itself a form of abuse. As the English Department for Education's *Keeping Children Safe in Education* (2018: 14) states:

> Abuse: a form of maltreatment of a child. Somebody may abuse or neglect a child by inflicting harm *or by failing to act to prevent harm.* [emphasis added]

REFLECTION POINTS

- When discussing ways of improving behaviour, how often do you and colleagues dive into the 'What shall we do?' instead of the 'Why are we doing this?'

- The next time you make a decision about behaviour ask yourselves 'How is this consistent with our values?'

What kind of school do we want to be?

This question is a useful way to frame discussions and decisions about how your values translate into the culture you're looking to foster in your school.

A school with unconditional positive regard

Unconditional positive regard is a concept developed by Carl Rogers (1902–87), a humanistic psychologist. As a key component in the development of a culture that commits to improving the behaviour of children who find schools difficult places to be successful I don't think it can be beaten, and indeed it is the cornerstone of some successful schools that work with children with social, emotional and mental health needs (Springwell Learning Community, 2016).

Without an unconditional positive regard for the children in your care, they are only accepted under certain conditions that you get to decide (conditions that may well be unknown to the children) and this positive regard is withdrawn when the children behave in ways that breach those conditions. As an example, you might say that a child can only rejoin their class once they have learned the necessary social skills. This is akin to saying that you'll add the water to the swimming pool only when they have learned to swim.

Unconditional positive regard means accepting that the children in your school, and the adults too for that matter, are doing their best to deal with the situations in their lives as best they can. Is their behaviour inappropriate? Maybe. Is it destructive? Possibly. Unconditional positive regard does not mean that when children behave poorly you cock your head to one side, wrinkle your nose up and say, 'Aw, bless 'im'. It does not mean letting children get away with things. It means that your approach to improving the behaviour of children, especially those whose behaviour may be the most intense, starts from where the child is at and seeks to improve from that position rather than simply reaching without thinking for the tired and ineffective punishment escalator to ratchet up the unpleasantness until the child complies.

A school where it is safe to fail

'We're here to catch you, not catch you out', has become a mantra of mine over the past few years as I work with other teachers to improve the behaviour of children. After I and my colleagues had worked with a significant number of children who had left mainstream secondary schools, largely because of their behaviour, it became clear to me that this was a message that we simply had to convince them was true. They had learned that adults in schools were not to be trusted because, as they saw it, they would give them work that they couldn't do and then have a go at them when they didn't do it. They had learned that school was a place of inevitable and repeated and public failure, and the way they generally learned to cope with this was to avoid it wherever possible.

This meant sometimes fetching a child from the woods at the back of the school because they refused to go to a lesson, or finding a child sat atop the climbing frame in the middle of the playground after storming out of lesson, maybe ripping their work up in the process. You may resort to exclusion to deal with such situations, but we were never going to help those children to feel safe enough to learn in our classrooms if we continually rejected them, for that is how they perceived exclusion. We had to help them to move from a position of safety. Believe it or not, what they were doing was protecting themselves; sanctions held no fear for them at that stage and in fact could be preferable as they got them away from whatever they were trying to avoid in the first place. A sanction loses all its power if it has no deterrent effect or becomes desirable.

The late Donald Winnicott (1896–1971), paediatrician and psychoanalyst, did influential work developing the concept of what he called 'holding environments' (Winnicott, 1960) – that is to say, caring and supporting environments that lead to a firm sense of trust and safety. Winnicott suggested that it is a duty of parents to slowly but surely disappoint their children; knowing when to say no and being clear with their children that they are not their friend. This is also true for us as teachers. We mustn't indulge our students, but nor can we ignore their feelings entirely.

Winnicott suggested that emotional problems develop when a person had been deprived of such holding environments in childhood. The children referred to above came to regard schools as risky places to be, full of adults who were risky people to be around. Of course, we need to instil in all of our students that same sense of trust and safety, but it is doubly important for children with behavioural difficulties.

Before they have learnt that we are safe and trustworthy we need to be the ones who put the work in. Simply waiting for them to change won't bear any fruit and this is where I see some schools running out of patience, so the child leaves.

Wilfred Bion's (1897–1979) concept of 'containing' (Bion, 1962) – that infants become overwhelmed by experiences as they lack sufficiently well-developed internal control and that a parent's containing function involves assisting the child to develop their capacity for self-regulation – can be a helpful way of thinking about our role too. Early Years teachers regard this as obvious, but I firmly believe that those of us who teach teenagers could benefit from thinking more deeply about this too. Our responses to children when they become overwhelmed should be a well-understood feature of our behaviour policy.

A central part of our role as educators of still-developing young people, and something that we have in common with their parents, is to make sure that they can thrive (I initially wrote 'manage' and decided that wasn't ambitious enough) when we're not around anymore. Overly restrictive school policies or practices of individual teachers where having a go or risking failure is a high-stakes affair, or where getting into trouble results in public shaming, run the risk of hindering this quest for independence and may not, to borrow Winnicott's term, foster good holding environments. In such environments, failure avoidance can become a goal in itself. Failure (and be aware that failure as defined by you, the teacher, may not be the same as failure as defined by the child) is not seen as a chance to learn, to develop, to grow; it is something to be ashamed about or to avoid come what may, even in the full knowledge that it will result in consequences of a different kind such as punishment.

We need to reassure our students that making a mistake is not a failure and that, instead of criticism, they will be met with unstinting support.

We need to communicate to them through our actions and our words that we are there to catch them, not catch them out.

A school *for* the community

I've always viewed the role of schools as servants of their local community as vital. When I led a school through the process of becoming an academy (an English state school that is funded directly from central government and not via its local council (House of Commons Library, 2019)) one of the things I was concerned about was that we would lose the word *Community* from our title. This is not a minor point. It was a clear statement that we placed great importance on being a part of our community. Schools cannot and should not stand alone from their community; the more connected to and the more reflective of their local community they are, through things like representation on their governing body, the better.

On matters of behaviour, there are three main community groups that I feel need special attention (there will be more detail on this in Chapter 4): your neighbours, your neighbouring schools and your parent community.

Your neighbours

All schools need good relationships with their neighbours, be they businesses, homeowners or other organisations. Things may not always be rosy as neighbours may object to the behaviour of some of your children when, for example, coming to and from school or that litter is dropped over their fences into their gardens.

Your neighbouring schools

Schools are likely to have relatively intimate relationships with their neighbouring schools, and indeed many are literal neighbours. Collaboration between Headteachers, departments and individual staff; feeder schools; siblings from the same family in your respective schools, executive Headteachers running more than one school, multi-academy trusts, are all positives. There may be difficulties too at times when, for example, groups of children from different schools clash as happened close to my school recently with some children badly hurt as a result. Such things are almost always carried out in full glare of the public and some reputational damage can arise, with some rebuilding of trust needed.

Your parent community

I am a firm believer in working as equal partners with parents. I am interested in their views, listen lots and do my best to communicate often.

'Who isn't?' you might ask. Well, where behaviour is concerned, we sometimes run the risk of communicating, either inadvertently or deliberately, that parents' views are of little or no importance when we say things like, 'We hold parents to account as well and insist that they support their child by supporting our rules' (Mercia School, n.d.). Of course we want parents to support us, but we must ensure they can tell us when they disagree. If they are unable to tell us because we are unwilling to listen then they will tell somebody, and that will almost certainly be via social media and, occasionally, the press. To paraphrase Benjamin Franklin, in this world nothing can be said to be certain, except death, taxes and tabloid newspapers in September running stories of children put into isolation because of uniform violations. We can't say that we'll hold parents to account (that's not our job anyway) and not expect to be held to account by them. We are, after all, a public service. With that in mind we should avoid over-reach by, for example, deciding that we can tell students and parents about when children should go to bed (Hosie, 2017). We can't and shouldn't.

A school with a strong sense of belonging

A positive culture that supports good behaviour from the children can be helped tremendously by a strong sense of belonging for the children and an equally strong sense of belonging or collegiality from amongst the staff.

One of my major worries when I taught in a comprehensive school of 1,200 students (that's about average for an English secondary school) was that some children were to all intents and purposes invisible. They were the children that rarely, if ever, came to the attention of many adults either for positive or negative reasons. They kept their head down – The Grey Man as the army would describe them – and just got on with things, with few adults knowing their name. I worried about them, partly because one of my own personal aims in secondary school had been to do just enough to stay out of bother and remain unnoticed.

I worried that they felt, in common with the children known to almost all adults in the school because of their seemingly continual behaviour problems, that they had little or no stake in the school.

> I want all children to feel that they are someone important in their school.

Not important in a self-obsessed sort of way, more that they know the school is a better place for having them as part of it, that they contribute positively, that they matter, that people would notice if they weren't there anymore.

It should come as no surprise to you to learn that research indicates that students who feel a greater sense of belonging tend to be more motivated and engaged in school and classroom activities, and more dedicated to school (Osterman, 2000). Further, they tend to have higher enjoyment, enthusiasm, happiness, interest and more confidence in engaging in learning, whereas those who feel isolated report greater anxiety, boredom, frustration and sadness (Furrer and Skinner, 2003). There is research indicating that about a quarter of students, a worryingly high proportion, could have a low sense of belonging (Willms, 2003).

We can generate this sense of belonging – a form of emotional investment (O'Brien, 2015) – in many ways.

Form groups

Although I loved teaching physics when I worked in a comprehensive and in a school for boys with behavioural difficulties, the job I loved the most in those schools was that of form tutor. I regarded it as vital to a well-functioning school for a couple of reasons:

- In a school where a child may have well over ten teachers a fortnight, I could be that constant presence in their life, know them better than anyone else, spot issues early and keep in regular touch with their parents.
- I wanted to develop a strong feeling with my tutor group that they took pride in being part of a tribe and that they looked out for each other.

I enjoyed being part of a vertical tutoring system when I was at school. I loved being friends with older children who looked out for me if I was in bother and we had a policy of siblings being together too, so that my brother, a year younger than me, joined B5 with me when he went up to secondary school.

The house system

I was humbled recently to be invited to present the awards at the annual prize-giving evening at my *alma mater*. I told the assembled children that I was very proud to be an alumnus of the school, but that I would have died for my house, Basildon House. The house system is one successful way that schools foster a sense of belonging. It cuts across year groups, provides opportunities for student leadership, builds competition between houses and students can take a fierce pride in representing their house. This extends too to representing the school at sporting events and performing in school productions, both good signs of a school with a healthy extra-curricular life.

I will never forget the final assembly for Basildon House. Our much-loved Head of House cried openly in front of us as we marked the demise of this adored institution – a victim of the 1988 National Curriculum that made our school decide to form into year groups instead.

Fundraising

One of the things I miss most about teaching in a comprehensive secondary school was sixth form fundraising week. Every year we gave the sixth form free rein and every year they impressed us with their ingenuity. I loved the buzz around school in those weeks and you could see how the enthusiasm spread throughout the school to the younger students. I have fond memories of having one of my shins waxed on stage in the main hall two years in a row, without pain relief I'll have you know. The following year, I and another teacher wrestled in inflatable sumo suits. Sure, it was a bit of fun, but those aspects of school are part of their lifeblood as vibrant places for young people to grow up in and thrive.

I've got your back

A sense of belonging for the adults in a school can have significant benefits in terms of mutual support for behaviour. One of the inherent weaknesses of our job is that we work in isolation from our colleagues for most or sometimes all of the week. In a school where you don't feel that you have the support of your colleagues and/or senior managers, this feeling of isolation can be magnified and makes dealing with behavioural challenges significantly harder. When I worked in a school exclusively for children with behavioural difficulties, our team spirit and mutual support was solid. Even though I was the deputy I had no hesitation in calling on any of my colleagues for support at times, and they were the same. There was no hierarchy when it came to behaviour support and this sense of security meant that we felt that, between us, there wasn't anything that we couldn't handle. There were no utterances of *the* most unhelpful phrase in the teachers' behaviour lexicon, 'Well, *I* never have any problems with him'.

A school that doesn't write off children

Teachers are, on the whole, very positive people. It's part of the self-selection process when people make the decision to enter the profession. We believe deeply in the inherent goodness of the role and of the glorious possibilities for children if we do the job to the best of our abilities and, as such, we're generally an upbeat bunch to be around. I've had my moments, but I confess that not every day in my classroom has been, '*Carpe diem*' and '*Oh, Captain, my Captain!*'. Being positive people in a profession that is positive by definition does not mean that we aren't negative at times about government policy, our leaders, certain children or certain parents, and any or all of them may be negative towards us too. We are also prone to fatigue, fear and insecurity just like all other human beings and we can become ground down by persistent poor behaviour such that our own behaviour can be affected and our judgement and perspective impaired. I'm not stating here that we need to fix a forced smile on our face and just get on with it; although teachers are past masters at this. I am going to examine the creeping, sapping negativity that can spread like a mould in a damp store cupboard about certain children, families or year groups if we don't eliminate it. As Dave Whitaker, a special school executive principal, says:

> Schools work best when adults believe in children and children believe they believe in them. (Whitaker, n.d.)

Leaders therefore have two subtle tasks: separating genuine concerns about behaviour and ensuring they are dealt with so that colleagues are well supported, and then dealing with what is left. This requires good listening skills and some subtle questioning with colleagues to elicit sufficient information to work out what precisely the problem is. What is left is likely to take the form of one of the examples below, and deal with it we must. It is a vital part of school leadership that we address behaviours from adults that can erode the culture we're continually building.

I have been heavily influenced in managing this aspect of the leadership of behaviour by the work of Dr Aaron Beck, an American psychoanalytic therapist, on depression and on ways to recognise and deal with negative thoughts that lead to emotional responses (Beck, 1976). This form of thinking is called 'cognitive distortion' or faulty thinking. There are many features of cognitive distortion, but the main ones I see that school leaders need to eliminate are detailed below.

Predicting failure (also known as the 'fortune teller error')

'Harvey is going to cause chaos in my lesson today.'

The fortune teller error is a response to a situation where you have already set your mind to failure. At the beginning of Chapter 2, I use the particularly egregious example of when I used to start certain children further up the ladder of warnings before lessons had even begun. You can immediately see why this is dangerous. No amount of support or new ideas to improve behaviour will be worth it because a lack of success is inevitable, the outcome decided.

As leaders we have to challenge this prediction of failure, but we cannot then leave our colleagues bereft of support because, as in the situation above, they still require help to deal with the situation and to see it more positively. Underlying the overt writing off of a child or class may well be a lack of confidence as to how to proceed, or an insecurity on the part of the teacher, and this is unlikely to improve without our help.

A colleague of mine developed a scripted response to this prediction of failure each and every time she came across it. 'We plan for success in this school', she would say. It didn't have to become an argument; she would repeat that to make her point and then offer to support with that planning.

Ignoring positives and focusing on negatives

'My class have been an absolute nightmare all week.'

This form of cognitive distortion is in effect a filtering of reality and leads us to over-generalise. We can apply this to ourselves too as teachers tend to be our own harshest critics.

No child generates negatives all the time, so as leaders we do need to help colleagues retain some balance here. Looking for positives is not a way of minimising the impact of things that have happened that were bad. On the contrary, it can allow us to seek ways in which to improve things. This is the heart of solution-focused thinking. As Dr Geoffrey James says in his book *Transforming Behaviour in the Classroom: A Solution-focused Guide for New Teachers*, 'The solution is the key, investigating the nature of the problem is unnecessary' (James, 2016: 25).

An unfortunate side effect of this way of thinking is the labelling of children. which we come onto next.

Labelling

'Ciara is unteachable.'

Some children develop reputations that manifest themselves as a label that describes the whole child, and once a label is attached to a child in a school it tends to stick. Describing a child as a nightmare, unteachable, or 'the worst kid I've ever taught' may seem on the surface like a teacher blowing off steam, but it is damaging. The language involved in labelling is inevitably emotionally loaded and ultimately unhelpful. The child and their family may be unaware of the precise label itself but children, especially as they get older, tend to be keenly aware of what the adults around them in a school really think of them. Perversely, this can lead to a positive reinforcement of the child's behaviour. Some of the children that I worked with in a special school for boys with social, emotional and behavioural difficulties revelled in their reputation as impossible to handle. This was the sorry end to a long conflict between them and adults, and it became their only way to be successful. Before you scoff at the idea that they were successful, I'll briefly mention Dr Ross Greene (more of him in Chapter 8). An American clinical psychologist, he contends that children do well if they can, and if they're not doing well it is because they are lacking the skills to be successful. Well, in the examples above, these children found ways to be successful. Not ways that we would agree with, but by that stage our views on the matter may be irrelevant to those children.

All-or-nothing demands

'One more step out of line from you and you're off the school football team.'

This is a tactical glass hammer that seems to get pulled out of the toolbox as a last resort. The logic behind an all-or-nothing demand is that the child is extrinsically motivated to behave because the stakes are so high. This logic is flawed as it is based on the notion that previous misconduct was simply a premeditated choice to be naughty and, by bringing the child to the proverbial cliff-edge to see how steep the drop is, this will incentivise them to sort their life out.

It is likely to be inequitable as other children won't be placed in the same position, even though they are likely to find it easier to be successful, and the child is likely to see this too.

We can also make the mistake of dangling incentives in front of the child that are actually entitlements such as going on a trip or swimming and this is where, as a leader, I have had to intervene in the past to insist a child goes on a trip or swims and is not left at school as a punishment.

A different example of all-or-nothing is where a child is told, 'This is your last chance. One more mistake and you're out of this school'. Any school leader that says this to a child is communicating that they have already largely made their mind up. Do they really mean that? What if a child has years left in their school?

Fallacy of control

'He just does that from time to time. There's nothing you can do. It's not your fault.'

When applied to a class teacher, the fallacy of control amounts to them rendering themselves powerless. They may have come to the view that they have exhausted everything and are on a treadmill of dread with a child or class that has drained their confidence. This is a dangerous situation and requires us as leaders to shore up our colleague's confidence with as much support and encouragement as we can muster. Ideally, though, we are better leaders than this and we don't let situations get this far as we spot problems earlier.

There is, though, a cousin of this fallacy. It is the fallacy of control applied by the senior leader onto the class teacher. Undoubtedly done to be helpful – I've done it – but it has precisely the opposite effect. It looks like this: a teacher endures a difficult lesson or day with a child or class and, in a ham-fisted attempt to be supportive, I say, 'Look, he/she/they just goes like that from time to time. There's absolutely nothing you can do about it. It's not your fault'. The only helpful bit of that statement is the last sentence. The rest tells the teacher that they are helpless in the face of this inevitable onslaught.

No teacher is helpless. There is always lots they can do, but in situations such as these they may need our support to see what that might look like.

Emotional reasoning

'This school is a warzone.'

When we assume feelings reflect fact, regardless of the evidence, we are engaging in emotional reasoning, and nowhere in schools is this more likely to happen than when dealing with behaviour. Because of the intense emotions that discussions of behaviour bring about, we need to guard against this really carefully and use good sources of evidence upon which to base our opinions and inform our decisions.

A colleague of mine, a highly respected Headteacher in a great school, told me recently about just such a discussion in his school: 'I can find you two people within three minutes, one of whom will tell you that behaviour here has never been better, and the other will tell you that it's never been worse'.

Working on removing these forms of thinking from schools – intensely human organisations where the thousands of daily interactions inevitably lead to problems at times – is no mean feat. But, if you want the culture to be right, it needs to be an aim that colleagues all agree on and then tenaciously pursue.

At the heart of cognitive distortion is at least some level of insecurity from adults about their own confidence in dealing with some issues.

In Chapter 3 I will consider how working to improve colleagues' perception of their own expertise in behaviour can improve their sense of self-efficacy, and I know that this is a major step in eliminating cognitive distortion from your school.

REFLECTION POINTS

- Can you think of a time or times when you have had to challenge negativity amongst your colleagues?

- Did you identify the root cause(s) of the negativity?

- What kind of things did you say to your colleagues?

- Would a script have helped? For example, to make a situation less confrontational you might use a response that all leaders have agreed to, such as, 'We plan for success in this school'.

Risks to values and culture

This chapter has been almost exclusively about how leaders form, develop and sustain a school's values and culture. There are, however, things that school leaders can do, sometimes deliberately, sometimes inadvertently, that erode a school's ethos or indicate when a leader's principles become compromised and need resetting.

Before we get to the specifics, I want to introduce the concept of complexity reduction. Complexity reduction amounts to deliberately reducing the number of available options for action in any particular system or organisation. It is not inherently a bad thing; indeed, as I will remind us in a moment, schools require hefty amounts of this in order to function effectively. An example of complexity reduction might be the filtering process on the automated phone handling system of a satellite TV company where you are met with limited options – 'Press 1 for sales. Press 2 to report technical problems. Press 3 to try unsuccessfully to cancel your subscription' – with a catch-all option ('Alternatively, hold [for infinity] to speak to the operator') if, as is sometimes the case, none of the above seem to be what you're after.

Schools engage in complexity reduction in many ways so that they can function. Organising children into classes in various ways (by age, by attainment), timetabling discrete lessons and organising the curriculum into discrete subjects are just a few examples. Sometimes this complexity reduction is done deliberately even though it is of no advantage to the children, or is even detrimental. Methods of assessment for particular subjects and the timings of exams are decided nationally irrespective of how any particular child could best display how much they have learned and when it is best for them to show this to you.

Biesta quotes Bruno Latour's work *The Pasteurization of France* in his paper referenced right at the beginning of this chapter as a good example of the pitfalls of complexity reduction:

> In his book on Pasteur, Latour argues that the success of Pasteur's approach was not the result of the application of this particular technique across all farms in the French countryside. Pasteur's technique could only work because significant dimensions of French farms were first transformed to get them closer to the laboratory conditions under which the technique was developed. (Biesta, 2010: 499)

Biesta goes on to say that:

> Again and again Latour argues that this is not the result of bringing facts and machines into the world 'outside' but of the transformation of the world outside so that it becomes part of the laboratory conditions under which things can work and can be true. (Biesta, 2010: 499)

One of my biggest fears for the education systems as they currently stand in the UK, Australia and the USA is that the culture of performativity, that is to say the pressure imposed by a heavy system of accountability in which the end-point narrative, the narrow definition of success as dictated by grades and attainment, can encourage school leaders to compromise their principles to do what they think is necessary to be successful. When leaders feel that their job is on the line and that the reputation of the school automatically attaches to them personally, this urge can be overwhelming. I've been there and felt its weighty presence. Ball (2003) discusses this pressure and contends that performativity: 'requires individual practitioners to organize themselves as a response to targets, indicators and evaluations. To set aside personal beliefs and commitments and live an existence of calculation' (Ball, 2003: 215). He continues: 'performativity produces opacity rather than transparency as individuals and organizations take ever greater care in the construction and maintenance of fabrications' (Ball, 2003: 215).

For a period of 15 months, my school was the only one of our county's 23 special schools to be rated less than good by Ofsted. Our school officially required improvement and, therefore, so did I. I felt that keenly every time I sat in a room with the other 22 Headteachers. They were lovely, supportive colleagues, but getting rid of that official grade couldn't come soon enough, and this can be where bad things happen in the name of progress.

To borrow from Biesta above, the transformation of a school so that it gets closer to the laboratory conditions under which things can work more easily can be done, but it comes at an inevitably human cost. As Biesta says, this, 'only tends to work under very specific conditions' (2010: 499) and I remain gravely concerned that we as leaders can be corrupted into trying to create those specific conditions, especially when it comes to behaviour. Rather than seek bespoke solutions to individuals' behavioural challenges, we tend to impose blanket policies, partly for ease of organisation and occasionally to mask the fact that we really don't know what to do to help this child. To continue the analogy, we risk creating something rather sterile by removing anything, and anyone, that is a perceived risk to being successful. Before you respond with, 'Who would do such a thing?!' I need to remind you that it sadly does happen. As I write, Ofsted (Bradbury, 2018) and the House of Commons Education Select Committee (2018) are both voicing concerns about a practice known as 'off-rolling' where children deemed to be a risk to the performance of a school are removed from the school's roll. Education Datalab have done some powerful work on this issue (Nye, 2017) and Warwick Mansell, a leading education journalist, has been reporting on this issue for a number of years too (Mansell, Adams and Edwards, 2016; Mansell, 2018). The House of Commons Library (2018) has produced a useful summary too.

This pressure to change a school to more closely resemble what the leader perceives a more successful school to look like can result in some, in my view, unnecessary conditions in the name of improving behaviour.

A policy where children move from lesson to lesson in silence is becoming more popular in England. I regard this as a sad situation. The logic is seductive – schools want vulnerable children to feel safe as they move between lessons and for children to get to their next lesson swiftly. No teacher, parent or child seriously disputes either of those things, but the way of achieving them says something about that school. If there are problems at lesson changeovers in my school then there is much that I can and will do about it, but a blanket ban on talking is not one of them. We miss opportunities to teach children responsibility when we insist on silence at these times. We communicate to children that we believe them to be incapable of succeeding at this safely, so we remove their agency.

Go back to your values – is this consistent with our aims of, for example, producing independent, considerate adults? I don't believe so and, further, policies such as this are more about meeting the needs of adults than they are about meeting the needs of children.

We engage in complexity reduction when we, ironically, make minor uniform infringements a major issue because uniform rules have become excessive. My current favourite rule about school uniforms is the one that allows long-sleeved shirts or short-sleeved shirts but children will be in trouble if they roll up their long-sleeves. This need to hyper-control children's clothing and their hair creates far more problems than it solves. Ultimately, we risk losing sight of what we're trying to achieve, what our school vision is, and we focus on the very short term when we try to micromanage situations or when we outlaw things that are neither disruptive to learning nor offensive to others – for example, a school rule that outlaws, 'saying "okay" when told off' (Sutcliffe, 2017).

No leader is without ego, and the culture of performativity – chasing that *Outstanding* badge from the inspectors, or seeking the *imprimatur* of the current Schools Minister – can infect the true, honest culture we all started out aiming for as naïve, inexperienced leaders. Staying firmly rooted to your values and living by them publicly and openly can protect against the temptations and pressures that you'll inevitably encounter in this highly challenging job. Don't end up like the Headteacher I once met who wanted one of his students to leave his school for mine. The boy had arrived in the September of Year 7 and within three weeks (15 days, 90 lessons) had been placed on a part-time timetable. This arrangement, going home at midday no matter how successful his day had been, lasted until the February when I visited him for an assessment for entry to our school. 'He cannot keep up at the pace we teach', I was told. Well, of course not. He's in school half as long as everyone else and already has learning difficulties. What did they expect? He came to our school I am pleased to say, and I reported the Headteacher to the local authority for illegally excluding the child daily for five months (more on exclusion in Chapter 12). My conversation with the local authority officer was brief. 'They're an academy', she told me. 'There's nothing we can do. Besides, the Headteacher is petrified of losing his [sic] outstanding grade from Ofsted and his [sic] Teaching School status and money along with it'.

> As Gert Biesta says: 'When children become a liability for their school's performance, education has come to an end' (n.d.).

TAKING IT FURTHER – QUESTIONS AND ACTIVITIES FOR YOU AND YOUR COLLEAGUES

- What kind of school do we want to be?
  - A school with ...
  - A school for ...
  - A school that ...
  - A school where ...

- Is the culture in our school by design or by default?

- What do we believe are the biggest risks to our school's sustained success?

- Are there solutions available to us that could compromise our values?

- How will we, as a group of leaders, collectively ensure that the values of our school are central to our decision-making?

- How will we, as a group of leaders, help each other to prevent knee-jerk decision-making when it comes to behaviour?

- Have we gone too far with complexity reduction in any aspect of our behaviour policy, such that we may be creating problems where there needn't be?

Notes

1. *Knowledge deficit* – the inevitable structural gap that exists between the knowledge that can be generated through experimental research and the ways in which we can use this knowledge.
2. *Effectiveness deficit* – the acceptance that in fields such as education there is no mechanistic or deterministic relationship between an intervention and its effect. At best the relationship is probabilistic.
3. *Application deficit* – we can think of this as the conditions that need to be present in order for something to work. In medicine, for example, it could be that a drug is only effective if the patient abstains from alcohol. The outside world has to be transformed in some way to allow the knowledge to become applicable.

References

Ball, S. (2003) 'The teacher's soul and the terrors of performativity', *Journal of Education Policy*, 18(2): 215–228.

Beck, A.T. (1976) *Cognitive Therapy and the Emotional Disorders*. New York: New American Library.

Biesta, G. J. J. [@gbiesta], (n.d.), Twitter.

Biesta, G.J.J. (2010) 'Why "what works" still won't work: From evidence-based education to value-based education', *Studies in Philosophy and Education*, 29(5): 491–503.

Bion, W. (1962) *Learning from Experience*. London: Karnac Books.

Bradbury, J. (2018) 'Off-rolling: using data to see a fuller picture', *Ofsted blog*, 26 June. https://educationinspection.blog.gov.uk/2018/06/26/off-rolling-using-data-to-see-a-fuller-picture/ (accessed 17 September 2019).

Department for Education (2018) *Keeping Children Safe in Education: September 2018*. Reference: DFE-00248-2018. www.gov.uk/government/publications/keeping-children-safe-in-education--2 (accessed 17 September 2019).

Finnis, M. (2018) '33 ways to build better relationships', *Independent Thinking*, 6 April. www.independentthinking.co.uk/blog/posts/2018/april/33-ways-to-build-better-relationships (accessed 30 September 2019).

Furrer, C. and Skinner, E. (2003) 'Sense of relatedness as a factor in children's academic engagement and performance', *Journal of Educational Psychology*, 95(1): 148–162.

Hosie, R. (2017) 'Children should be in bed at 9pm and up at 6:30am, says new headmaster at one of UK's worst schools', *The Independent*, 11 September. www.independent.co.uk/life-style/health-and-families/children-bedtimes-9pm-wake-up-6-30-am-headmaster-school-worst-performing-great-yarmouth-high-charter-a7940146.html (accessed 17 September 2019).

House of Commons Education Select Committee (2018) *Forgotten Children: Alternative Provision and the Scandal of Ever Increasing Exclusions*, 25 July. https://publications.parliament.uk/pa/cm201719/cmselect/cmeduc/342/34202.htm (accessed 17 September 2019).

House of Commons Library (2018) *Off-rolling in English Schools*, Briefing Paper 08444, 10 May 2019. https://researchbriefings.parliament.uk/ResearchBriefing/Summary/CBP-8444 (accessed 17 September 2019).

House of Commons Library (2019) *FAQs: Academies and Free Schools*, Briefing Paper 07059. researchbriefings.files.parliament.uk/documents/SN07059/SN07059.pdf (accessed 17 September 2019).

James, G. (2016) *Transforming Behaviour in the Classroom: A Solution-focused Guide for New Teachers*. London: SAGE.

Mansell, W. (2018) 'Are schools flouting the exclusion laws to protect their reputations?', *Times Educational Supplement*, 14 February. www.tes.com/news/are-schools-flouting-exclusion-laws-protect-their-reputations (accessed 17 September 2019).

Mansell, W., Adams, R and Edwards, P. (2016) 'England schools: 10,000 pupils sidelined due to league-table pressures', *The Guardian*, 21 January. www.theguardian.com/education/2016/jan/21/england-schools-10000-pupils-sidelined-due-to-league-table-pressures (accessed 17 September 2019).

Mercia School (n.d.) 'Are we right for you?'. www.merciaschool.com/page/?title=Are+we+right+for+you%3F&pid=27 (accessed 17 September 2019).

Nye, P. (2017) 'Who's left: The main findings', Education Datalab, 31 January. https://ffteducationdatalab.org.uk/2017/01/whos-left-the-main-findings/ (accessed 17 September 2019).

O'Brien, J. (2015) 'Emotional investment will pay dividends', *Times Educational Supplement*, 28 August. www.tes.com/news/emotional-investment-will-pay-dividends-0 (accessed 17 September 2019).

O'Brien, J. (2016) *Don't Send Him in Tomorrow*. Carmarthen: Independent Thinking Press.

Osterman, K.F. (2000) 'Students' need for belonging in the school community', *Review of Educational Research*, 70: 323–367.

Springwell Learning Community (2016) 'Unconditional positive regard – podcast', 12 September. https://springwelllearningcommunity.co.uk/news/unconditional-positive-regard-podcast/ (accessed 17 September 2019).

Sutcliffe, R. (2017) 'Huddersfield school introduces extreme rule book to crack down on behaviour', *ExaminerLive*, 8 September. www.examinerlive.co.uk/news/huddersfield-school-introduces-extreme-rule-13592779 (accessed 17 September 2019).

Whitaker, D. (n.d.) www.independentthinking.co.uk/associates/dave-whitaker/ (accessed 17 September 2019).

Willms, J.D. (2003) *Student Engagement at School: A Sense of Belonging and Participation: Results from PISA 2000*. Paris: Organization for Economic Co-operation and Development.

Winnicott, D. (1960) 'The theory of the parent–child relationship', *International Journal of Psychoanalysis*, 41: 585–595.

2

POLICY

Don't handle 99% of cases based on the 1%.

Patrick Skinner, former CIA officer (2018)

THE HEADLINES

- An opening policy statement sets the scene for what a school is trying to achieve, both on a day-to-day basis in school but also in the longer term for when children leave the school, and should be informed by the statement of principles from the governing body (or trustees in an academy or trust). It is effectively a restating of the vision and aims of the school with a specific focus on behaviour.

- A good policy stresses the importance of the foundations of a healthy school that promote high standards of behaviour. These include:

  - how the school fosters a strong sense of belonging
  - what the school does to make students feel safe and secure, not just in terms of their physical safety, but also to ensure they know that the school is a place where they can give anything a try without fearing the consequences of failure
  - the importance of recognising when children do well, and not simply relying on rewards and the enticement of material gain to persuade children to work or behave well
  - a commitment to recognising when children make progress with their behaviour, no matter how difficult things may have been previously
  - placing a premium on communicating with parents early and when things go well, not simply getting in touch when things go wrong, and also ensuring communication within school is strong
  - working with parents as equal partners when working together to help their children.

- Mistakes to avoid when formulating a behaviour policy include:

  - giving insufficient thought to those affected by the policy – the children and staff – and what implications it has for their life in school

- o producing a policy that is purely or almost entirely reactive, i.e. it only comes into effect when things go wrong and omits all of the positive and preventative things that make for better behaviour
  - o not aligning the behaviour policy with other policies of the school such as special educational needs.

- A graduated approach to improving behaviour requires:

  - o school- and classroom-wide systems that apply to all children and adults
  - o specific interventions for identified groups (such as those with literacy difficulties)
  - o an individualised approach for a small number of children.

- A thorough annual review of the effectiveness of the policy that takes into account the views of parents, gathers information on whether behaviour is improving, declining or is stable across the school and in particular places, and whether particular groups of children may be disadvantaged by the policy.

Have you ever heard of a desire path? If not, you'll definitely have walked on one. Also known as desire lines or social trails, these are unplanned paths that are created when we take repeated shortcuts on the grass resulting in a worn or beaten track instead of using the footpath that was designed and built to take us the long way round.

I'm sure you've seen these in many places, but these desire paths also have a habit of appearing metaphorically in schools' behaviour policies.

I don't mean because children sometimes intentionally pervert behaviour policies, such as when a child deliberately displays a certain behaviour in order to be removed from a lesson because that is their aim; their definition of success being to avoid something or someone, for example.

I am thinking of situations where a teacher feels forced to manipulate a behaviour policy beyond what it was designed to sustain in order to make it work for them. I'm not proud of it, but I have done this before – quite a lot when I first starting teaching – and it can be indicative of a behaviour policy that needs to be reviewed. (It could also be indicative of a teacher that doesn't like your policy, but I'll leave you to deal with that.)

If a policy is not achieving what you designed it to do, your colleagues may, and most likely will, manipulate the policy to work for them. Not out of deviousness, but out of necessity. This means that a carefully designed eight-stage intervention process ends up in real life as a two-stage shortcut to isolation. I've done it.

In my first school the behaviour policy was based on a warning system. Each misdemeanour from a child was met with two things, a warning and an instruction of what was required to improve and, if necessary, action by

Figure 2.1 User experience versus design – when teachers shortcut behaviour policies

the teacher such as moving the child to work in a different location within the classroom. Each warning came with an associated sanction and these escalated in response to non-cooperation. The warnings ran out at five when the child would be removed from the classroom by a member of the senior management team. The first warning carried with it a success reminder; the second resulted in losing a small amount of time at break or lunch with the teacher; the third a faculty detention (we staffed these on a rota basis); the fourth resulted in an after-school detention (senior colleagues staffed these on a rota basis too); and the fifth meant that the child was removed from the lesson and remained in isolation for the next lesson you had with that child (which could be up to a fortnight away by which time the situation that led to the removal was long forgotten, so this resurrected negative feelings nicely). Five warnings is, in my view, too much, but the way the policy was designed almost guaranteed escalation with some children, especially as warnings were usually given publicly.

I recall a couple of lessons in the early days with some classes where I had many names up on the board with tally marks against them to keep track and this was the most obvious indicator to any visitor that I had lost control of my lesson. I am disappointed now that I resorted to writing the names of the children on the board. I was relying on the public shame to help to positively modify the children's behaviour and it of course did nothing of the sort. It escalated the situation, breaking my personal mantra of, 'First, do no harm'. This resulted in aggravating a child who might respond overtly with anger, or they may simply have taken the hit and seethed inwardly with resentment. Some of the children amassing warnings found it amusing (or seemed to in an overt denial of the induced shame, perhaps deciding that I'd already made my mind up about them, which I certainly had in some cases) and others whose learning was being disrupted would become exasperated by my lack of control. I could, of course, have kept track on a piece of paper, but had stupidly decided that the public display would communicate to the children the seriousness of what was happening.

Here is where I began to corrupt the policy. I started putting certain children on two or three warnings before the lesson started. I even wrote them up on the board before they walked in. I remain profoundly ashamed that I ever did this, and it happened quite a few times. I am sure that I reasoned with myself that I was being tough and sending a firm message to the child, 'Look, this is serious now. You've got fewer chances so sort yourself out. I'm helping you and being kind by doing this to you'. In reality the ink was already dry on the exit ticket. It is a lame excuse to plead with you that I heard about this from one of my colleagues regarded as somewhat of a behaviour expert, but I have no one to blame but myself. The fact that it came from such an esteemed source indicates how little we discussed behaviour, our policy or such flagrant subversion of our own system, not that I would have admitted to it. I said in Chapter 1, on faulty thinking, that some children become aware over time of what the adults in their school really think of them, and it must be so damaging for those children to walk into a classroom knowing that the dice are loaded against them from the start. These were precisely the group of children that needed more of me, and instead I blatantly, and to their face, gave them less.

Clearly, you want to avoid teachers in your school feeling the need to do something like I did by having behaviour policies that are clearly understood by the adults and that are flexible enough to cope with the differing circumstances and contexts that are inherent in all schools. This is easier said than done for a number of reasons, so this chapter appears early on in order to support the production of effective policies that are resistant, as far as is possible as none are bulletproof, to inadvertent or deliberate corruption.

Potential pitfalls

Before we get to the possible make-up of a policy, I want to lay out the three most common pitfalls I see in policy construction that should be avoided.

Behaviour policies that are designed with insufficient regard to the users

Sounds unlikely, right? This can happen when policy is created in a hurry, such as when responding to an adverse Ofsted inspection judgement, and can be driven by deciding that a school should get on top of behaviour by coming down incredibly heavily on the smallest things. Policies that, for example, suggest that poor behaviour from children arises because lessons aren't engaging enough leave teachers as hostages to fortune; policies that make it very easy for children to get into bother can create unnecessary friction between children and adults; policies that make unreasonable demands on teachers make everyone's life harder and certainly make it more challenging to uphold high standards of behaviour.

Behaviour policies that are reactive

This type of ineffective policy essentially amounts to a list of things that adults must do when children misbehave and the shiny rewards on offer to children if they comply. There is no context, no aspiration, no embedding of the policy in the values of the school to enable the children to thrive and the adults to develop that warmth and sense of belonging and success. These policies fail to take into account everything that wraps around children's behaviour and contributes to it. If your behaviour policy only really kicks in when something bad happens then it's too late. You may as well write, 'Do your best and if that doesn't work call one of the SLT on duty' on a post-it note and use that as your behaviour policy.

Behaviour policies that are not aligned with the other policies in the school

If you have a behaviour policy that insists on, for example, a blanket ban on children using the toilets during lesson times then this will inevitably contradict your policy for children with special educational needs (the policy that I see most at odds with schools' behaviour policies) and your policy for supporting children with medical conditions at school. You just end up having to make a series of concessions for individuals such as the child who uses a proxy talker being allowed to use their mobile device or tablet during the day, or the child with a tracheostomy not being required to have their top button done up on their shirt. These are easy examples for schools to accommodate, but most reasonable adjustments will break a highly stringent behaviour policy. It is far better to know how to make policies inclusive from the start. This is not a minor point as I know many parents of children with special educational needs worry about this and spend time when choosing schools learning about their respective policies to see how inclusive they are. You certainly don't want to put off prospective parents (or do you?) with an inadvertent message that differences won't be accommodated, and besides, parents shouldn't have to ask for concessions.

REFLECTION POINTS

- Do any of the pitfalls identified above apply to your current policy or any policy you have been subject to in the past?

- In what ways, if any, did those issues hamper efforts to promote good behaviour?

- What would you have done differently?

What's in a behaviour policy?

For schools in England there is law in the form of statutory guidance (I've always been slightly bemused by that seeming oxymoron) that mandates what a school must do when writing a behaviour policy (Department for Education, 2016: 4–5). You will note that it makes a distinction between what maintained schools and academies must do (see 'A school *for* the community' in Chapter 1 for a basic explanation of the difference between the two types of school), but that difference is largely immaterial for the purposes of this chapter.[1]

Governors' statement of principles/Opening policy statement

When formulating a behaviour policy, you must take account of the statement of principles of the school's governing body. (For the avoidance of repetition, I will use 'school's governing body' to mean both the governing body for a maintained school and the board of trustees for an academy from now on.)

To avoid over-complication, the governors' statement of principles can also amount to the opening policy statement that sets the scene by describing in a couple of paragraphs or so what the school is trying to achieve and how the behaviour policy contributes to that.

This is an ideal opportunity to align, right from the very start, the behaviour policy firmly with the school's values. Those shared values can once more be made crystal clear and a strong message follows that the policy is a natural outcome of those values. For example, the statement of principles can explicitly state the school's commitment to inclusion by declaring that the policy will be flexible enough to ensure that reasonable adjustments *must* be made so that children with special educational needs and disabilities (SEND) are not disadvantaged by the policy (O'Brien, 2018) – there's no *maybe* about this; the Equality Act (2010) is a law not a choice (see Chapter 11 for more on this) – or to account for gender diversity so trans children aren't falling foul of uniform rules that are too rigid to accommodate their needs.

Don't underestimate the power of this alignment with values because, without it, the risk increases that we end up with policies that demand zero tolerance with the premise that any allowance for individuals amounts to indulging feckless children, and statements from school leaders stating that, 'reasonable adjustment destroys positive discipline and destroys effective schools' (Parker, 2018).

The statement of principles can encapsulate the right of all children to be safe and to be free from disruption to their learning; it can reaffirm the school's commitment to helping children improve their behaviour (in the truly educative sense as opposed to the punitive 'That'll teach 'im' sense) and, crucially, it can make it clear that the school will work with parents to achieve this.

The statement of principles can also provide guidance to you from the governing body on the following (although, in my opinion, these are better covered separately later in the policy in Tier 1 [see below] in order for the policy to flow better):

Screening and searching pupils

- There is detailed guidance available from the Department for Education (2018a) on this matter and this must be well understood by school leaders.
- Here you can identify what, beyond the standard list of prohibited items including obvious ones like knives and alcohol, you as a school regard as prohibited. 'Headteachers and authorised staff can also search for any item banned by the school rules which has been identified in the rules as an item which may be searched for.' It is worth considering the use of this freedom carefully as defining hoodies, trainers or other such relatively inoffensive items, but ones which schools sometimes tie themselves in knots over trying to control, as prohibited is one thing (and therefore giving you the power to search for them), but actually choosing to exercise that power and search for relatively innocuous items may be a step too far.

- You can provide guidance to parents on confiscation in this section too. The temptation to create a system where, for example, mobile phones are confiscated by your school for an extended period of time (e.g. weeks on end) as a deterrent is, in my view, inadvisable as it may be considered disproportionate by any reasonable person.

The power to use reasonable force and other physical contact

- There is guidance available from the Department for Education (2013) on this matter and this must be well understood by school leaders.
- No school should have a no-touch rule as this is both unrealistic and potentially negligent.
- Despite the guidance that states, 'It is good practice for schools to speak to parents about serious incidents involving the use of force and to consider how best to record such serious incidents. It is up to schools to decide whether it is appropriate to report the use of force to parents', I cannot conceive of a school that would not consider it absolutely necessary to inform parents if their child has been involved in a serious incident involving the use of force against them. As a parent, I would be appalled to discover some time after the fact that this had happened to my child, perhaps multiple times, or to hear it from them first hand when they came home.

The power to discipline beyond the school gate

- This is the place to lay out the school's response to non-criminal behaviour when a child is, or children are:

  - taking part in any school-organised or school-related activity
  - travelling to or from school
  - wearing school uniform
  - in some other way identifiable as a pupil at the school.

- Or misbehaviour at any time, whether or not the conditions above apply, that:

  - could have repercussions for the orderly running of the school
  - poses a threat to another pupil or member of the public
  - could adversely affect the reputation of the school.

When to work with other local agencies to assess the needs of pupils who display continuous disruptive behaviour

- You can cover this more effectively when you detail the tiered responses (see below in Tier 2 and, more likely, in Tier 3) that make up the graduated approach that forms the basis of your policy.

Pastoral care for staff accused of misconduct

- It is an unfortunate fact that there are, thankfully rare, occasions when an allegation is made by an adult or a child against an adult that they have behaved in a manner that amounts to a misuse of their powers. As leaders we have a duty of care to all involved in such situations, including the person who is the subject of the allegation, irrespective of whether the allegation is subsequently proven. Our colleagues need to know that we will support them and we can state here how we will do that. This can include the provision of a named colleague to discuss matters, and to keep in touch with if they have been suspended (a good local authority or private human resources service will provide you with solid advice and a risk assessment template if you're also the Headteacher who has to decide whether to suspend someone). You can also detail here any services that your school or local authority provides for teachers, often called employee assistance services.

Vision and aims

This section of the policy is your chance to aim high. Of course you want classrooms, corridors and playgrounds where children are safe and learning is disruption-free. It's not enough, though, to just settle for aiming for a school where teachers can teach and children can learn. That's the bare minimum. Surely you are also looking to the medium and long term by supporting children to develop the lifelong ability to manage their own behaviour and to recognise that they have a personal responsibility to their fellow humans by fostering a culture of mutual respect. Lastly, you can also communicate that you have an inclusive ethos by making it an explicit aim that you will work with children and their families to support them to improve their behaviour. A well-written opening policy statement will skilfully include the vision and aims within it and avoid duplication.

Foundations

There are a number of important features of positive culture that reinforce and encourage good behaviour in schools and they can be stated here.

Building a sense of belonging

This was raised in Chapter 1 and is sometimes underestimated in developing a strong culture of good behaviour. The easier bit is to list all the key things you do to construct a school that your students are proud to attend. It's more challenging to go one step further – would you consider watching out for things that can damage a sense of belonging? By that I mean when we prevent access to a favoured aspect of school life for a child when they have done something wrong in another unrelated part of school. For example, it is decided that a child is to be excluded from the rugby team as punishment for misbehaviour in an art lesson. Withdrawal of a child's favourite thing in response to misbehaviour is very superficial and carries with it a risk of deepening resentment rather than improving behaviour. 'Right! For that behaviour you are banned from maths homework for the rest of the term!' said no teacher ever.

Safety and security

'A school where it is safe to fail' was, just like a sense of belonging, covered in Chapter 1 so I won't rehearse the main thrust here, but a statement concerning the importance of adults' understanding when children fear school, fear the adults or their peers or fear the work they are expected to do, and that the school recognises this, and outlining what they can do about it conveys a powerful message.

Recognition

The more experienced I become the more convinced I am that we are mistaken in our rush to reward children for good behaviour. We should aim for recognising good behaviour (see Chapter 7). Offering inducements to comply and do work is setting a low bar for our children, and I believe that a culture of recognition as opposed to reward is the way to go. And that recognition may well be low key and private as some children are uncomfortable with very public and grandiose displays of appreciation.

Progress

Policies where the positives only kick in once a child has crossed a certain threshold of 'goodness' will be very limited in their ability to improve the behaviour of those who are finding it hardest to behave well in school. The importance of recognising progress from the child's starting point, just as we do when assessing the progress children make with their academic study, is crucial. We don't continually label a child a failure until they become a free reader or until they attain a certain grade at GCSE, and a similar, developmental approach with behaviour helps everyone to keep going when signs of progress become evident.

Communication

A common, and legitimate, complaint from parents is that teachers can sometimes leave it too late to get in touch with them when there are behavioural issues, or that their contact with them is wholly negative.

Communicating early, frequently and when things go well as well as when they don't are good foundations for maintaining strong working relationships with parents. We shouldn't forget the importance of communicating well with our colleagues either. Poor communication kills organisations so a clear system is vital for communicating things such as behaviour plan changes and agreed strategies, key information that all staff need to know, and when new children join the school and have had issues with their behaviour in the past.

Parents

In addition to communicating with parents, a healthy system involves them in the solution when there are concerns about a child's behaviour, at an informal stage, when a child goes on report and when behaviour support plans are required. Parents are naturally keen to ensure that their children do well in school, even when we perceive that they are disinterested or at odds with us, and we should use this energy to everyone's benefit. I have known tensions surface at times like these because a school can sometimes take the view that it's 'my house, my rules', but this is a missed opportunity. This working in partnership will be entirely consistent with your community values.

REFLECTION POINTS

- What does your school currently do to instil a sense of belonging in its students?

- What would the students who find it hardest to behave well say about this?

- What is the balance of recognition/reward strategies in your school?

- How effective do you believe them to be relative to each other?

- How involved are parents when it comes to working to improve a child's behaviour?

Graduated approach

A policy that fails to take into consideration the complexity and variation present in its student community with a one-size fits all approach is a policy that will fail. (As the staff at St Andrew's School in Derby say, 'One size fits one'.) On the other hand, no policy can reasonably cover all scenarios or eventualities, so a graduated approach is required in order to cope with the inevitable range of behaviours and needs present in any school, no matter how small.

Tier 1: School- and classroom-wide systems for all children and adults

Rules

Your behavioural expectations, stated in a positive way (i.e. 'Do …' as opposed to 'Don't …'), in simple, limited language and kept to a small number that can be easily remembered and recalled by staff and children.

Modelling

All the things you want to see from the adults that reinforce the positive social norms that you are striving to engender in your children.

Routines

Aspects of school life that you insist on for all staff and/or children. You may have routines for the beginnings and endings of lessons. You may have routines where children line up in classes at the end of breaks and lunchtimes and are collected by their teachers, or you may insist that all children stand up when the Headteacher, or any teacher, enters the room. (I dislike this idea as it seems to suggest that an act of deference is deemed important enough to interrupt children's learning.) A school I am familiar with insists on what it calls 'silent starters', where the first few minutes of every lesson, marked with a starter activity, is conducted in silence.

Recognition

The importance of recognition was mentioned in 'Foundations' above and here you can go into the detail of how you will recognise good behaviour and improvements in behaviour. There should be some different aspects to this – recognition by the teachers of individual children and classes; in groups such as house activities, and at a whole-school level.

Sanctions

Your generally agreed responses to incidents of poor behaviour. Whilst retaining a level of flexibility (a missed homework hasn't always been eaten by the dog) you can indicate the differences in response to a uniform infringement or to bullying or physical abuse.

Specifics

I'm thinking of mobile phones here, especially for secondary schools given their near universal presence amongst this age group. Whatever your policy, you can leave everyone in no doubt here as to what you will and will not accept.

Tier 2: Specific interventions for identified groups

In some 'universal → small group → individual' tiered systems, this middle section is devoted to *behaviour* interventions for groups with issues they have in common. My experiences over the past 18 years have led me to think we're missing a trick here. Whilst behavioural interventions are not unimportant, we mustn't forget the evidence that tells us about the significant contributory factors that can lead to behavioural difficulties in schools too, and I believe there is much to be gained by identifying groups of children with particular needs in common and seeking to address those as a preventative measure. I detail three below, but this list is not exhaustive.

You may well involve external support within this tier, such as educational psychologists (see below in Tier 3 for a bit more on them).

Speech, language and communication difficulties

Studies have shown that children with speech, language and communication needs (SLCN) are more likely to develop behavioural, emotional and social difficulties than typically developing children, with prevalence rates as high as 35–50 per cent (Lindsay et al., 2007; Van Daal et al., 2007; St Clair et al., 2011). Although this is well established in the research evidence, it is not a well-known association amongst teachers. Given this association it would make sense for schools to take a preventative approach by providing support in this area. The vast majority of children with some form of SLCN will have no guaranteed right to formal speech and language therapy (SALT), so this need is almost certain to be only partially met at best, unless a positive decision is made at a school level to prioritise this as a preventative behaviour measure. In the absence of a speech and language therapist who, without the legal weight of an education, health and care plan (EHCP) will be as rare as hens' teeth, you may be able to obtain expertise and support with meeting speech, language and communication needs from a local special school's outreach service which is, at the time of writing, often free at the point of use. SALT work is often carried out in small groups in any case, so this intervention lends itself well to working with small groups of children. My experience of working with speech and language therapists and members of support staff with certain skills in this area has shown them to be very adept at using their work to support improvements in communication that address specific areas of a child's life. Therefore, this work could be used to help with areas of difficulty such as turn-taking, listening, following lists of instructions, scripts for dealing with more unstructured times such as breaks and lunchtimes or how to talk through disagreements with their peers – all sources of problems for some children.

Literacy difficulties

Research findings suggest a significant association between literacy difficulties and emotional and behavioural problems in childhood (Hinshaw, 1992; Meltzer et al., 1999; Willcutt and Pennington, 2000; Arnold et al., 2005; Carroll et al., 2005). This association is, though, unlikely to be one way, with findings, which chime with common sense, suggesting that behavioural difficulties impede progress in literacy and that literacy difficulties lead to behavioural difficulties. I've yet to meet a school that does not provide support, often significant ongoing support, for children with literacy difficulties, but the research findings suggest that schools should effectively screen children who are experiencing behavioural difficulties for both literacy difficulties and, given what I have said in the previous subheading, speech, language and communication difficulties in case aspects of either, or as is sometimes the case, both of these difficulties have been missed. Schools are naturally more likely to be well set up to support children with literacy difficulties than they are for speech, language and communication issues, but advice and guidance can also be obtained from local authority literacy and language support services.

Transition for those with known behavioural difficulties or those deemed vulnerable

In my 19 years as a teacher I have seen a gradual and determined improvement in efforts dedicated to transition between schools, most notably between primary and secondary education. Children who are already experiencing difficulties with their behaviour in their current school represent an obvious group to focus on in the often months' long transition process into their future school. However, I have worked with a fair number of children who would have been defined as 'vulnerable' in one school become, over time, labelled as a 'behaviour problem' in the next. I am reminded of a conversation I had in my early days as a senior leader with a civil servant from the Department for Children, Schools and Families (DCSF was a previous incarnation of the DfE) when we were working on the original *Achievement for All* programme. He described an apparently well-known graph he kept on his office noticeboard, which showed the relative proportions of children in Year 6 with SLCN and of those with behavioural difficulties next to the relative proportions of children with the same needs in Year 7. In Year 6, he said, it showed that children with SLCN far outweighed those with behaviour difficulties, yet the situation seemed to be magically reversed in Year 7. His conclusion was obvious. (A quick glance at the DfE's own statistics [Department for Education, 2018b] does show very crudely that the proportion of children with SEND who have SLCN as their primary need drops from 29.8 per cent in primary to 11.3 per cent in secondary schools. However, I am sure that a clear plan to ensure that children deemed by their current school as vulnerable have a bespoke transition plan – many schools already do this well – can go a long way to preventing behaviour problems, or related issues such as attendance issues, arising later on.)

Transition between schools for large groups at planned times (Year 6 to Year 7, for example) is well covered, but what can be less well planned is transition for individuals at other times. Reasons for this vary widely – family relocation, permanent exclusion (or managed moves), bullying, parental dissatisfaction to name just a few. The process is inevitably disruptive and you could make a case that all such transitions make children vulnerable. Sometimes these moves happen very quickly, but any preparatory work a school can do will help make the process just that bit more manageable for the child.

Tier 3: Individualised approach for a small number of children

For the overwhelming majority of children in any school, with the possible exception of some specialist schools, the strategies, approaches and practices that arise out of Tiers 1 and 2 will support leaders, teachers and support staff to maintain good behaviour. However, there will be a very small minority of children who will need a planned approach that is specific to them to support them to behave well.

How this is formulated and who is involved – it may be unfeasible in a secondary school, for example, for all adults working with a child to be involved in agreeing a strategy – is down to individual schools, but they may feature some or all of the following.

Parent consultation

I am sorry to say that I have caught myself a few times when I've been ground down saying to a child in a moment of difficulty, 'Right! That's it!

I'm getting your parents in!'. It was used as a clear threat and, unsurprisingly, it was an ineffective one. Involving parents as equal partners is crucial, both in terms of reassuring them that you value their child and the family and that you're serious about helping their child to improve their behaviour, but also because they will have a lot to offer in terms of potential solutions. Bringing them in to berate them, or, as I did, to use them as a threat to stun the child into behaving better is likely to be ineffective or could make things worse.

Solution-focused work

By nature, solution-focused work is done with individuals and is characterised by being goal-directed, whilst regarding time invested in looking at problems as being unnecessary. (This last point about not seeking to analyse problems seems counter-intuitive and this is the main reason, I think, that solution-focused work is often dismissed by colleagues as a soft option that indulges naughty kids in a cosy chat.) There are three fundamental beliefs that underpin solution-focused work:

1. The child is successful.
2. The child is resourceful.
3. The child is hopeful.

This set of beliefs clearly communicates that the child has both an awareness of what they want their future to look like and of what would improve their current situation. The process validates the importance of their view, and this is something that can be missing from more standard approaches to behaviour improvement that are done unto children. It also maintains that the child possesses the skills necessary to make the changes, and the process is designed to support children with this if they need assistance in describing the details of the improvements they wish to see by the use of questions like, 'Suppose things were going better for you in science. What would you notice that's changed?' or follow-ups such as, 'What might you change a bit to get you there?'.

This is not a method about which I feel comfortable just picking up and giving it a go and seeing how it pans out. I feel the same about using restorative approaches to resolving conflict, and recommend that there is a level of training provided to colleagues before considering its use.

Special Educational Needs Coordinator (SENCo) involvement

Children with SEND are far more likely than their peers to be excluded from school either for a fixed-term or permanently (Department for

Education, 2019). The use of fixed-term and permanent exclusion should be reserved for the most serious behaviour issues in schools (although I remain concerned that fixed-term exclusion is used far too liberally for minor things in some schools), so it is likely that children with SEND are also regulars on the lists of children receiving sanctions at the levels below suspension – detention and isolation, for example. The involvement of the school's resident expert on SEND should be a given at this stage for at least one of two reasons: either the child is already identified as having some form of special educational need and, if so, it would be perverse not to involve the SENCo in plans to improve this child's behaviour (indeed, they may well lead the process); or the SENCo can assist with screening for literacy, speech, language and communication issues or other needs that may be contributing to the difficulties that the child is experiencing.

The SENCo can also be the person to assist with securing the services of other professionals too such as the local authority's behaviour support team or an educational psychologist (EP).

Educational psychologists

EPs or ed psychs, as educational psychologists are often known, are colleagues who are well used in the field of special educational needs but, in my experience, far less when schools are looking to improve behaviour. They bring a wealth of experience around the areas of child development, the psychology of learning and teaching, and the psychological aspects of teaching children with SEND. They carry out work at different levels: they can be used on a consultancy basis by schools for particular issues (and as such have their own place in Tier 2 too), such as the assessment of individual children; they can undertake intervention work such as a school-wide approach to reducing bullying or on transitions for vulnerable children; they can carry out training on specific issues, and this could be for groups such as support staff or lunchtime staff or for the whole team; and lastly they also conduct research.

Behaviour plans and reports

It is inevitable that if an individual child requires a specific, planned approach that involves multiple adults to help them improve their behaviour then there will be a need to keep track of how that child is progressing. This is needed in order to gauge the effectiveness of what has been put in place to support the child, and of the advice given to their teachers. That way changes can be made if needed, or if successful, you can build confidence in what you're doing and do more of it. Behaviour plans (the agreed strategies that all staff will use) and behaviour reports (the collation of the evidence to gauge effectiveness) need to knit together and are, I hope, not used as punitive devices any more. You can read more about them in Chapter 6.

Positive handling plans

In the extremely rare event that consideration needs to be given to physically restraining a child because there is a serious threat of harm to themselves or to others, a positive handling plan should be considered. No adult wants to have to hold a child, but if violent behaviour puts people at risk, we need to give careful thought as to how we can best protect the child, their peers and adults. Positive handling plans can detail all the strategies the school can use to prevent behaviours occurring, how best to de-escalate and what are the agreed approaches if they don't work. It can also highlight training requirements. A good behaviour plan will do all of these things anyway, so a handling plan is effectively an extension or appendix to a behaviour plan because there is no way that a child will have a handling plan without a pre-existing behaviour plan.

Policy review

Reviewing policies can sometimes be a task that senior leaders loathe, and I admit to being one of those people on occasion. At its worst, policy review amounts to a change of the date at the bottom of the cover page and a task successfully shelved for another 12 months at least. Policies date quickly under these conditions and I recall after six years as a Headteacher reading our behaviour policy and realising that our day-to-day practice had diverged quite markedly from the words I was reading on the page (and, importantly for parents including prospective ones, that appeared on our website).

Policy review is not just a cosmetic rewrite or a chance to add in new legislation or statutory guidance. For behaviour policies, it is a golden opportunity to test how the policy is faring and adjust accordingly.

Evidence-informed policy review helps schools improve, and to spot where practices and strategies may have lost their effectiveness over time. In order to do this, though, the school does need good evidence from a range of sources. If reporting to governors is a strong feature of the school (see Chapter 13), and it really should be, then the information provided to them can form part of this process as it is the governing body that ultimately signs off the policy.

Parents

Schools should involve parents in reviewing the policy, resisting the 'my house, my rules' approach that I mentioned earlier by committing to listening to what parents really think about your approach to behaviour in your school. DfE guidance states that, for maintained schools, 'The headteacher must publicise the school behaviour policy, in writing, to staff, parents and pupils at least once a year' (Department for Education, 2016: 5), so this presents an ideal opportunity to involve parents in the process rather than informing them after the ink is dry on the policy.

Information

Schools are replete with data these days, but these data are not always translated into useful information. When it comes to reviewing the effectiveness of a behaviour policy, there are two key strands of information that are required. Firstly, evidence that behaviour in the school overall is improving, stable or declining, and where in the school it is improving, stable or declining. This needs consistent, reliable evidence over time in order to make solid inferences (nothing is absolute). It also needs sufficient breadth and depth – too little (a school I am very familiar with records fixed-term and permanent exclusions but nothing else) leaves you relying on opinion and if that's the case you may as well not bother. Secondly, a thorough review needs to look deliberately at the presence of particular groups within the data. This is vital as we have been aware for a long time that particular groups of children are far more likely to receive fixed-term exclusions or be permanently excluded and, I contend, this is also likely to be true for all other aspects of behaviour sanctions. Strand and Fletcher (2014: 18) – in the most comprehensive English study I know comprising a cohort of over 500,000 children tracked over the five years of their secondary education – found variations that they describe as, 'consistent with a degree of systemic discrimination'. Given that this is common knowledge, a school should go out of its way to show how it measures up against these national trends.

REFLECTION POINTS

- What range of information do you currently use to gauge the effectiveness of your behaviour policy?

- How widely is this information shared? Would staff know about this information to allow them to come to a more-informed view about behaviour in your school over time?

**TAKING IT FURTHER – QUESTIONS AND ACTIVITIES
FOR YOU AND YOUR COLLEAGUES**

- Is our policy clear enough or detailed enough on the foundations and preventative work we do to promote good behaviour?
- What do parents think of our behaviour policy?
- How has that fed into our review process?
- Are we using enough information when we review our behaviour policy?
- If not, what is missing and who is going to get it?
- Do we know for sure that particular groups of children aren't disadvantaged by our policy?
- If not, what information do we need and who is going to get it?

Note

1. Within the fragmented schools' landscape in England, there exist maintained schools (funded via their local councils and whose staff are employees of that council) and academies (funded directly from central government and whose employees are employed by a trust that runs the academy or group of academies) and, unhelpfully and irrationally, demands placed on them by the Department for Education seem to be different. One example being that, while maintained schools are required by law to publish their behaviour policy in writing to staff, parents and pupils at least once a year, bizarrely, no such compulsion exists for academies.

References

Arnold, E., Goldston, D., Walsh, A., Reboussin, B., Daniel, S., Hickman, E. and Wood, F.B. (2005) 'Severity of emotional and behavioral problems among poor and typical readers', *Journal of Abnormal Child Psychology*, 33(2): 205–217.

Carroll, J., Maughan, B., Goodman, R. and Meltzer, H. (2005) 'Literacy difficulties and psychiatric disorders: Evidence for comorbidity', *Journal of Child Psychology and Psychiatry*, 46: 524–532.

Department for Education (2013) *Use of Reasonable Force: Advice for Headteachers, Staff and Governing Bodies*, July. https://assets.publishing.service.gov.uk/government/uploads/system/uploads/attachment_data/file/444051/Use_of_ reasonable_force_advice_Reviewed_July_2015.pdf (accessed 17 September 2019).

Department for Education (2016) *Behaviour and Discipline in Schools: Advice for Headteachers and School Staff*, January. https://assets.publishing.service.gov. uk/government/uploads/system/uploads/attachment_data/file/488034/ Behaviour_and_Discipline_in_Schools_-_A_guide_for_headteachers_and_ School_Staff.pdf (accessed 17 September 2019).

Department for Education (2018a) *Searching, Screening and Confiscation: Advice for Headteachers, School Staff and Governing Bodies*, January. https://assets. publishing.service.gov.uk/government/uploads/system/uploads/attachment_ data/file/674416/Searching_screening_and_confiscation.pdf (accessed 17 September 2019).

Department for Education (2018b) *Special Educational Needs in England – January 2018: National Tables*, Table 8. www.gov.uk/government/statistics/ special-educational-needs-in-england-january-2018 (accessed 17 September 2019).

Department for Education (2019) *Permanent and Fixed-period Exclusions in England: 2017 to 2018*, 25 July. www.gov.uk/government/statistics/perma nent-and-fixed-period-exclusions-in-england-2017-to-2018 (accessed 17 September 2019).

Hinshaw, S.P. (1992) 'Externalizing behavior problems and academic undera- chievement in childhood and adolescence: causal relationships and underlying mechanisms', *Psychological Bulletin*, 111: 127–155.

Lindsay, G., Dockrell, J. and Strand, S. (2007) 'Longitudinal patterns of behaviour problems in children with specific speech and language difficulties: child and contextual factors', *British Journal of Educational Psychology*, 77: 811–828.

Meltzer, H., Gatward, R., Goodman, R. and Ford, T. (1999) *The Mental Health of Children and Adolescents in Great Britain*. The Office for National Statistics. London: The Stationery Office.

O'Brien, J. (2018) 'How to build a behaviour policy with inclusion at its heart', *Times Educational Supplement*, 4 May. www.tes.com/news/tes-magazine/ tes-magazine/how-build-a-behaviour-policy-inclusion-its-heart (accessed 17 September 2019).

Parker, K. (2018) 'Big rewards and "really harsh" punishments – meet the man who says he has a behaviour silver bullet', *Times Educational Supplement*, 4 February. www.tes.com/news/long-read-big-rewards-and-really-harsh- punishments-meet-man-who-says-he-has-behaviour-silver (accessed 17 September 2019).

Skinner, P. (2018) https://twitter.com/SkinnerPm/status/103647994813394534 4?s=20 (accessed 30 September 2019).

St Clair, M.C., Pickles, A., Durkin, K. and Conti-Ramsden, G. (2011) 'A longitudinal study of behavioral, emotional and social difficulties in individuals with a his- tory of specific language impairment (SLI)', *Journal of Communication Disorders*, 44: 186–199.

Strand, S. and Fletcher, J. (2014) *A Quantitative Longitudinal Analysis of Exclusions from English Secondary Schools*. Oxford: University of Oxford.

Van Daal, J., Verhoeven, L. and van Balkom, H. (2007) 'Behaviour problems in children with language impairment', *Journal of Child Psychology and Psychiatry*, 48: 1139–1147.

Willcutt, E.G. and Pennington, B.F. (2000) 'Psychiatric comorbidity in children and adolescents with reading disability', *Journal of Child Psychology and Psychiatry*, 41: 1039–1048.

3

STAFF CONFIDENCE AND SELF-EFFICACY

True intuitive expertise is learned from prolonged experience with good feedback on mistakes.

Daniel Kahneman (2011)

THE HEADLINES

- Each of us brings to the profession a legacy of attitudes, practices and values from our own extensive and significant experiences as schoolchildren observing teachers. This so-called 'apprenticeship of observation' can be influential, yet unrecognised, and lead to derivative or imitative approaches to dealing with behaviour, especially at times of indecision or stress.

- As leaders, we need to discuss this with colleagues to allow them to recognise where this may be the case, and to allow them to develop a self-assurance that is the result of successful experience of behaviour improvement.

- Developing a sense of confidence and self-assurance in teachers and support staff requires consideration of four main areas:

  o Experiences of success – achievement builds a solid sense of one's personal efficacy. Experiences of failure, on the other hand, can damage this especially if encountered early on before a level of confidence is secured. Easy success, though, provides only a veneer of confidence as this leads to an expectation of swift trouble-free results and little experience of negotiating hurdles along the way. Lasting self-efficacy comes from successfully overcoming difficulties, learning from them and persevering.

  o Social modelling – learning from others is a powerful way to build self-efficacy, but systematic and longer-term work with colleagues can be hampered by the organisational demands of the school day, term and year. Significant attention needs to be given to how easy it is for colleagues to learn from each other or what it will take to make it work – how can a particular strategy be transferred from one context to another or from one teacher to another?

o   Social persuasion – sharing successes, the overcoming of challenges and what it took to defeat them, and reminders of past achievements are all good ways of sustaining colleagues' commitment and energy to improving behaviour. Sharing early signs of progress with colleagues is also a good way to maintain belief in the team that strategies are working and that persistence will pay off.

o   Stress reduction – behaviour is an inevitably emotional matter in schools. Leaders need to pay close attention to the emotional demand it places on staff as it can get out of hand. Stress, fatigue and tension can influence colleagues' perceptions of their own capabilities, so efforts to manage this through supervision, support and mentorship are important.

My daughter, Hannah, happens to be a student in the same school in which her mother teaches (although my wife is not her teacher as both she and Hannah value each other's sanity). Because of this it is common for Hannah to spend some time in her mum's classroom at the beginning and end of the day. I recently tentatively asked Hannah what she learned about teachers during this time that she didn't already know and her immediate response was to express amazement at the amount of chocolate teachers eat.

Hannah is in the middle of serving an apprenticeship of observation. This term was coined by Dan Lortie in *Schoolteacher: A Sociological Study* (1975) to reflect the thousands of hours that new teachers spent as children in close proximity to teachers, observing their actions and forming opinions and judgements about who teachers are and what they do. (Hannah's apprenticeship is slightly broader than most because of the overtime she's putting in every day before and after school.) This apprenticeship means that we don't all arrive into the profession fresh; we arrive with a set of strongly formed views in our minds, whether or not we are aware of them and different for each of us, of course, of what teaching consists of and what teachers do.

Lortie says that children see, 'the teacher frontstage and centre like an audience viewing a play' (Lortie, 1975: 62) and this chimes very much with our oft-stated description of teaching as performance. By extension, what they don't see, unless they get a glimpse like my daughter, is the backstage work and this is well worth considering when thinking about the legacy of new teachers' observations and experiences of how behaviour was dealt with when they were children at school. They saw the immediate, overt behaviours and reactions from teachers in their classrooms in response to poor behaviour but little, if any, of the other work that teachers undertook to try to resolve individual issues or their wider foundational work that we went through in Chapter 2. Additionally, their experience of school like everyone else's is partial. Teachers are generally academically able people so at least some of us will have spent most of our time in groups set by ability, certainly at secondary school, or in grammars or selective independent schools, and the differences in behaviour evident in top sets or bottom sets may well be stark.

Given how we as experienced professionals can sometimes find it tough to describe what results in exceptional teaching when we think we see it in front of us, new teachers stand no chance, based on their childhood experiences, of appreciating the subtleties of all that teachers do to promote good behaviour. Thus, teachers and support staff new to the profession bring strong intuitive or derivative ideas about how to manage behaviour that are unlikely to have been subject to analysis or forethought. Indeed, a number of studies (John, 1996; Richards and Pennington, 1998; Virta, 2002) have highlighted the lasting power of this apprenticeship on teachers, with teachers sometimes reverting to type even after a period of training. I contend that apprenticeships of observation are not limited to children, but apply to teachers too. Teachers spend lots of time around those of us who lead on behaviour in schools, seeing us perform on Lortie's stage as it were, but much of the work is conducted behind closed doors. This is a problem, especially if we take issues away from colleagues to solve them – this can be supportive for obvious reasons, but risks never allowing those colleagues to see or be involved in a situation from beginning to end. Thus, early career teachers can be forgiven for wondering what it is precisely that senior leaders do all day, even if they, as I always did, publicise their diary for all to see. I am sure that this, in part, explains some teachers' reluctance to take on the jobs of school leadership.

REFLECTION POINTS

- When thinking about your own experiences of school as a child what are the strongest memories of how behaviour was dealt with?

- Is there a legacy evident in how you have approached behaviour in the past, or still do now?

- Could examination of the apprenticeship of observation be a useful aspect of induction training for teachers and support staff new to your school or of a behaviour refresher session?

Self-efficacy

The inertia in the apprenticeships we all served is strong, but we want teachers and support staff to move from a position of relying on their instincts to developing a self-assurance when dealing with behaviour, which is borne out of the experience of successful behaviour improvement. We could simply let teachers learn from experience, which was my main method when I worked in a comprehensive in my first few years of teaching, but we will undoubtedly lose colleagues from the profession and damage some of those who remain, or we as leaders can take a more deliberate approach to helping colleagues feel confident about managing and improving behaviour.

When thinking about how to develop that confidence in others, I have been influenced by Bandura's work on self-efficacy (1994). It has been helpful because, even after all these years of experience, I constantly worry about doing enough to support colleagues appropriately – backing off too much means deserved criticism, but piling in too quickly or heavily can result in either a dependency that stifles that sought-after confidence, or more likely, a feeling from colleagues that I don't trust them to get it right. Neither is good.

I have written much in various places about the behaviour issue of work avoidance from children. I regard work avoidance as failure avoidance – the task at hand is not the main issue, it is the seemingly inevitable shame, failure or sanction that goes with it that the child is avoiding. The fact that punishment, however severe, will surely follow is irrelevant. It is preferable to failing at the task at hand. This is a lack of self-efficacy at work, and similar underlying emotional drivers can influence our own feelings as teachers if we feel we're struggling with behaviour. As the nineteenth-century American philosopher and psychologist William James said, 'With no attempt there can be no failure; with no failure no humiliation'.

A high degree of self-efficacy means that difficult tasks are regarded as challenges, but ones that can be overcome. The difficulties present in those challenges are not ignored or minimised, but understood. The process, although tough, is seen as a learning experience and a chance to grow. Setbacks are expected as a natural part of the process and, when they do arrive, are regarded as opportunities to improve. The person will see that at that point in time they lacked certain skills and/or knowledge, but they are committed to acquiring the skill or knowledge in order to be more successful next time. They do not see failure, if it does occur, as a personal deficit and are slow to lose heart or commitment, maintaining a focus on their goal.

As I read this paragraph back to myself I realise that there is a danger of it sounding like a description of supreme confidence that is usually the pre-serve of Old Etonian cabinet ministers. There is a big difference between an inner determination, which is what the paragraph above is really describing, and a pig-headed insistence on bluffing your way through a problem, even when all around is in ruins. This high degree of self-belief is something I have seen over and over again in friends who are military officers. And one of the reasons for this, which I will come on to below in more detail, is the vicarious experiences provided by social models – their peers and mentors – and this is, I am convinced, a major factor in success in collegiate professions.

Conversely, a lack of self-efficacy leads to difficult tasks being regarded as insurmountable or as threats to be avoided. Setbacks can quickly derail the process and persuade someone to quit, and can be put down to personal deficiencies. This can become chronic, with people less likely to attempt something in the future if previous experience has taught them that the chances of failure are too high. This is something that I have battled with my entire life, so I can attest to how debilitating it can be as it has overwhelmed me on a great number of occasions. Given the number of teachers that leave the profession relatively early on (there will be many of us too, and I am certainly one, who came close to quitting teaching), and some departures unfortunately will be because of behaviour, it seems worthwhile to try to increase this sense of self-efficacy where possible to help reduce this loss.

Bandura (1994) details a number of different, complementary ways to improve self-efficacy.

Mastery experiences

Bandura (1994) uses this term to describe one key area in building self-efficacy, but I dislike it in the context of teaching as it implies superiority. I prefer to think about the experiences of success rather than of mastery, as teachers, being a modest bunch, have an aversion to concepts such as mastery for their own practice. If you've ever suggested to a colleague that they should apply to become an Advanced Skills Teacher or Specialist Leader of Education you'll know what I mean: 'Me? Good Lord, no! I'm just an ordinary teacher!'.

There's another reason I prefer 'success' to 'mastery' and it is to do with a feeling of messiness that can arise when dealing with behaviour difficulties. I am reminded of the officer safety training that was a key part of my training to be a Special Constable. Learning to deal with potentially dangerous situations in role-play scenarios was a low-stakes affair – fellow constables tend to be relatively cooperative when you're learning to handcuff them, strike them with a baton or spray them in the face with PAVA – but real life is different. Arresting someone who doesn't want to be arrested, who wants to hurt you or is armed with something dangerous, whilst maybe being under the influence of drugs and/or alcohol (all fall under the rather dry and understated label of 'someone with a positive mindset') could sometimes feel very chaotic. The outcome could still be a safe, competent arrest that was managed well and everyone got to go home in one piece. I never came out of those situations feeling masterful, but I did eventually realise that in those times I had been successful. The same is true of some situations where behaviour has been difficult – it's hard to feel good about a situation that seems inherently bad, such as when one child bullies another.

It is self-evident that you can build a sense of your own competency and confidence by experiencing success, but Bandura notes that easy successes can lead to over-confidence or an expectation of quick results and thus you can be more easily discouraged by failure. Self-efficacy, if it is to be lasting, requires the successful resolution of problems through perseverance.

Failure, however, can undermine self-efficacy if it is experienced enough before that confidence is established. This was certainly a problem for me as a student teacher and I'm glad my tutor removed me from one placement where I was left to sink or swim, and I was sinking like a brick wrapped in lead. New teachers and support staff need to experience some success early on and will need support with that if they encounter problems. If problems are consistently taken away from colleagues, they won't learn how to solve them. Rescuing people is of no help to anyone as it creates dependency, which is dangerous as it provides an illusion of comfort and support, but also contributes to the lasting appeal of the Behaviour Guy – the hero leader who swoops in to save the day, perhaps boosting their own ego in the process. (As an interesting aside, I have encountered more than once colleagues who proclaim that, 'I am the only one who can make him behave'. My response has always been the same – 'I bloody well hope not'.) Further, given that behaviour improvement takes time, a lasting sense of efficacy needs teachers and leaders to gain experience and understanding of the entire process as much as is possible, including the inevitable setbacks.

Support can be in the form of in-class mentoring or allowing colleagues to see effective practice elsewhere. In-class mentoring is not a veil for being the muscle in the room who hovers expectantly to sort out any problems if they arise. It is more of a spot-coaching role that can be combined well with being a member of the support staff at the same time. When it comes to learning from others, simply getting a colleague to observe someone else is not enough. As stated above, just watching someone else, especially someone with a high degree of self-confidence, is no good as 'Just be more like me' or 'Do what I do' are unhelpful messages. (See below for more on social modelling and the importance of feeling that you are like the model you are observing.)

I worked with one school a while back that had got to the end of the road with a number of children over time, feeling that they weren't able to improve their behaviour to a level they could manage. I know that they were able – they had overcome significant problems to improve teaching, for example – but because they had never persevered enough with behaviour, they lacked the inner confidence that comes from getting to a good place and seeing that all your effort, and that of the child and their parents, did bear fruit. I asked them a few times, 'What is going to be different about your school now to avoid this situation happening again?'. Each time they struggled to answer, mainly because they had yet to experience the success that would give them the confidence to think, 'We can do this!'. They had come to a settled view that this sort of behaviour was the sort of the thing that their school wasn't set up to deal with, and they had unfortunately given up any hope that they could improve it. The journey I describe briefly in the Introduction, at the school where I was first a Headteacher, meant we developed an institutional confidence that we could overcome challenges because we had successfully negotiated setbacks before, so we were less likely to give up. I came to realise a few years into my headship what a powerful source of energy and confidence this institutional confidence can be.

My military friends, mentioned earlier, encounter mastery experiences early on as part of their selection process. Some units have exceptionally challenging entry criteria so passing the selection course and becoming part of the organisation means you are one of a highly select few. This elitism, in the most positive and meritocratic sense, is very powerful (although there is an anachronistic, over-privileged dark side in some of the more class-ridden regiments of the army). There is a loose comparison in teaching when looking at the differing status of teachers in different countries. There is fierce competition in Finland and Singapore, for example, for places on their teacher training programmes, with Finns completing a five year master's degree to qualify and attaining a status to match. There must be a sense of competence that comes with that, which was missing from my nine-month PGCE. (That is no criticism of those who provided my teacher training – they squeezed a lot in and did it well, but the course was over before it really began.)

REFLECTION POINTS

- What is already happening in your school to support colleagues to feel successful with behaviour matters?

- What more could be done?

- Could this involve other schools?

- Could this involve others such as parents or educational psychologists?

Social modelling

I described teaching above as a collegiate profession. Although this is shared with military personnel, firefighters, police officers and prison officers, one big difference is that much of our work at the chalkface is carried out in isolation. Yes, we are surrounded by 30 or so other humans, but they aren't our colleagues, with the exception of a teaching assistant (TA) or two for probably part of the week. We rarely actually see our colleagues teaching once we're out of training. This is a major problem as the social model of learning from our peers is a significant way to improve self-efficacy and a belief in our abilities. This isolation can be compounded by the way we retain a high level of individual accountability over students' results. Between us we may teach the same sixth former, physics with me and maths with you, yet, despite the fact that each of us will contribute significantly to the other's subject because of their overlap, we retain full accountability for the outcome in our own individual subject and none in the other.

I referred earlier to the high degree of self-belief present in my friends who are military officers and soldiers. Having spent a long time with them discussing leadership, culture, teamwork, training and many other things, I am struck by a number of factors that contribute strongly to their collective self-assurance. The extreme challenge of passing the Special Forces selection course I mentioned above is one such example. Military personnel spend most of their working life training and building competency from their peers yet relatively little time operationally active. This is in direct contrast to teaching where much of our time is spent performing the job for which we spend precious little time training. I had a fascinating discussion with my closest friend a while back on the link between competency and time served. He was adamant that there is a direct link between how good a soldier is and how long they've been doing the job, yet that is not well established with teachers at all. More experienced soldiers are expected, indeed it becomes their main job in many cases, to teach less experienced colleagues.

As you can see, much of what contributes to this self-assurance is down to factors that we cannot replicate in our profession or that are out of our control as school leaders, such as the cultural view in some countries that teachers come from the top tier of graduates rather than the tiresome, 'Those who can't, teach' that I sometimes hear.

Given the limitations of our working practices – I'm teaching most of the time you are and I can't use all of my relatively small planning and preparation time to watch long sequences of your lessons, and even if I do, I'll miss the ones in between – we have to think hard about how we can use what time we do have to our best advantage.

Bandura states that, 'Seeing people similar to oneself succeed by sustained effort raises observers' beliefs that they too possess the capabilities to master comparable activities required to succeed' (1994: 72). A key part of that sentence are the words 'people similar to oneself'. Bandura emphasises this by stating that the impact of modelling on perceived self-efficacy is far weaker if the person being observed is seen as being very different from themselves. I find this interesting as it seems to me that there are two forces at play here. Firstly, there is an inverted magnetism – opposites repel and likes attract – such that I am less likely to feel that I can learn more from a colleague whose practice and persona seem far removed from my own. This is 'similar to oneself' in the literal sense when thinking about style, personality and values. Secondly, 'similar to oneself' could be related to context such as teaching the same class or the same topic. These make intuitive sense as social learning involves a lot of imagining and planning of how you will be different and if that leap is too great you're more likely to fall short or regard the gap as unbridgeable in the first place.

Before we go any further, I think it is worth considering the limitations and potential pitfalls of observing colleagues in order to learn from them. It is not a straightforward case of watching what they do and replicating it in your own classroom. The sheer number of intertwining and interdependent factors that contribute to effective teaching make this impossible, so we need to be more sophisticated in how we try to learn from this process.

There is a legacy we will be unaware of. We cannot know about past successes or failures for the teacher with a specific child in the class, the class itself or prior learning the teacher may have brought from other experiences, yet all of these are at play in front of us, but invisible and largely unknowable. Discussion with the teacher prior to the lesson may help to elicit some of this legacy and this could be a good starting point – 'What has happened with this class/child in the past and how has that affected how you work with them now?'.

I believe that discussion, both before and after a lesson, is as useful to learning as the lesson is itself, for this is where you can seek to understand from the teacher what was going on inside their head when they were planning or when they made split-second decisions in the lesson itself. Incidentally, this will be beneficial to the teacher themselves too as asking them to explain seemingly intuitive responses could be enlightening. 'Why did you move Joel and not Alex when they were messing about?' could form the start of a rich discussion on the acceptability, or not, of moving the child most likely to comply with your request. 'I notice that Jess had her phone out for a minute. Why did you choose to ignore it?' can help teachers talk through what is acceptable to let pass (we each have our own threshold) or the occasions when we might do that, and what needs to be tackled every time without fail. Simply seeing a teacher ignore mobile phone use and then translating that back into another classroom is no help at all.

It would seem immediately obvious to double up and look for similar colleagues in similar contexts. This is likely to be fruitful, but I think it is too limiting an approach on its own. As a secondary science teacher by training I know that I can certainly learn a lot from colleagues working in early years, but I need to know, or be assisted to understand, how I can make what I see work in my context. I will miss all of the subtleties that go into effective teaching in early years and the time will be wasted.

Social modelling when applied to direct teaching could involve a couple of different approaches:

- *Direct observation* of other teachers to learn from them (bearing in mind Bandura's advice above about taking into consideration the similarity to oneself). If this doesn't involve some sort of pre-lesson discussion on what's to come and a post-lesson discussion on what happened then this will be of limited value. This does not have to be limited to their department, key stage or even school.
- *Team teaching* a sequence of lessons in a Lesson Study style (planning together, one teaching while the other observes specific areas that the teacher wants to improve such as getting the lesson started, struggling to get a class to be quiet or an issue with a particular child, and then reviewing together). This could follow on naturally from direct observation – a teacher learns from a more experienced colleague and then uses that new knowledge to translate that into their context with the support of that colleague.

In addition, there is a lot of work that goes on behind the scenes with behaviour that may remain a mystery for some teachers, especially early on in their career. Making time for them to be a part of these approaches helps to improve their skill in these areas but also crucially helps to demystify what goes on. Effective conflict resolution to solve bullying, for example, is an approach that requires a certain level of skill and confidence. Enabling colleagues to see how it is done – how the sessions are planned, how they are run and then allowing time for questions afterwards to tease out some of the subtleties – is important. Simply expecting colleagues to observe and then do it themselves in a 'monkey see, monkey do' fashion will be of limited value. Other aspects of behaviour that can occur out of sight of many colleagues, and they may therefore benefit from being involved in, may include:

- meetings with parents
- strategies to improve behaviour that require structure and planning such as conflict resolution, restorative approaches and solution-focused work
- drawing up of behaviour plans
- analysing any information the school holds on the behaviour of a child in order to inform those behaviour plans or to gauge their effectiveness when reviewing them
- analysing information on groups of children, or the whole school
- meetings with allied professionals such as educational psychologists or speech and language therapists.

REFLECTION POINTS

- What is already happening in your school to support colleagues to learn from others through social modelling in the field of behaviour?

- How much thought is given to learning from colleagues 'similar to oneself'?

- What more could be done?

- Could this involve other schools?

- Could this involve others such as parents or educational psychologists?

Social persuasion

I came to see after the first few years of my first headship how important our institutional confidence was. It wasn't sufficient, though, just to have experienced success in the past. I had to feed it by a number of deliberate actions. I used to continually remind colleagues of past successes, either with previous students or with a particular child we were currently working with to improve their behaviour. I hear this sometimes described as story-telling, but don't be fooled by its soft-sounding label. It falls under Bandura's social persuasion. Describing what things were like and what it took to make things better can be very powerful as it sustains effort. It doesn't have to put a gloss on history as it can also include times when things didn't go so well, when heads went down and what the team did to get back on track. It can feed that key component of self-efficacy – to keep going when things seem too tough. I also made a big deal of highlighting early signs of improvement – the green shoots as it were – to sustain and propel effort. It is easier to maintain effort if you can see that your early efforts are working.

Crucially, Bandura notes that successful efficacy builders, 'structure situations for [others] in ways that bring success and avoid placing people in situations prematurely where they are likely to fail often' (1994: 72). This places a duty on us as leaders to ensure that things like timetabling, deployment of support staff and duty rotas don't contribute negatively to a teacher's wellbeing. I still remember the year I was given my break and lunch duty on the same day each week and this was a day when I taught all day too. I also remember the conversation with the Assistant Headteacher where I pointed this out, which ended with me being told to just do it as the timetables were all finished.

REFLECTION POINTS

- Is social persuasion a feature of leadership in your school by:
    - reminding colleagues of past successes?
    - reminding colleagues of times when they overcame adversity and what it took to achieve their goals?
    - keeping colleagues informed of the early signs of progress to sustain effort?
- Does the planning of the organisation of the school support colleagues' wellbeing and prevent, as far as is possible, the creation of conditions that make success more difficult?

Stress reduction

I referred earlier to the emotional turbulence that could come from arresting someone safely and competently in a seemingly chaotic and disordered situation, because it left an inevitable sense that it could have been handled more effectively and therefore I hadn't done well. I believe that something similar exists in schools because of the inherently emotional nature of dealing with behaviour, and that this is a major contributor to teachers' feelings of vulnerability or occasional feelings of a lack of proficiency in this area of school life. It will never be, and cannot be, a stress-free affair, but I don't believe we talk about this side of dealing with behaviour anywhere near enough. I don't mean that we should just accept that it is inevitably stressful and so we should just suck it up and get on with it as part of our job. That way leads to burn out. I mean that we must acknowledge that dealing with behaviour will never seem like plain sailing, and that we should ensure we do all we can as leaders to minimise this and to help colleagues manage the emotional load that remains. Bandura states that people, 'interpret their stress reactions and tension as signs of vulnerability to poor performance' and that, '[m]ood also affects people's judgments of their personal efficacy' (1994: 72). If we as leaders were able to explicitly recognise this and discuss it openly with our colleagues more often, and make dealing with it a priority, then our collective confidence could be improved.

One thing that I have become better at over the years, especially since becoming a Headteacher, is recognising how my emotional state impairs my ability to communicate, both with adults and children. I am now far more prepared to say to someone else that I am dealing with something badly and that I need their help, rather than try to save face but make a situation worse. I have a fairly high level of tolerance to stress when dealing with behaviour in schools, especially in the more extreme situations, but I know when I'm making things worse and I also know that my judgement will be compromised. I am now OK with initial reactions that I am weak or that I am ducking out of dealing with a difficult problem and I know that I must then explain why, at this point, I need support myself. This is usually, but not universally, met with understanding.

This arose out of the experience of working in a school exclusively for secondary-aged children with emotional and behavioural difficulties (EBD back in the day, now known as SEMH [social, emotional and mental health]). At the end of each day, the entire staff got together for a debriefing. Every child in every lesson was discussed (it was a small school) and this was a great way of dealing with situations early, maintaining support for colleagues, information sharing and of sharing responsibility – my problem became everyone's problem. Initially, I thought this daily meeting to be excessive, but it quickly became invaluable to me. I know that this is not practical in almost all schools, but some form of supervision or regularised support is vital to reducing stress.

REFLECTION POINTS

- Do leaders and colleagues discuss the inevitable emotional demands that dealing with behaviour places on each other?

- Do leaders and colleagues discuss how this can be managed?

- Is there a form of supervision or organised mentoring for colleagues dealing with the greatest behavioural challenges?

Recall, too, the faulty thinking or cognitive distortion I mentioned in Chapter 1. Emotional reasoning, the fallacy of control, the prediction of failure and ignoring positives and focusing on negatives are all perpetuated by stress. A colleague with a high degree of self-efficacy is less likely to engage in this form of thinking.

'I came to get you …'

One of the most satisfying aspects of being a Headteacher has been to observe colleagues flourish over time. I will never forget two colleagues who changed radically in a few short months from a position of visible low confidence to a quiet, solid self-assurance.

I was in the staffroom one lunchtime when a colleague came in and said to me, 'Zara is stood on a bench in the playground and is refusing to come down', to which I replied, 'And what did you do?' My colleague replied, 'Well, I came to get you'. My colleague didn't lack the skill to deal with the relatively minor situation, indeed she remains one of the most inspiring colleagues I've ever worked with, but have had little chance to do so. Her skill wasn't low, but her confidence was. This changed quickly and it was a joy to watch someone become so comfortable in their own skin with a confidence that spread to the support staff who spent time with her (an obvious social model of learning in action).

I remember my other colleague being emotionally paralysed after being called a 'bumlicker' by a student. This is obviously more serious than a child stood on a bench, and my colleague really struggled to think about how to move on from this. As with her colleague above, offering support whilst not removing the problem and fixing it out of sight paid dividends over time. She soon took on a full-time behaviour role in our school, an outcome I couldn't have predicted a few months previously.

TAKING IT FURTHER – QUESTIONS AND ACTIVITIES FOR YOU AND YOUR COLLEAGUES

- As school leaders' what have we inherited in our work on behaviour from leaders we have served under previously? What remains of that apprenticeship of observation in terms of habits, policies and practices?

(Continued)

- Consider the four areas of Bandura's sources of self-efficacy. For each one – mastery, social modelling, social persuasion and stress reduction – list out what is currently working well in our school and what you can do to improve.

- Do the same with the staff team and compare the results.

- Reconcile the two to come up with a sharp, concise action plan.

- Within the senior leadership team, pay particularly close attention to stress reduction. Do we emanate signals to colleagues by our body language, our words, our actions at times of stress or fatigue that may communicate the wrong messages to our colleagues?

References

Bandura, A. (1994) 'Self-efficacy', in V.S. Ramachaudran (ed.), *Encyclopedia of Human Behavior* (Vol. 4). New York: Academic Press, pp. 71–81.

John, P.D. (1996) 'Understanding the apprenticeship of observation in initial teacher education: Exploring student teachers' implicit theories of teaching and learning', in G. Claxton, T. Atkinson, M. Osborn and M. Wallace (eds), *Liberating the Learner: Lessons for Professional Development in Education.* London: Routledge.

Kahneman, D. (2011) *Thinking Fast and Slow.* London: Penguin.

Lortie, D. (1975) *Schoolteacher: A Sociological Study.* London: University of Chicago Press.

Richards, J.C. and Pennington, M.C. (1998) 'The first year of teaching', in J.C. Richards (ed.), *Beyond Training.* Cambridge: Cambridge University Press.

Virta, A. (2002) 'Becoming a history teacher: Observations on the beliefs and growth of student teachers', *Teaching and Teacher Education*, 18(6): 687–698.

4

SUPPORTING OUR COLLEAGUES

Serve to Lead.

The motto of the Royal Military Academy, Sandhurst

THE HEADLINES

- Supporting colleagues well with behaviour requires leaders to work alongside them to improve their confidence and sense of competence.

- Leaders who constantly rescue colleagues from situations may feel good about themselves, but run the risk of creating a dependency culture and a frustrated staff team.

- The planned presence of senior leaders in key areas before, during and after school helps staff feel supported. It helps children get to the right place at the right time, reduces the likelihood of issues arising or escalating at unstructured times and reduces the chances of issues spilling over into lessons.

- As well as ensuring there are numerous ways in which children can build their sense of belonging in the school community, leaders can use tools such as the Psychological Sense of School Membership (PSSM) scale to seek explicit information on areas where it may be weaker, both across the whole school and for individuals, particularly for those whose sense of belonging is weaker or seemingly non-existent.

- A high-quality ongoing training programme will feel more supportive for colleagues than one-off training days.

- Give careful consideration as to how timetabling can affect teachers, including rooming. Ensuring teachers teach in the same room as far as is possible, and that they are not ricocheting from room to room if that is not possible, will be appreciated by colleagues.

- Have a pack ready for supply teachers, constructed in consultation with them, so that the key behaviour information for your school is at their fingertips.

- Ensure senior leaders drop by supply teachers' lessons more frequently than for established colleagues so they feel well supported.

- Take a critical approach to the adoption of ideas from other schools. Ask yourself what your school needs and how this approach helps, and what is different between the two schools that might make implementation difficult.

I am a strong advocate of leadership as service to others. It is a happy coincidence that my neighbours, the Royal Military Academy, Sandhurst, have as their motto precisely this invitation. This world-famous establishment, whose beautiful training area I am fortunate to be able to run around, has woven this into the fabric of the training and conditioning of their Officer Cadets as public servants. There is undoubtedly a similar commitment to public duty by school leaders, but the visibility of it in our training, such as it is, is far less overt. (There is, by the way, a whole book to be written on how the armed forces have an infinitely superior approach to leadership development than the education sector.) Leading in this manner requires a selflessness and a commitment to trusting and supporting colleagues. It also demands a cast-iron determination to uphold the values and integrity of the organisation, and this can mean challenging underperformance and making tough decisions in the full knowledge that as leaders we will be unpopular.

Supporting staff with behaviour in schools is one such area of servant leadership where the best leaders excel. But what does this support actually look like? It is not about taking problems away from colleagues as this can create a dependency culture, or worse, leaders develop a saviour complex where they continually rescue people. Benevolent on one level, but fatal for organisational effectiveness – we met this in the form of the Behaviour Guy in the Introduction. Recall from Chapter 3 Bandura's mastery experiences where leaders sensitively support colleagues over time such that their sense of confidence and competence improves. This way of working with and supporting colleagues can be a helpful antidote to the assumption that senior leaders will automatically be better at behaviour (whatever that means) because of a natural authority that comes with the job title. But there is much more to supporting colleagues than that.

Presence

I confess to an ever-present nervousness as a school leader that I'm never doing enough to support my colleagues. One way in which this manifests itself is that I am desperate to make sure I and my fellow leaders are always visible in and around the school at key times. This nervousness is soothed by the surefire knowledge that visibility of senior leaders at those important times where supervision can be looser and the chances of problems arising higher – at the gate before and after school, on the corridors at lesson changeovers, on break and lunch duty, in and around the local area outside the school gate – helps the rest of the school day in lessons go better. Fewer issues at those unstructured times, or issues addressed far earlier, means less disruption or conflict brought into lessons. I strongly recommend a duty rota for these key tasks. I have tried and failed twice to rely on the general commitment of senior colleagues to ensure through self-discipline that they are out and about regularly. You will see that it is obvious that this lack of planning leads to gaps in coverage (I don't know why it took me two attempts to realise this), so far better to plan out where and when you want senior leadership presence.

Psychological school membership (aka a sense of belonging)

We looked at the importance of building a sense of belonging and some of the research underpinning it in Chapter 1 so I won't rehearse the general case other than to reiterate how crucial it is and how often it can be over-looked for the group of children we struggle most with. I will, though, highlight a couple of other interesting aspects of research, particularly for those children who may find it the hardest to feel a healthy attachment to a school. (It's worth noting that the absence of a sense of belonging can result in active and aggressive rejection, which can be very difficult to reverse.)

The results of the Organisation for Economic Co-operation and Development's PISA (Programme for International Student Assessment) report into student wellbeing in 2015 make for interesting reading. They report that, '[o]n average across OECD countries in 2015, 73% of students felt that they belong at school' (OECD, 2017: 118). Worryingly, therefore, over a quarter of students self-report that they do not – a far bigger fraction than the group of children you may have in your mind who could be considered the disaffected few in any year group. Furthermore, they note that the pro-portion who lacked a sense of belonging had increased in each of their surveys since 2003. Their findings also show that a substantial contributor to the differences within countries is influenced by the socio-economic status of the students. But fascinatingly, and counter-intuitively to me, in a number of countries, including the United Kingdom (which, overall, has a negative sense of belonging index and one that is below the OECD average), 'boys were more likely than girls to report a greater sense of belonging at school' (OECD, 2017: 119). Crucially, this report and others they cite indicate that students' self-reported sense of belonging seems understandably tied to, as the OECD term it, a school's disciplinary climate. (By this they mean how well the students behave as opposed to how strict the regime is in a school.)

Creating the conditions upon which a strong sense of belonging is likely to grow is a major achievement. Leaders can go further, though, and seek the views of the student community explicitly to inform and refine their work in this area. Carol Goodenow (1993), in a study on psychological school membership among adolescents, provides us with a great tool in the form of 18 questions from which we can elicit in some depth what students feel about their place in their school. Goodenow notes that, '[e]ven in generally supportive schools some individual students may feel socially marginal or excluded ... Especially for young people who feel unsupported or "disinvited" by school adults or academically striving fellow students, the appeal of peer groups with antiacademic norms may be strong and may result in gradual disidentification with the school and disinvestment from academic or achievement goals' (1993: 81).

Table 4.1   The Goodenow Psychological Sense of School Membership (PSSM) scale

---

1. I feel like a real part of [NAME] School.
2. People here notice when I am good at something.
3. It is hard for people like me to be accepted here. (R)
4. Other students in this school take my opinions seriously.
5. Most teachers at [NAME] School are interested in me.
6. Sometimes I feel as if I don't belong here. (R)
7. There's at least one teacher or other adult in this school I can talk to if I have a problem.
8. People at this school are friendly to me.
9. Teachers here are not interested in people like me. (R)
10. I am included in lots of activities at [NAME] School.
11. I am treated with as much respect as other students.
12. I feel very different from most other students here. (R)
13. I can really be myself at this school.
14. The teachers here respect me.
15. People here know I can do good work.
16. I wish I were in a different school. (R)
17. I feel proud of belonging to [NAME] School.
18. Other students here like me the way I am.

The statements are answered on a Likert scale[1] (Goodenow used a five-point scale originally with choices ranging from *not at all true* [scoring 1] to *completely true* [scoring 5]) and can provide valuable information to leaders both on an individual and cohort level. (The '(R)' after approximately a third of the questions indicates that they are reversed, that is to say that they are phrased deliberately in the negative sense to avoid a *response set* from students, i.e. providing the same answer such as *not at all true* to each question.) Goodenow finds that, '[t]he quality of psychological membership in school was found to be substantially correlated with self-reported school motivation, and to a lesser degree with grades and with teacher-rated effort' (1993: 79).

Steiner et al. (2019) looked to see if there was an association between this, as they put it, connectedness and multiple health-related outcomes in adult life. Their findings suggest that there may be long-lasting protective effects in the areas of, 'mental health, violence, sexual behaviour, and substance use'.

Cockerill (2019) used the PSSM scale in a small study when examining the sense of belonging of a group of children attending a shared placement between their mainstream school and an alternative provision. This is inevitably a small group of children in any school, but a group that requires a significant amount of support, so a focus on this group, and others who are at risk of being part of that group, is likely to be worthwhile. He found that, 'for some pupils, shared placements led to greater engagement with mainstream education and improvements in behaviour, whilst for others, a shared placement led to further disengagement from the mainstream education system. Sense of school belonging was highlighted as a strong predictor of positive outcomes and this was linked to various school attitudes and practices' (Cockerill, 2019: 23).

REFLECTION POINTS

- If you were to carry out the Goodenow PSSM scale survey with your students now, what do you predict would be the main headlines?

- What do you think the findings would be if you were to conduct a slightly modified survey with your staff?

Staff training and development

I hope that as a profession we are on the cusp of ridding ourselves of the scourge of the one-off, one-day whole staff training session. Too often we package up training and development in this way. This is understandable on one level as our five annual training days are precious and, if you are anything like me, you will have an aversion to twilight training sessions for tired colleagues after a hard day of teaching, although I've made use of them many times – there is only so much time in the year, so you squeeze it in where you can. These one-day events have major downsides, and for behaviour training usually a supposed expert turns up and, in fairness, there may be some good stuff in what they say, but the day is too often not part of a coherent process of school improvement. (As an interesting aside, I went through a phase of being asked to deliver mental health training to some schools. I have no idea why as I have no expertise in this area at all. Obviously I refused, but I could have said yes, taken the money and winged it. How much consideration are leaders giving to credibility and credentials when they approach people to deliver training in their schools?) School leaders can do better in supporting our colleagues by improving the quality and the design of our training and development.

Induction

Aside from the standard elements that schools include on induction (please ensure you include teaching assistants in this; too many receive no induction at all, which I find negligent) concerning your expectations, routines, policies and procedures, I believe it is vital that, before you even get to that stage, new staff understand the ethos, values and history of your school. New staff won't pick up by osmosis how the school has evolved to the point it is at now. I recognised the importance of this too late. The process of improvement in our school was extremely good, albeit painful, professional development for all of us (a colleague of mine said that 'we grew up together'). However, I failed to realise that newer staff wouldn't and couldn't fully appreciate why we had ended up doings things in a particular way, so a potted history for new staff is needed.

Ongoing and specific training

It is incumbent upon school leaders to ensure their staff have the necessary skills and knowledge to meet the needs of their student population. There must be a basic level of knowledge amongst the team about certain difficulties where it is proven that the likelihood is far higher of behavioural issues arising if needs aren't well met, the main needs being literacy difficulties, speech, language and communication difficulties, and sensory processing difficulties. There is more on this in Chapter 11, and far more detail for class teachers in my companion publication, *Better Behaviour: A Guide for Teachers* (O'Brien, 2018).

It is not enough to offer an occasional day on behaviour – this is too broad a topic to do well in seven hours. It may even be counter-productive as you are likely as a team to feel frustratingly that you are no further forward.

Occasionally, individual colleagues or small groups will require training that is specific to their role. Examples might be restrictive physical intervention (it would be a rare thing for a whole school to need this) or to enable some colleagues to carry out some forms of behavioural assessment.

Timetabling

I am writing this particular section at the end of an academic year, a time that is particularly challenging for those senior colleagues responsible for timetabling. In some smaller schools, the job seems relatively straightforward – it won't be, by the way – and in others, especially larger secondary schools, it can be fiendishly difficult. Yes, it is a technical job getting the right people in the right places at the right times without double-booking anyone or forgetting that a particular class or subject exists, and solving the puzzle still doesn't guarantee satisfaction. It may be efficient, but not effective. For example, in my first year as a Headteacher I inherited a timetable for two Year 10 classes that looked like this on a Tuesday:

Table 4.2   Timetabling example

Class	Period 1	Period 2	Break	Period 3	Period 4	Lunch	Period 5	Period 6
10a	Art	Art		Art	PE		PE	PE
10b	PE	PE		PE	Art		Art	Art

We had one art teacher and one PE teacher, so between them they spent the day with Year 10 (the year group that I struggled the most with, by the way). From a timetabling point of view, this was convenient and efficient. From any other point of view, it didn't work. The students hated it and ran out of steam, the staff found it wearing – the breaks interrupted the flow of their lessons, plus three lessons in one go was too many in any case – and both groups swapped in the middle, each arriving agitated to a teacher that had probably had a tough morning. It also meant that I needed Tuesdays clear in my diary as I soon learned that the likelihood of disruption was far higher than in the rest of the week.

The other major consideration for teachers is where they are expected to teach, especially in secondary schools. Wherever possible teachers should remain in the same room, or if that is difficult, remain in the same room for as long as possible. Colleagues who teach more than one subject can sometimes be found sprinting to get to lessons before their class if they've had to go from the English block to the Humanities block and then back again an hour later. This is made doubly difficult if schools mandate that, for example, teachers are at their door greeting students as they come into the lesson. This is a good policy, but teachers need to be in with a fighting chance of being at the door to make it work.

I don't underestimate the difficulty for timetablers in getting all of this right, but the critical consideration of how the timetable plays out in real life must take place because, without it, a school may well be stuck for a year with that problem before it can be fixed. The timetable may be stuck for the year, but the teacher doesn't have to stick around with it; they're free to work elsewhere if they feel it makes their job unmanageable.

Supply teachers

There is one group of teachers that will attest to receiving less support than the rest of the profession and they are our supply teachers. They provide a vital service and their job is a very tough one. By definition they often step in at a moment's notice to support schools and have little or no time for preparation. They are past masters at picking up information as they go along that we could and should have provided them with at the start of their day or time with us. School leaders need to pay particular attention to supporting supply staff, and this begins with providing them with a pack of information to help them during their time with us. When looking specifically at behaviour they need the essence of the policy so that they can enforce our rules and know what sanctions to apply if rules aren't followed. Similarly, they will want to use the positive side of our policies too, so providing them with the information to offer recognition in whatever form your school chooses will help them to swiftly build relationships with their classes.

Leaders also need to ensure that we drop by supply teachers' classes with greater frequency than with our own staff to ensure things are in good order and that they feel well supported. I mention in Chapter 5 about how we can obtain valuable information from supply staff regarding their views on the behaviour of the children in our schools, and offering them good support, especially early on, helps them and the students get off on the right foot.

REFLECTION POINT

- What information are supply staff provided with when they arrive at your school?

Uncritical adoption of ideas

One of the biggest services we can provide to our colleagues is to slow down our decision-making, especially at times of great stress and urgency when the pressure to do something, anything, can be over-whelming. When behaviour is not as good as we want it to be, we as leaders can be prone to rushing in new ideas or policies in an attempt to improve things, and there are a number of examples throughout this book and its companion publication, *Better Behaviour: A Guide for Teachers* (O'Brien, 2018) where I have been guilty of that. I have now learned through painful experience that I need to listen more, talk to people, test my thoughts against the values of the school and then make decisions, communicating them carefully to everyone affected. The last bit there is crucial; even when I've felt sure about the correct course of action there have been times when I have communicated poorly and this has affected the support I've received from colleagues and/or parents for changes I've known needed to be made. I'm now much more careful to ensure everyone knows why decisions are being made. People may still, and will, disagree but I want there to be no doubt as to the reasoning behind my decisions.

Sadly, as a profession we can be prone to uncritically 'magpie-ing' ideas from elsewhere that have an allure about them. I have seen it time and again. A school struggling with behaviour looks elsewhere for inspiration and lifts tactics from another school with a seemingly stellar reputation. Examples include a uniform overhaul – always a tightening of policing, interestingly, as the smartness of a uniform is used, erroneously, as a proxy for behaviour and standards – or the enforcement of silent corri-dors, without careful consideration of the sources of the original school's problems that the policy addressed or of the collateral damage, such as a large number of parents withdrawing their children, that may have taken place, which those of us outside the school will not have been privy to. A more stringent approach has an obvious appeal, but this uncritical implementation of ideas, either from other schools or from a general crackdown, runs the risk of destabilising the school by alienating groups of staff, parents or students. Christy Kulz's *Factories for Learning* (2017) provides some interesting examples from one high-profile school such as the outlawing of visits to the local fried chicken shops after school and the perception from some of their students that there was a clear racial disparity in the policing of haircuts. We should seek to lead by consent, by convincing others with the force of our evidence, by the vision we have for the organisation and how these improvements we wish to make align with that vision. It is no use, for example, proclaiming that your school

is highly inclusive whilst continuing to exclude children grossly disproportionately with special educational needs. Without this careful
approach, people can be left waiting with dreaded anticipation for our
next policy lurch (which is how my initial leadership style was explained
to me once).

**TAKING IT FURTHER – QUESTIONS AND ACTIVITIES
FOR YOU AND YOUR COLLEAGUES**

- Conduct the PSSM scale with either a particular group of children that
  are of interest or with the whole school.

- Analyse the findings and come up with a plan to improve the collective
  sense of belonging for the whole school, and to inform behaviour
  improvement planning with particular children.

- If you don't already have one, consider the construction of a welcome
  pack for supply teachers to your school with the necessities to help
  their time with you go more smoothly.

- Ask supply teachers what they would like included in this welcome
  pack.

Note

1. The Likert Scale, named after its inventor Rensis Likert, is a rating system
   used in questionnaires to measure people's attitudes, opinions or perceptions. Respondents are presented with a statement and they are invited to
   decide the extent to which they agree or disagree from a range of options
   such as: *strongly agree, agree, neither agree nor disagree, disagree, strongly
   disagree.*

References

Cockerill, T. (2019) 'Pupils attending a shared placement between a school and
    alternative provision: Is a sense of school belonging the key to success?',
    Educational & Child Psychology, 36(2): 23–33.
Goodenow, C. (1993) 'The psychological sense of school membership among ado-
    lescents: Scale development and educational correlates', *Psychology in the
    Schools*, 30(1): 79–90.

Kulz, C. (2017) *Factories for Learning*. Manchester: Manchester University Press.

O'Brien, J. (2018) *Better Behaviour: A Guide for Teachers*. London: SAGE.

OECD (2017) *PISA 2015 Results (Volume III): Students' Well-being*. Paris: PISA, OECD Publishing, p. 118. https://read.oecd-ilibrary.org/education/pisa-2015-results-volume-iii_9789264273856-en (accessed 19 September 2019).

Steiner, R., Sheremenko, G., Lesesne, C., Dittus, P., Sieving, R. and Ethier, K. (2019) 'Adolescent connectedness and adult health outcomes', *Pediatrics*, 144(1).

5

HOW GOOD IS BEHAVIOUR
IN THIS SCHOOL?

Man is only fitfully committed to the rational – to thinking, seeing, learning, knowing. Believing is what he's really proud of.

Martin Amis (2002)

THE HEADLINES

- Deciding how good behaviour is in a school requires careful consideration of a range of sources of information, both positive and negative.

- Questionnaires can place limitations on the fullness of the information that schools can receive. On the one hand, they provide information in tightly controlled categories (strongly agree, disagree, etc.), but they close off any chance of providing detail. Deeper replies elicited via free text responses provide a richer evidence base, even if the responses are fewer.

- Information systems are susceptible to datafication – an unhealthy process whereby the prioritisation and harvesting of data can corrupt people and practices in schools. A culture of performativity can increase the danger of this occurring.

- School leaders should explicitly discuss how they can gauge what they value, as opposed to valuing what can be measured or trying to measure simply what cannot or should not be measured.

- Soft information can be noticeable by its omission in the sources of evidence on behaviour in schools. The views of the school's parents, staff, students and visitors and the local community are all valuable sources of evidence, as are soft indicators such as the rate of students leaving the school at times other than their expected leaving date.

- Hard sources of information (fixed-term exclusions, isolations, etc.) still require careful analysis and should also be used by schools to look for evidence of potential systemic discrimination.

- Leaders should evaluate their evidence over a number of years. Lasting cultural change in schools, and with it lasting behaviour change in children and adults, takes time and this will be more evident when looking back over a period of time.

- Leaders should share information with staff, parents and governors or trustees to demonstrate improvement, build confidence and sustain effort, or where standards may be deteriorating, to justify reasons for change. Transparency also builds trust.

- A peer review process can be powerful for school leaders to test the strength of their sources of evidence and their evaluation of what the evidence tells them, and to identify what they may have missed.

School leaders and teachers live in an age of performativity and heavy accountability, and in our current system the reputational difference and the implications for schools and their leaders between the neighbouring judgements that describe our schools in the English system as either *good* or *requires improvement* are enormous. That is, of course, precisely why they were designed that way. This cliff-edge creates an immense pressure for school leaders to rid themselves of the shame of the label of *requires improvement* which, it is weakly argued, aids school improvement. It may do, but the collateral damage can be dreadful in the same way that being hunted by a shark can do wonders for your 100-metre freestyle personal best. The implications for school leaders of adverse inspection judgements are significant, and when someone's job and reputation are on the line, that can impair our judgement and influence our behaviour. With this in mind, you will see how it is not simply a cool, low-stakes objective matter to gauge how good behaviour is in your school. I desperately want to believe that behaviour is good enough in my school and anything less reflects badly on me, so it automatically follows that I am the easiest person in the school to persuade that it is so. It takes serious effort for the rational part of me to grapple with and overcome my emotional self to enable me to make reasoned judgements.

In my first Ofsted inspection as a Headteacher, the opening morning meeting between the inspection team and me and my leadership team went like this:

'You've put in your self-evaluation that behaviour requires improvement.'

'Yes.'

'You do know what that means for your school don't you?'

'Yes.'

It is not the opening to an inspection that any Headteacher plans for, but I had no choice. If I felt that behaviour was good in our school, I would have said so. I took no joy in making that judgement. I was accused by some colleagues of deliberately talking the school down so that I could claim credit later if it improved. Given that the governors and local authority had to decide at one point whether to back me or sack me, it would have been a very risky strategy had I been stupid enough to do it. It was my judgement and it was the right one. Anyway, people forget that I was also saying that my leadership required improvement, which was definitely true. In my opinion, there is nothing worse for a school leader to be told, 'Your school is not as good as you think it is', and that is why self-evaluation needs to be done formatively and with brutal honesty to drive school improvement and not as an aspiration to tenaciously defend to an inspectorate despite glaring evidence to the contrary.

In spite of what I've written above, this chapter will not provide an algorithm or matrix to enable you to gauge where your school is on the Ofsted scale of gradings, nor is it about how to gain an outstanding grade from them. Rather, its aim is to help you collate and weigh up sufficient information to come to a reasoned judgement about how things are in your school. Those simplistic matrices do exist, but they encourage a spreadsheet approach to self-evaluation that can be conducted entirely behind a desk. I want you to resist the temptation to assign a single word to describe behaviour in your school for as long as possible. Our system encourages school leaders to think this way, but it is horribly reductive. If you're a school leader like me who has known nothing else other than the inspection system under which we operate, it can feel reckless not to put a single word like *good* or *impeccable* (for those who want to appear to reject the Ofsted system, but who have simply used a thesaurus to avoid using the word *outstanding*) in a box on your self-evaluation. It is akin to saying, 'The air quality in England over the past five years has been good'. On its own it is of very limited value.

Information, data and tracking systems

Leadership of behaviour in a school can sometimes feel like one long slog where you're ricocheting from one incident to another without respite. This takes its toll on everyone and can make the task of coming to a reasoned judgement about how good behaviour is in a school a difficult one. Arriving at these judgements should involve a sophisticated consideration of a range of evidence, but it is common for me to see judgements in schools' evaluations of their own performance that rest entirely on narrative and feel.

I suspect that this is partly due to the emotive nature of behaviour in a school. If you've just dealt with a nasty bullying incident it can be difficult to reason that behaviour in your school is brilliant. Similarly, behaviour in schools is much more than simply good order and compliance, and so the absence of any reported incidents is also not the sole indicator of good behaviour either. A colleague of mine who claimed that, because his school hadn't excluded anyone for three years, behaviour was no problem was skating on very thin ice. I'll split evidence into two here – that gleaned from soft information and that from hard information – but first I want to raise something that is not talked about anywhere nearly enough: the corruption of people and their practices by the misuse of information.

Beware datafication

I hope that as an established or aspirant school leader you are familiar with the management adage that should serve as a warning to us of the dangers of datafication in education:

Measure what you value instead of valuing only what you can measure.

In organisations where data is king, it attains a power well beyond that which is reasonable. Datafication is a process by which the importance, significance and prevalence of data is magnified to such an extent that the values and the practices of an organisation become corrupted. And sadly schools in the current culture of performativity are particularly vulnerable to being perverted by such pressures. Any teacher who has been told by a senior leader that their assessment data, their judgement about how a child in their class that they have taught all year long and know better than anyone else is doing, is wrong (presumably because it ruins the senior leaders neat spreadsheet) will know what I mean. In such systems the urge to enumerate human qualities promises an accuracy and precision that is simply not warranted, but can be under- or unappreciated by the generators and consumers of the information. Every time I see a child's report along the lines of, 'Chas progressed 82 per cent of Level 3 in French this year' a bit of me dies inside. As Williamson and Piattoeva (2018: 68) note, 'quantification came to be allied with objectivity not because it mirrored reality more accurately, but because numbers were easily transportable'.

Within such systems it is *always* partial as to which data is selected as being important or rejected as unimportant, and a crucial part of this is who has the power to decide. Persons in control of data in schools get to decide, often arbitrarily and rarely understood publicly, how that data is used and what weighting is attached to it. Which is worse? A child that is five minutes late ten times in a row for a lesson, or a child that bullies another child once? The knock-on effects of those behaviours are hard to quantify, but they are not unimportant. The tardy child may well disrupt the learning of 29 other children repeatedly. Is that worse than the bullying of one child, and who gets to decide? Is a school that has cut exclusions in half actually improving in terms of its behaviour? Maybe the previous incidents were relatively minor, but were still dealt with by way of exclusion, but the school now has a significant drug or knife problem. Maybe big incidents are down, but low-level disruption (not recorded anywhere) is endemic. Bald numbers are not enough.

Systems that track, chart and analyse all have the potential to present information in a way that influences these judgements and I worry that schools can adopt such systems uncritically. How critical are we of the information we receive from such systems? How much thought do we give to this when we present information of this nature to governors or trustees? Another danger with the datafication of behaviour is that it can situate the responsibility for behaviour entirely with the students, and Manolev et al. (2019: 47) tackle this persuasively, warning that, 'this form of psychologised discipline ... [is] problematically decontextualising and erasing the complexities of behaviour, in particular those influenced by structural and contextual components of schooling'.

Finally, datafication plays right into the hands of the behaviourist approach of reward and punishment. Reward systems such as ClassDojo or Vivo are especially prone to this as they rest entirely on the thoroughly depressing approach of racking up points that are monetised and can then be cashed in for real-life prizes later on. (There is more in Chapter 7 on precisely why I find that approach to be wrongheaded.)

REFLECTION POINTS

- Take a fresh look at the information you receive from any information systems you use for behaviour. How were the decisions made as to what information is entered into the system by staff? Did you buy the system off the shelf or was there a process of deciding what was important and tailoring it to your school and its context?

- Is there a weighting attached to different behaviours? By that I mean are staff able to differentiate levels of seriousness or does one uniform infringement carry equal weight compared to, for example, one incident of serious violence?

(Continued)

- Take a fresh look at the information that you present to governors or trustees. Are they able to get a feel for behaviour in the school from a range of carefully considered information or are they presented with charts, graphs and percentages?

- Who decides what information governors or trustees receive? Why did they decide on this? Perhaps they get no information. If not, why not?

Soft information

Good school leaders get through a lot of shoe leather. They make it their business to be highly visible in, around and outside of their schools for three main reasons – they want to stay close to the chalkface to see what life is really like in their classrooms; they want to offer good reassurance to their colleagues in classrooms (and playgrounds), and residents and businesses nearby that they are there to support and that they care about how everyone is getting on; and thirdly, so that the students fully understand that behaviour is of prime importance to the leaders in the school. Leaders pick up a lot of soft information about what behaviour is like in their school, and in the local community before and after school, by doing this. I've just started a new job and recently I went to the local supermarket after school and stood outside the entrance for half an hour. The shocked faces on some of my students as they came out was a picture – 'Er ... what are you doing here, sir?!'. It is something that I will be doing regularly and the message to our students is clear – you're in our uniform representing our school, and I care about you all and how you're behaving even after school has finished for the day.

This softer evidence, so-called because it cannot and *should not* be enumerated, quantised or subjected to some other mathematical abuse to mistakenly measure it, is no less important than harder information that can be measured genuinely and correctly. Unfortunately, it is often either treated with less respect or missing entirely from the considerations that leaders make about how their school is faring.

Here are some of the different sources of softer evidence you could consider when gauging how good behaviour is in your school.

The views of parents

This *can* be measured in a very rudimentary way. For example, you can ask parents what they think of behaviour in the school and some will respond. You can then go on to say, as I have done before I'm sorry to admit, that

'100 per cent of parents strongly agree that children behave well in this school'. Hmmm, really? 100 per cent of respondents, maybe. (And that could well be a small minority of the parent population.) But even then, what is their view based on? I have absolutely no idea how children behave in either of my children's schools. Any information I do have comes from my own children, who are a very unreliable source of evidence, so my opinion would essentially be theirs and should carry little weight on its own. Tick-box questionnaires are appealing because of the ease with which they can be completed and because we can restrict responses (strongly agree, agree, etc.), and compare year-on-year, but with ease comes an inevitable bluntness in the information you receive. Even within paper-based tick-box questionnaires, respondents still try to finesse their responses. On many occasions I have seen respondents place their tick at one end of the *agree* box, for example, to let you know that they were very close to ticking *disagree*, or in some cases, placing the tick so it straddles two options. That nuance is lost in the totting up of responses. I think it is better to have a richer evidence base, even if the response rate is lower. Of course, it is also important to ensure you maximise response rates (without resorting to simple tick boxes), as an absence of a response should not automatically be taken as implied satisfaction.

Think carefully as to what information you are trying to elicit from parents. The softer information that could come from asking parents, 'Please write in the box below what you think about how children behave in this school', could be a richer source for your team to pore over. It won't produce a pie chart at the end, but you'll survive without that and you'll know a lot more at the end too. I can see useful information coming from questions like these:

- If you are in or around our school at the start and/or the end of the day, what kinds of behaviours do you see from our students?
- What do your children tell you about what behaviour is like in our school?
- Our values are [insert here]. Do you see examples of our students displaying these? If so, where and what did you see?
- If your child has been bullied, how do you think we dealt with it?

The views of staff

I have yet to meet a school leader who has struggled to elicit the views of their staff on the behaviour of their students. Thirty minutes sat in the staffroom at the end of the day should do it. As with parents above, what questions you ask and how you go about securing the information are the keys to this being meaningful. One important point of view that you cannot secure from any other source is how well staff feel they are supported with behaviour from senior leaders. This perception is crucial and is a major aspect of the foundations of staff morale. This evidence can also be helpful in informing training and development activities, especially around areas such as special educational needs (SEN). The senior leadership team, as a subset of the staff, need to ensure that they keep a log – one for the entire team – of their views on behaviour as they get around the school on a daily basis. This longitudinal source of evidence is a useful tool to reflect on months or terms gone by where the collective memory will prove fallible.

The views of supply teachers

This group of colleagues are a sadly underused source of information. Granted, some of them may only be in your school for a day, but their view should be taken seriously for at least three reasons: they get around a lot of schools, so their view will be benchmarked against other schools; they will tell you if they felt supported by school leaders; and a good test of a school's culture of behaviour is how the students conduct themselves when taught by supply teachers. In my experience, supply teachers are usually more than happy to provide their view, so have some simple questions on a pre-prepared sheet, given at the start of the day so they know it's an expectation at the end of the day (or longer if they're with you past that). As with parents, give some thought as to the information you want from the supply teachers and avoid the temptation of tick boxes. You will also get an immediate view rather than at a fixed point in the year as is the case with most other questionnaires.

The views of visitors (interview candidates, prospective parents, fellow professionals)

These colleagues may well be in the building for a shorter duration than supply staff, so you may attach less weight to their views, but the volume of them makes their views a decent source of information. I can remember after time spent doing parent tours that I realised that I kept hearing similar comments from the parents – 'Your students are so confident and articulate', they would say. This was important precisely because *confident* and *articulate* were two of the elements of our school vision (*When students leave [this school] they should be ...*)'. This was superb evidence that our vision was becoming a reality, so it needed capturing and sharing with the staff.

The views of the students

As a profession we seem split on the matter of eliciting the views of students. Some of us find it abhorrent that they are involved at all in the interview process for teachers, for example. I think it would be a missed opportunity were a school not to take in the views of its own students on behaviour, especially on the school's effectiveness in dealing with bullying. It is relatively straightforward to get the basic views of almost the entire student population with a questionnaire, but this can be supplemented by deeper questions on the things that are important to your school with groups of students, and conducting these in person may well be more productive than in paper form. I also like the idea of exit interviews with students near to the time they are leaving to gauge their views on how things have changed in their few years with the school. This can be powerful as we often use the questionnaire/interview technique to understand the state of the school as it is today and lose sight of the progress, or sadly the decline, the school has made over the course of a few years.

The causes of unexpected leavers

A child or children leaving a school at a time other than at their expected end-date is not unusual. Families relocate, service personnel get deployed to a military base somewhere else in the UK, for example. The rate of turnover in a school, though, is worth keeping an eye on, especially as a governor or trustee (see Chapter 13 for more on this). A higher than expected turnover should prompt questions from school leaders. Perhaps the behaviour policy is too stringent and families are dissatisfied? Perhaps bullying is not being dealt with effectively enough and parents are withdrawing their child to protect them? Whilst the numbers leaving will be precise, the reasons will be varied, which is why this soft information is useful to school leaders and governors or trustees. (This will be straightforward to put into context – for example, my local comprehensive is next door to the Royal Military Academy, Sandhurst, and as a result, has a larger than average number of service families, which in turn leads to a larger than average turnover of children. Other schools without a similar context will have to work harder to reassure themselves and their governors that there isn't an issue in their school.)

REFLECTION POINTS

- How refined is the information you currently seek from parents, teachers, etc.? Is it tightly categorised via questionnaire or do you gather richer views and opinions?

- What steps are you taking to maximise the response rates from parents?

(Continued)

- How do you currently record and review the observations that leaders make as they spend time around the school each week?

- What do supply staff say about behaviour in your school? Do you systematically seek their views?

- Is there anything for you to be concerned about in the numbers of children leaving your school at times other than their expected leaving date? Does this group of children contain a higher proportion of children with special educational needs and disabilities (SEND), for example?

These softer sources of evidence are vital, but they must be supplemented by harder sources of evidence that schools can gather.

Hard information

I've written earlier about my time as a first-time Headteacher and the problems we had with behaviour. One problem was entirely of my own doing and that was the system of recording behaviour incidents. When I joined the school there was no established system, statements were simply written down and filed. As behaviour deteriorated I acted, unwisely, in haste. I brought in a paper-based recording system that was entered into a database so we could analyse it. The trouble was that the paper just mounted up and we were never able to get on top of it and therefore couldn't get anything meaningful from it. (You can imagine how irritated the admin team were carrying out a task that turned out to be pointless.) I recall the lead inspector in our first inspection sitting at the front desk wading through a pile of green slips (so-called as we printed the slips on green paper) and I could see how it looked – this was a school that was not on top of behaviour or its systems. Hard information that you gather has to be both useful and used.

You could go to town on gathering data on behaviour in your school, asking for ever-finer details, but you will be up against the law of diminishing returns. The list below is long, I admit, but you need that level of detail, especially in a large school and certainly in one with a heterogeneous population, to be sure that you know the effects of your policies on the students. I am also painfully aware of the potential to contradict myself on the dangers of datafication here. The warning needs to be reiterated in terms of the influence it can have on the behaviour of leaders. For example, if a school leader is determined to reduce the use of fixed-term exclusion then it is a simple matter to achieve that – they simply stop deciding to exclude children. What is not simple is to do something to effectively address behaviour problems in its place. It is the effectiveness of the actions that are important, rather than the action itself.

Permanent exclusions

I will presume very small numbers here, which only really allows for a year-on-year comparison.

- Number in year to date.
- Of those, number of students on SEN Support, number of students with an education, care and health plan EHCP, number of children looked after (CLA), number of students from black, Asian and minority ethnic (BAME) backgrounds, and other protected characteristics relevant to your school.
- Breakdown by reasons for permanent exclusion.
- Number that went to independent review panels (with outcomes).
- Year-on-year comparisons of all of the above.
- Local, regional and national comparisons (available annually from the Department for Education [Department for Education, 2019]).

Fixed-term exclusions (FTEs)

- Number of incidents of FTE in year to date (for example, a five day FTE is one incident).
- Number of days of FTE.
- Number of children receiving FTEs.
- Number of children receiving multiple FTEs (detailed by number).
- Breakdown by reasons for FTEs (both for number of incidents and number of days).
- Proportion of FTEs (both for number of incidents and number of days) given to students on SEN Support, with an EHCP, from BAME background, children looked after and other protected characteristics.
- Year-on-year comparisons of all of the above.
- Longitudinal study of year groups (i.e. how Year 8 compare to when they were Year 7).
- Further analysis to search for sources of systemic discrimination (see more in Chapter 12 for the evidence from Strand and Fletcher (2014) on this)

Isolation

- Number of occurrences of isolation (for example, a one-hour isolation or a three-day isolation both count as one occurrence).
- Analysis of duration of isolations (periods, days, etc.).

- Number of children receiving isolations.
- Number of children receiving multiple isolations (detailed by number).
- Proportion of isolations (both for number of incidents and number of days) given to students on SEN Support, with an EHCP, from BAME background, children looked after and other protected characteristics.
- Year-on-year comparisons of all of the above.
- Longitudinal study of year groups (i.e. how Year 8 compare to when they were Year 7).

Detentions

- Number of occurrences.
- Breakdown by reasons, year groups, protected characteristics.
- Year-on-year comparisons.
- Longitudinal study of year groups (i.e. how Year 8 compare to when they were Year 7).

Managed moves via in-year fair access panels

- Number of occurrences.
- Year-on-year comparisons.

Longitudinal analysis

- In their time at the school, how many children receive at least one:

  o   fixed-term exclusion?
  o   isolation?

- Break this down by protected characteristics (Strand and Fletcher [2014] found significant differences with the number and duration of FTEs between children of different ethnicity, for example).

REFLECTION POINTS

- How does the evidence base you currently rely on compare to the list above?

- What further information do you now need to start gathering to improve your evidence base?

- Do you carry out any longitudinal analysis to look at the effects of your policies over time rather than relying on isolated annual data?

Positive information

In the rush to gather all of this information about behavioural incidents, schools can lose sight of the need to consider too when things go well. Schools are great at celebrating success and progress and this is good evidence of the system working well, but it can be omitted when considering how good behaviour is in schools. Children working hard as a team in the inter-house netball competition and still losing graciously, children striving to overcome challenges in their learning, children picking up litter, children helping a supply teacher who is lost, these are all instances that should all be recognised for what they are – signs of children with a strong sense of belonging, children developing perseverance and resilience, children who respect their environment, children who are keen and willing to help others. Too often we do what Dr Aaron Beck highlighted in Chapter 1 – ignore positives and focus on negatives – or as Bill Rogers (2006) describes it, we focus on the small black dot in the middle of the big white square.

Each school is different in the details of its positive systems, but careful consideration of what this positive information tells you is important. As an example, I was once asked by a very astute governor to convince her that we as a school didn't have a downer on the children who found it hardest to be successful in our school. This is a brilliant challenge from a governor, so I set to work. Intuitively I felt we didn't, but I went into the process fascinated to see what the information would say. In a rather blunt way, I simply took the ten students who had the highest number of behavioural incidents and set that information against how those students fared in the positive aspects of the school's system. The crude outcome was that every one of them seemed to receive far more positive recognition than negative. As I said, crude, but this analysis was not the end of the story. I am not one of these teachers who believe in the mantra that praise and positive comments should outweigh anything negative by at least a 5:1 ratio – this is way too simplistic and forced for me – but we do need to know if the experience of school for some of our children is one long telling off. If you, as an adult, has ever worked for a boss where your life is a series of criticisms and reprimands, you will know how quickly you develop a desire to tamper with the brakes on their car.

Triangulation

Now you are armed with a lot of information, but does it smell right to you? The information that leaders collate from different sources cannot always say the same thing, but it needs to be assimilated and, as a whole, has to make sense with what your eyes and ears tell you. Low levels of reporting of behavioural incidents cannot be reconciled with lots of observations of disrupted lessons. Repeated use of tactics such as isolation or fixed-term exclusion are not consistent with a belief that these systems effectively improve behaviour. A school that claims to be inclusive will struggle to explain a high level of behavioural incidents for children with SEND.

This careful consideration of the evidence also allows for leaders to spot gaps in their evidence base, given that all systems that collate behaviour information in schools, both positive and negative, are incomplete – not everything gets noticed, and not everything that gets noticed gets reported. Consider, for example, incidents at break times, lunch times, before and after school. I contend that they are systematically under-reported in schools because of the lower levels of supervision at those times compared to lessons. This lower level of supervision can also contribute to a greater chance of incidents occurring at those times, so it is doubly important that schools look more carefully at what information they do have and ensure that they seek out softer information from duty staff to fill their potential knowledge gap.

Sharing information

The collation and analysis of the information above is potent, and this can be boosted by careful sharing of the information with the governors or trustees, with the parents and with the staff of a school. It can achieve a number of different things.

It can help to build confidence to show that things are improving. This can encourage people to sustain their efforts, and this is especially important in the earlier stages of implementing a new policy when people will take more convincing that tactics and strategies are working.

It can be used to challenge negativity if and when people doubt that things are better than they were before. I faced this situation myself and I could see then how vital it was to convince people that, although behaviour was still not good enough, it was better than it was before. It did also make me reflect on the perspective of those less convinced than I. I had to remember that the class teacher who spends most of the week in their corner of a school is likely to see things differently from a member of the senior leadership team who gets around the school on a daily basis. It is important to acknowledge this with colleagues, otherwise we run the risk of invalidating their opinion and, whilst they will continue to have an opinion in the future, they are less likely to share it with us as we've communicated that we don't value it sufficiently.

It can help everyone to see when a change of direction is needed. This transparency buys goodwill with staff as they can see when leaders admit that change is needed. (It is easier as a new leader to turn up and correct what you perceive to be the mistakes of others; far harder to admit that your own decisions were wrong.)

In the past I have produced a *How Well Are We Doing?* report for staff after it struck me one day when I was producing a report for governors that I should also be sharing that information, albeit in a different format, with staff. Sharing does, however, come with pitfalls. I have made the mistake of sharing information in a format that looked liked teachers were being ranked on a particular aspect of behaviour. Two seconds' worth of fore-thought would have told me that this was a terrible idea, but I gave it none. I repented at leisure after that.

REFLECTION POINTS

- What do you currently share with parents and with staff?
- What improvements can you make in information sharing to build confidence?

External moderation

I mentioned earlier the difficulties leaders face to remain objective when gauging how good behaviour is in their own school. This is why the case for seeking a peer review of leaders' judgements is compelling. Sometimes it is a mandatory part of being in a multi-academy trust of schools, or it can be conducted voluntarily between school leaders in the same local area or where a school leadership team seek a particular external professional or professionals to provide the peer review because of the expertise they have.

Peer review is categorically not about inspecting schools, those horribly named 'Mocksteds', but it is about testing the strength of the evidence that school leaders use to arrive at their judgements. It is a moderation process, not a process of inspection. With that in mind, I see the role of peer review as seeking answers to the following questions:

- What evidence does the school rely on to arrive at its judgement about behaviour?
  - This allows the peer reviewer(s) to probe the quality of the evidence that the school uses.

- To what extent does the school's evidence support its judgement about behaviour?

  o Peer reviewers make judgements here to either agree or disagree with the school's evaluation of the evidence.

- What further evidence about behaviour does the school need to gather?

  o Peer reviewers can be helpful here in providing advice on what they feel is missing from the evidence base.

There is an ever-present danger with peer review that it can become a process of mutually assured safety whereby school leaders implicitly offer each other a guarantee that they won't go too hard on each other, so peer reviewers who are chosen for their candour is an essential part of ensuring this process is meaningful. Done well, though, and it is a force for good, a valuable learning opportunity for leaders and it provides a strong source of evidence for boards of governors or trustees. It can also expose middle leaders and inexperienced senior leaders to scrutiny and challenge. I encourage you to build it into your school improvement work if it is not already an established feature.

TAKING IT FURTHER – QUESTIONS AND ACTIVITIES FOR YOU AND YOUR COLLEAGUES

- What sources of evidence do we currently use when deciding how good behaviour is in our school? What evidence are we missing? Is it easily accessible? If not, how are we going to obtain it?

- What questions are we currently asking parents, supply staff, visitors, staff and students about behaviour in our school? Are we relying on tick-box questionnaires? How can we improve the depth of information we receive?

- How are we as leaders collating the soft information about behaviour we pick up on our daily rounds?

- Do we as a school have a downer on the children who find it hardest to behave well in our school? How do we know this?

- How much information are we currently sharing with staff and parents? Could this be improved?

- What were the outcomes from the last time we obtained a moderation of our judgements on the behaviour of children in our school? What progress have we made with the recommendations since that time? When do we next need an external moderation of our judgements on behaviour? Who is going to do it?

References

Amis, M. (2002) 'The voice of the lonely crowd', *The Guardian*, 1 June. www.the-guardian.com/books/2002/jun/01/philosophy.society (accessed 30 September 2019).

Department for Education (2019) *Statistics: Exclusions*. www.gov.uk/government/collections/statistics-exclusions (accessed 19 September 2019).

Manolev, J., Sullivan, A. and Slee, R. (2019) 'The datafication of discipline: ClassDojo, surveillance and a performative classroom culture', *Learning, Media and Technology*, 44(1): 36–51. DOI: 10.1080/17439884.2018.1558237.

Rogers, B. (2006) *I Get By With a Little Help … Colleague Support in Schools*. London: Paul Chapman Publishing.

Strand, S. and Fletcher, J. (2014) *A Quantitative Longitudinal Analysis of Exclusions from English Secondary Schools*. Oxford: University of Oxford.

Williamson, B. and Piattoeva, N. (2018) 'Objectivity as standardization in data-scientific education policy, technology and governance', *Learning, Media and Technology*, 44(1): 64–76. DOI: 10.1080/17439884.2018.1556215.

6

BEHAVIOUR REPORTS AND PLANS

A behaviour plan won't work if it's an ultimatum dressed up as targets.

Mary Meredith, local authority inclusion service manager (2018)

THE HEADLINES

- Behaviour plans should be positive and supportive tools that aim for behaviour improvement through agreed actions and approaches, understood by the child and their parents.

- Plans should be rounded, well-considered documents that are informed by evidence from multiple sources of what has and has not been working well to date, and contain good contextual information.

- Good plans are constructed with the contributions of as many of the key people in the life of the child as possible.

- Effective plans aim for improvement, not for perfection. They do not hold children to higher standards than their peers.

- Strategies for success in plans are graduated in their approach, aiming for:
  - *preventing* behaviours occurring in the first place
  - *teaching* desired behaviours
  - *eliminating* the chances of poor behaviours occurring
  - *reinforcing* behaviours we do wish to see
  - *sanctioning* when necessary
  - and lastly, actions to ensure the *safety* of everyone if the worst occurs.

- Behaviour plans need to be reviewed regularly, informed by good evidence as to how well they are faring, refined where necessary and, when things are good enough, ceased.

- No child should be on a behaviour report without an accompanying plan.

- Behaviour reports should not be high-stakes, pass/fail documents.

- Behaviour reports should be a support schedule for the child, which captures simply the main aims of the behaviour plan and can then be used to gather information about how the child is getting on.

- Putting a child on report for their behaviour as a means of increasing the pressure on them is not worth it, and may be counter-productive as it could be a form of escalation.

- Reports should not offer further sanctions for not meeting the targets that wouldn't normally be given to any other child.

- Similarly, reports should not offer rewards as enticements for compliance, but should recognise when things go well and there has been progress.

Before this chapter really starts I want to conduct a little thought experiment. Please answer the following two questions:

- What would the effect on behaviour in your school be if you simply ceased all behaviour plans tomorrow?
- What would the effect on behaviour in your school be if you did the same for all children on report for their behaviour tomorrow?

The school where I first became a Headteacher is situated in a beautiful site in Surrey. The main building is two storeys high and a corridor along one side of that building looks out over a small courtyard below with some lockers for the students. Over these lockers and just below the windows on that top corridor is a lean-to roof to protect the lockers from the elements. It does this job very well, but for the first year of my headship it also served as the temporary resting place for dozens of deceased behaviour reports – those pieces of paper that some children take from lesson to lesson so that their conduct can be closely monitored. They ended up there, having been thrown out of the windows, often ripped into confetti, before being carried on their final journey, River Ganges-like, by the rain into the gutter, or blown away on the wind.

The frequency with which they were despatched indicated both the respect they were afforded by their owners and how useful they were in improving behaviour. This knowledge is what led me to posing those two questions at the start of this chapter. The reports we used had a number of fatal flaws, which resulted in me deciding to change them, and I know that there are many more poorly designed reports out there.

A flawed system

Firstly, our reports were used as a purely punitive measure. This is a common error I see in the use of behaviour reports. My children watch a superb fly-on-the-wall programme on children's TV that follows Year 7s through their first year in secondary school and I remember hearing a Head of Year on this programme exclaim at a child, 'Right! You're now on report and you'll see me at the start of every day!'. I'm sure it wasn't intended to sound quite as knee-jerk as that, but the use of a behaviour report as a shock tactic to stun, or worse, shame, a child into behaving better is as likely to succeed as making them wear a dunce's hat.

Secondly, the design of the reports made it difficult for them to be useful to the child and, sadly, increased the chances of failure. Here's why:

Table 6.1   Example of a behaviour report

Name: Fiona Marshall Form: 10R	Behaviour target(s): 1. No swearing 2. Arrive to lessons on time 3. Seek help from adults instead of walking out of lessons		
	Period		
	1	**2**	**3**
Monday	DH	RP	AS
Tuesday	/	/	LM
Wednesday	BC	/	/

The basis of the report was described to me by both staff and students as 'line or sign' – catchy but useless. If the child was good enough in a lesson, as judged by the teacher, they initialled the relevant box on the form. If the child wasn't good enough in a lesson, the teacher simply put a diagonal stroke in the box to denote this. One line or more in the course of the day meant that the child 'failed' the day – whatever that meant.

You can immediately see why this is problematic. Behaviour reports almost inevitably contained more than one target and these had to be distilled down in each lesson to a simple yes/no judgement on the acceptability of the child's behaviour. The child may have made great strides with two of the three targets, yet struggled with the third, but there was no acknowledgement possible in the design of the report so that progress or success was lost forever.

It was also possible to get a line for something that had nothing to do with the behaviour targets. It was possible, therefore, for a child to do well against their three behaviour targets yet still get a line. You'll see later when I describe the key purposes of a behaviour report that they are not there to judge everything the child does. A child on report for specific things should remain subject to the same treatment as the rest of the school for other behaviours. You'll also notice that the report only covered lessons so there could be issues at other times of the day – there often are at more unstructured times and when there is less supervision such as break times – yet the report could look pristine.

The pass/fail element was baked in even further by the failure of the whole day if a child got even one line. I'd heard more than once a child despair that it wasn't worth trying for the rest of the day if they got a line for Lesson 1. You can see now why so many reports ended up on that roof in pieces, as being on report was a high stakes affair.

Thirdly, the information was never actually logged or analysed over time, so we had no real idea if the reports were working beyond simply leafing through past ones. I recall picking up Dean's file before an annual review and finding it bulging with reports. Dean had been on report perpetually for at least a couple of years, clearly to little or no effect.

The last problem that this report system had was that there were often no behaviour plans preceding them to inform the teachers and support staff on the agreed ways that the adults were going to support the child to improve their behaviour.

This is the most important point in this entire chapter – a behaviour plan and a behaviour report are two parts of the same process. One, the report, should follow naturally from the other, the plan. If the plan does not inform the report then they are at best duplicating effort by accident, or at worst contradicting each other. A child may need a plan, but not need a report. The reverse should never be allowed to occur: a child put on report but without the backing of a plan, that is to say the careful consideration from the adults as to what is going to be different, is on a hiding to nothing.

Who needs a plan? Who needs a report?

I have a habit of describing the time when a behaviour plan is needed for a particular child as when the school's behaviour policy stops working. Actually, this is unhelpful and overly simplistic because all schools are skilled at making adjustments for individual children and much of this happens without school-wide planning or coordination as individual teachers, perhaps in conjunction with key stage managers or heads of year or department, iron out issues before they get too big. The need for a behaviour plan becomes more pressing once a behaviour issue is chronic or there is a deterioration and this requires the input, understanding and agreement of the adults working with a particular child about what they are going to do to support that child to improve. It also needs the involvement of the child and their parents, and we'll come on to that later.

Behaviour plans should only ever be for a small minority of children, even in a school specifically for children with social, emotional and mental health (SEMH) difficulties, because if the proportion of children requiring a bespoke behaviour plan grows then this is a strong indicator that it is the school's policies and procedures that need to change.

It does not automatically follow that a child for whom a behaviour plan has been written will also need to be on report. As I stated earlier, reports have a tendency to be used to exert some pressure on a child to perform because of the increased lesson-by-lesson scrutiny on their conduct – hence the, 'You're on report!' exclamation – and this tightening of the screw is probably either ineffective or counter-productive. A report is a good idea if it supports the child on a short-term basis to keep them on track. If not, if it simply makes them feel worse about themselves, then it is better not to bother. Indeed, the use of the phrase 'being put on report' itself suggests a punitive element to the setup, so I will refrain from using it from this point on in the chapter.

If there is a need in the school to gather information on a lesson-by-lesson basis for a particular child then this is probably more efficiently done without using the child as the carrier for the information, not least because of the tendency for reports to get lost or to get 'lost' on its journey around school each week. Schools have various electronic options for doing this these days so there is far less need for the child to mind the report for them. It may still be important to provide timely feedback to the child about how they are getting on, but the collation and transportation of the information does not have to rest with the child.

REFLECTION POINTS

- How many children in your school currently have a report as a means of monitoring their behaviour?

- Where does the information go once the behaviour report has been completed?

(Continued)

- Of those students on report, what is the longest period any one of them has been on report for?
- What improvements have there been in that time?
- How has the report helped to achieve those improvements?
- What would happen if that report was ceased tomorrow?

Behaviour plans

There is no one correct way to organise a behaviour plan, so I will resist the temptation to produce a template for your use, but any and all behaviour plans should have a number of essential elements that I detail below (use them as headings when constructing or reviewing yours if that helps). Before I go on to set them out, it is worth hammering home that behaviour plans should be positive and supportive in nature – as the former colleague of mine from Chapter 1 is fond of saying, 'We plan for success in this school'. If they go little further than listing the things that the child is failing at and setting out what the child needs to do, then progress is going to feel laboured or stuck. We, as the designers, must resist the tendency to build in those desire lines that we met in Chapter 2 because they are convenient for us, but not supportive to the child in improving their behaviour. Here I am reminded of Joe Bower's sage advice that in any situation there are two problems to solve – yours and the child's – with yours being by far the easier to solve. As he rightly says, 'The child must feel like you care about solving their problem as much as you care about solving your own' (Bower, 2012).

Informed by good prior knowledge (aka baseline information)

A plan that is written in haste because a situation with a child has become very difficult can only really be superficial because it is not informed by rich and broad information about the situation so far.

Good baseline information should not be limited to simply knowing in great detail what is going wrong, how often it is going wrong and where it is going wrong. More than anything, what you really need at the start is to know what is going well, how often it is going well and where it is going well. Identifying what is already working can provide better clues as to how to secure improvements in behaviour.

Other information that you may find useful includes: the intensity of behaviours, the duration of incidents, who else is present (both adults and children). But, again, this is also just as useful in the context of when the child is successful.

With good information on the situation to start with you stand the best chance of knowing where to focus your efforts because no child is badly behaved all of the time.

Contextual information, including strengths and things that need to improve or change

There will be contextual information about the child that should be considered when formulating a plan. For example, the child may be on SEN Support or have an education, health and care plan (EHCP). Given that children with special educational needs and disabilites (SEND) are far more likely to receive a fixed-term exclusion or be permanently excluded from school (Department for Education, 2019) it is vital that this informs the approach of a behaviour plan as that child will already have a plan of a different sort in the school and the two clearly need to complement each other. This will also be true of children who are looked after as they have personal education plans that are reviewed bi-annually.

You and your team will know what else is important in terms of context. I am reminded of a child, Sam, for whom we wrote a behaviour plan a number of years ago. His father had been ill for years and was slowly deteriorating, as was his mother's sight and heart. This was a source of much anxiety for him generally, but he became very stressed as a school trip abroad got ever closer because he was petrified that they might die while he was away. It was rather straightforward for us to support him with a phone call home every day, but without knowing this our job would have been much harder.

One interesting aspect of contextual information that I don't think is well known in schools about their students is if they have been born prematurely. I raise this in light of the extremely interesting EPICure (1995) longitudinal study, which is following over 4,000 children born extremely prematurely (i.e. between 20 and 26 weeks gestation), and its findings are fascinating. Of interest to teachers with regard to behaviour and learning are the findings at age 11 that, 'learning problems such as problem solving, thinking and reasoning were much more common: the EPICure children had lower IQ scores in general and 40% had scores that were moderate or severely impaired compared with 1.3% of their classmates'. Further, '[w] e asked parents and teachers of all the children to tell us about their feelings and emotions and about their behaviour. We found that the EPICure children tended to have more problems in these areas than their classmates. These kinds of problems tended to be fears and worries and problems sustaining attention and focusing on tasks. We also found that some of the EPICure children had more difficulties interacting with other children and adults' and that, 'the EPICure children tended to [do] better with things presented in order (sequential) compared to being asked to do several things together (simultaneous) and were less attentive when carrying out tasks' (EPICure, 1995). This kind of research information married up with the context of a child can be very helpful when putting a plan together. It can also be very reassuring to a parent to know that a behaviour plan will be an informed and considered document rather than a blunt tool.

Who needs to be involved in its construction?

In a primary school, it may well be possible for all the adults involved with a child on a day-to-day basis and a senior leader to get round the table with the parents and, for example, an educational psychologist or other professional(s), to construct a plan. In a secondary school, this is likely to be much more difficult as the child may have upwards of a dozen teachers a fortnight. It is for each school to decide who needs to be actively involved in the construction of a plan, but others can of course contribute remotely via a form of strengths and difficulties questionnaire, for example, and this is to be encouraged.

The child and their parents

I don't think we should produce plans without the involvement of the child (and I mean more than 'Sign here') and their parents. A plan imposed upon a child may well improve their behaviour over time, but there is a principle here, a relational one, that is important. It is at the heart of restorative practices and it is the belief that people are more likely to change their behaviour for the better when those in positions of authority do things with them rather than to them or for them. I know that some colleagues find this challenging as they hold the view that, as the child is not yet behaving well enough, they have a duty to tell the child what to do and that involving the child makes no sense given their poor behaviour. This is limiting and misses the solution-focused opportunity to elicit from the child their views about what is already working well and what their best hopes are. Similarly, for the parents, this is their chance to be part of the process – no one is more keen than they are for their child to be flourishing in school – and for the school to take their views and suggestions into account. It also helps bring the parents closer to the situation – because they are not in school every day almost all of their information is third-hand and filtered by either their child or the school, and potentially contradictory, and this cannot be easy for parents.

Class teacher (in primary) or form tutor (in secondary)

It is self-evident why the class teacher of a primary school child needs to be there, but it is likely to be difficult to get all of the teachers of a secondary school child round the table, so the form tutor is best placed to take on this role. The Head of Year or similar may well be involved too at secondary level.

Special educational needs coordinator (SENCo)

I would involve the SENCo from the outset. There is much more on the links between SEND and behaviour in Chapter 11, but one example will suffice to highlight the issue for now – the Royal College of Speech and Language Therapists (2018) quotes research indicating that, '81% of children with emotional and behavioural disorders (EBD) have significant unidentified communication needs' (Hollo, Wehby and Oliver, 2014). If, after an initial period, it is decided that the SENCo's involvement is unnecessary then that is fine. I would much rather positively rule out the need for SEND involvement than discover later that a specific issue around literacy, sensory processing or communication, for example, remained unsupported.

Teaching assistant(s)

Given the aforementioned intersection of SEND and behaviour and the fact that TAs spend a lot of time with children with SEND, I am sure they can offer a valuable perspective in addition to the SENCo.

Educational psychologist

Educational psychologists (EPs) can provide expert input in planning to improve behaviour. They can support schools in many ways, but the main ways that they could specifically help with behaviour plans are via:

- Consultation and assessment – consulting with and gathering information from others working with the child; classroom, dinner hall and playground observations; curriculum-based assessment and use of recognised assessment tools.
- Intervention – using that assimilated consultation and assessment information to inform what to do next.

Other professionals

The SENCo or education psychologist may recommend bringing in the expertise of colleagues such as a learning and literacy support advisor (or equivalent in your local authority or multi-academy trust) or a speech and language therapist or occupational therapist (OT), potentially for further assessment if issues in specific areas of need are suspected.

Targets and strategies for success

The section on 'Contextual information' above detailed what is already going well and what needs to improve. It can be tempting in a behaviour plan to aim to tackle all of the issues in one go. I advise against this and recommend prioritising the main things that need to be improved first.

The targets need to be in a language that the child can understand. As James McTaggart (2019), educational psychologist in the Scottish Highlands, says, progress will be hampered, 'if the targets are unattainable, incomprehensible, or personally irrelevant or designed around the needs of the adults rather than of the child/young person'. With that in mind, we need to recognise that the point of a behaviour plan is not to end up with a child that never puts a foot wrong. We can't expect 100 per cent perfection and shouldn't hold the child to higher standards than other children in the school. Targets are therefore aimed at improvement, not faultlessness.

I like a specific way of looking at planning for success. Once the priorities are agreed I recommend a graduated approach that begins with the least intrusive strategies aimed at prevention, and reserves the most intrusive approaches for emergency intervention. Many behaviour plans I see kick in after something bad has happened – typically they take the form, 'Child does this, you do that' and this purely reactive approach misses opportunities to prevent behaviours occurring in the first place, which is surely the entire point. With that in mind, we need to start with preventative strategies.

Prevention

What can be done to render the behaviour irrelevant because the problem it is deployed to solve doesn't arise?

- This may involve environmental changes such as where the child is seated if the issue involves conflict with others.
- If failure avoidance is an issue then an approach that allows the child to feel that attempting a task is safer than before could be beneficial.
- In the solution-focused approach (mentioned below under 'Reinforcement'), this would involve doing more of whatever is already working well.

Teaching

The aim here is to make the behaviour inefficient by teaching new skills so that the child finds it easier to have their needs met by behaving in a different way.

- Think about the way that for younger children, for example, we explicitly teach the pro-social skills of waiting, turn-taking and lining up. We need to do this because children can obtain things more swiftly if they don't do any of these pro-social things, but they need to learn that exhibiting non-pro-social behaviours is unacceptable, no matter how effective they may seem to the child.

Elimination

By minimising the recognition of a behaviour, we aim to make it ineffective and therefore eliminate it.

- A standard piece of behaviour advice – and one I will repeat here – is to ignore secondary behaviours. (For example, I tell you to put your phone away, which you do, but also mutter that you hate me under your breath as you do it. The muttering is the secondary behaviour, which follows the primary behaviour of having your phone out in my lesson.) Ignoring secondary behaviours prevents escalation of situations – always one of our main aims – but I accept that it is fiendishly difficult to do as you have to overcome the overwhelming urge to respond.

Reinforcement

In contrast to elimination, the aim here is to make desired behaviour more rewarding, satisfying or fulfilling.

- This does not mean offering an inducement to encourage the desired behaviour, although admittedly this may help in the very short term. It means that we make every effort to spot when things are going well and we immediately reinforce with recognition. We don't go over the top as children will spot when we're patronising them or are being inauthentic and the effect is diluted.
- We can follow up here too with further reinforcement by making contact with parents later on or by informing the child's form tutor and/or Head of Year.
- The solution-focused approach of identifying what is already going well and encouraging more of it fits in well here.

Sanction

You will all be familiar with this. Any sanctions you use in response to poor behaviour need to be proportionate (i.e. a child doesn't end up in isolation for a week for a minor offence), socially appropriate, aversive responses that are educative and not simply punitive.

Safety

In the most extreme situations you need to know what you will do to ensure the safety of all. This may involve evacuating a classroom and summoning help, or extremely rarely, may involve the use of physical intervention. (Most behaviour plans I know of have no need for this section, but there will be rare occasions where explicit planning and forethought is needed.)

Evaluation

A plan soon ceases to be of use if it is not subject to review on a regular basis. The purpose of reviewing the progress of the plan is twofold – firstly, to identify what is working well so that you can carry on with that; secondly, to refine or replace the strategies that are proving less effective. The review interval is important – too often and very little, if anything, will be different; too infrequently and the child and the staff will have long since moved on, and the plan will be out-of-date.

Evaluation needs to be informed by the evidence that the school has available, and if targets are written well, this will help. This is likely to involve harder evidence such as incidences of fixed-term exclusion, detentions, records of behaviour incidents on the school's recording system, but also qualitative, narrative evidence from the adults who work with the child and, importantly, the parents.

I was recently conducting a behaviour review in a school and one senior leader, new to the school, made a very enlightening comment. 'No one ever comes off a plan in this place!' she said. When we talked about this we could immediately see why. I asked her about the review process and she said that reviews of plans took place only when things got worse. One question to consider when reviewing a behaviour plan is if a plan is still required. This seems self-evident because plans are designed to support improvements in behaviour, but I can see the temptation to keep a plan in place for a child just in case.

Who owns the plan?

The person who knows the child best needs to be the owner and writer of the plan. This is likely to be the class teacher in a primary school or the form tutor in a secondary school. The upside is that it is written by the person, as said above, who knows the child better than anyone else, but the downside is that the quality of plans across a school will inevitably vary without some form of support or quality control. That is why they are best constructed with the group of people detailed in the section on 'Contextual information' above, but without a named owner, any plan runs the risk of gathering dust on a shelf somewhere.

Communication of the plan

Unless what is agreed is well understood by the adults who work with the child, who in some cases were not at the original meeting or at any of the reviews, then the plan will have a limited reach and impact. Further, the school risks variation in practice or, at worst, contradictory approaches by different adults to the same behaviour(s). A behaviour plan that makes a reasonable adjustment[1] for a particular child that is contrary to the expectations or rules for every other child in the school needs to be widely known to avoid placing the child in a very difficult position where they are sanctioned in one lesson for something that is allowed in another. This isn't a formalised permissive route to ignoring the behaviour of some children – clearly there are some things for which no allowance can be made – but could happen where, for example, a child is allowed to use a device such as a tablet or smartphone to type instead of write or to use dictation software. This is, of course, essentially no different from the consistent application of the school's behaviour policy by all teachers, but is doubly important for those children with behaviour plans, given the need for the plan in the first place. Careful consideration needs to be given, therefore, to how the implementation of the plan is communicated and that this in not just an email to all staff or a paper copy of the plan in everyone's pigeonhole.

REFLECTION POINTS

- How does your current behaviour plan compare to the suggested structure above?

- Where there are differences, what could be done to incorporate those into your practice?

- How well would your colleagues say they know the contents, expectations and targets in your behaviour plans?

- Can anything be done to improve communication of plans in your school?

- How rich is the information you use to review the progress your students are making against their behaviour plans? What may be missing and how could you go about securing it to improve the review process?

Behaviour reports: what is the point?

The 'line or sign' example used at the start of this chapter is a neat case study in ineffective behaviour reports. But before we look at how behaviour reports can be effective we need to be clear on their purpose. I indicated earlier that behaviour reports have the potential to be punitive tools that rely on increased pressure and scrutiny on a child to improve their behaviour. This punitive aspect should not be an explicit aim nor an inadvertent outcome, as this sort of coercion will not generate long-term behaviour change – so leaders do need to look out for this as it is a form of escalation. I also stated earlier that a report without a plan behind it is a waste of time. To that end, these documents are essentially more of a support schedule for the child, distilled from and informed by the behaviour plan, which we can use to gather information about how they are getting on, rather than a report in the old-fashioned, 'Was it a good lesson/bad lesson?' sense.

I see two main reasons for using a report for a child who needs support to improve their behaviour:

1. The child responds well to immediate reminders, especially at times of stress, about what they need to do and how they can be successful. The report can then be used as a form of checklist for the child.
2. The document can double as a tool that adults can use for formative conversations with the child (with the added benefit that it can remind them of what is explicitly in the plan).

If the main aim of a report is to collect information on a child's conduct during the course of a day then this can probably be achieved electronically by adults without using the child to carry the information around with them all day long.

I was working with a colleague last year to support her efforts in improving the behaviour of Seb, an 11-year-old boy with learning difficulties in her class, around two specific issues – playing with other children on a one-to-one basis and lining up. When playing with another child, Seb would often get physical and the other children became very wary of being near him. Similarly, when lining up, Seb simply went to the front, even if pushing and shoving were required. Seb was keen to play with the others and struggled to understand why they didn't reciprocate. The teacher used a behaviour report for Seb serving two purposes: firstly, a reminder for the adults working with Seb (there were five adults in that class) about what he needed to do, and as a tally chart so that they could keep track of the times he did well or didn't manage it, which they could look at daily and then weekly; and secondly, as a reminder for Seb of what a good friend did (sharing, no hitting, etc.) and what good lining up looked like. It was essentially a distillation of his behaviour plan. Both were done with pictures as well as with language that Seb understood, and were put on a plastic triangular prism (think of the shape of a Toblerone box), which was unobtrusive, but which the adults could refer to easily and could use as the basis of a conversation with Seb.

When done well, this kind of support benefits everyone and doesn't look too dissimilar from other learning supports that may appear on the desks of children, like the small laminated reminders about grammar I sometimes see in primary schools.

When reports are constructed in haste, and I see this often, they resort to using systems very similar to the 'line or sign' model, often with things like smiley or frowny face emojis. This is because the class teacher has spent their previous evening on their laptop knocking the report up and that, understandably, is the best that can be done because there simply must be something, anything, in place for tomorrow morning. It is better not to bother.

Features of effective behaviour reports

Low-stakes documents

Reports that carry with them big consequences end up on the lean-to roof I described earlier. Sadly, I think that making them high stakes, punitive affairs is one of the foundations for using behaviour reports in schools today. It is unsurprising as it aligns well with the behaviourist logic of reward and punishment, such that there is a need for consequences if the report is not good enough in addition to the natural consequences that there would have been for any misdemeanours anyway. To avoid this, design reports that do not detail what punishment or sanction will occur if the report is deemed to be not good enough. There is no reason to double sanction someone. (Incidentally, this is why the 'line or sign' or smiley face/frowny face reports are attractive. They allow teachers to say things like, 'If you don't get four smiley faces today then you'll lose your break time'.)

There is a similar version of these high stakes reports that is quite common, but which is worse. These reports are seemingly positive in that they are designed so that a child begins each day with a certain amount of credit in the behaviour bank – this comes in the form of something like ten ticks or smiley faces or gold stars. For each misdemeanour the child loses one (or more) tick or star or smiley face. The flawed logic at play here is that the child will try progressively harder to hold it together as the gold stars disappear. I've seen what really happens a number of times. The removal, sometimes done publicly, is an escalation as the chances of failure are heightened so that there comes a point when the child decides that failure is inevitable and takes matters into their own hands, perhaps telling the teacher that they, 'DON'T GIVE A SHIT!' or ripping up their work or leaving the lesson or all three. With that in mind, avoid making reports pass/fail devices.

Avoid rewards

In the same vein that reports should not hold the threat of further sanction over the head of the child, nor should they dangle enticing rewards for improvement either. This is consistent with the thinking about rewards that you will read about in the next chapter in that we want to encourage and support children to behave well because it is the right thing to do, rather than just because it results in them receiving something nice at the end. We do, however, want to recognise when things go well and there are improvements. Recognition, as you will read in Chapter 7, is not the same as reward and, as was stated earlier in this chapter, recognition is a great way to reinforce what you do want.

Specific

No child is perfectly behaved all of the time, and no child is poorly behaved all of the time. Ask yourself, therefore, if you really need to be monitoring the behaviour of particular children at all times. There may be some children for whom this is entirely appropriate and necessary, but for some their issues will be specific and it is sensible and consistent with the principle of being least intrusive to maintain a sharper interest in areas of concern and then subject the child to no more scrutiny than their peers for the rest of the time.

This is also true in terms of what we are monitoring. There is no need to monitor everything about the behaviour of a child if our concerns are only about one aspect. For example, there is no need to report on uniform and punctuality if neither of those things were a bigger problem for this child than for anyone else in the first place. Any misdemeanours outside of the scope of the report are then dealt with as you would with any other child in the school.

Achievable

It may seem self-evident, but a child must feel that they are capable of meeting the expectations that have been set for them. This sense of self-efficacy (remember that from Chapter 3? It is as true for children as it is for us) is crucial in securing lasting behaviour change, for without it the chances of the child quitting are high. If school life already feels tough and success seems out of reach, which means failure is inevitable, then it can seem pointless to put yourself through the pain of disappointment.

The report is the distillation of the behaviour plan so it is important to translate the aims of the plan into achievable steps for the child. In doing this we must *never* hold the child to a higher standard than the rest of their peers. We aren't after perfection here; we're aiming for things to be good enough.

Shared with home

All parents are desperate for their children to do well at school and, no matter how indifferent or hostile the parents may seem on the rare occasions you think otherwise, if there are problems they will want to know firstly that we are on top of the situation, secondly how they can support us and lastly, they'll want to be well informed as to how their child is faring.

I do recall a particular example of a parent who was very supportive and worked well with us, yet we had a major disagreement on what we were doing. His son had done something at home and the father brought him in one Friday morning asking that we keep him off that day's trip as a punishment. I disagreed, as one strong principle of mine is that children aren't subjected to double jeopardy for one incident. Things that happen at home are dealt with at home, and things that happen at school are dealt with at school. A colleague who works in a boarding school tells me that they work in this way too. The father and I couldn't agree, but the child went on the trip. It can be tempting for parents to punish at home if the report is not good enough, but this should always be avoided.

REFLECTION POINTS

- How does the structure of your current behaviour reports measure up against the advice detailed above?

    o Are they pass/fail documents?
    o Do they help the child focus on what needs to improve?
    o Are there further sanctions if the report is not good enough?
    o Are rewards offered for good progress?
    o How involved are parents currently?
    o Are children on report held to a higher standard than their peers?

TAKING IT FURTHER – QUESTIONS AND ACTIVITIES FOR YOU AND YOUR COLLEAGUES

Behaviour plans

- Can you think of a child or children for whom a behaviour plan was a very successful part of improving their behaviour?

  o What was it about the plan – its contents, how it was constructed, shared, reviewed and refined – that made it successful?
  o What did the child say about how the plan helped them?
  o How can this information be used to inform behaviour planning across the school?

- Now do the same for a child or children for whom a behaviour plan proved ineffective in improving their behaviour.

  o What was it about the plan – its contents, how it was constructed, shared, reviewed and refined – that meant it wasn't as successful as you had hoped?
  o What does/did the child say about what they think was missing that could have helped them?
  o What lessons are there in this to help improve behaviour planning across the school?

Behaviour reports

- Remind yourself what your main aims are in running a behaviour reporting system in the first place. Is it a device to impress upon a child how serious the situation is, or is it truly supportive?

- How does the way the system is currently set up help you achieve those aims?

- Are there any changes you now need to make to better help you achieve those aims?

Note

1. As defined by the Equality Act (2010). www.gov.uk/guidance/equality-act-2010-guidance (accessed 19 September 2019).

References

Bower, J. (2012) 'Solving problems collaboratively: The Ross Greene approach', *For the Love of Learning blog*. http://joe-bower.blogspot.co.uk/2012/04/collaborative-problem-solving.html (accessed 19 September 2019).

Department for Education (2019) *Permanent and Fixed-period Exclusions in England: 2017 to 2018*, 25 July. www.gov.uk/government/statistics/perma nent-and-fixed-period-exclusions-in-england-2017-to-2018 (accessed 19 September 2019).

EPICure (1995) 'EPICure at eleven years: Findings'. www.epicure.ac.uk/epicure-1995/epicure-at-eleven-years/findings/ (accessed 19 September 2019).

Hollo, A., Wehby, J.H. and Oliver, R.M. (2014) 'Unidentified language deficits in children with emotional and behavioral disorders: A meta-analysis', *Exceptional Children*, 80(2): 169–186.

McTaggart, J. (2019) https://twitter.com/JamesEdPsych/status/10974648626938 22465?s=20 (accessed 30 September 2019).

Meredith, M. (2018) https://twitter.com/marymered/status/10549833460 21896194 (accessed 30 September 2019).

Royal College of Speech and Language Therapists (2018) *Understanding the Links Between Communication and Behaviour*. www.rcslt.org/-/media/Project/ RCSLT/rcslt-behaviour-a4-factsheet.pdf (accessed 19 September 2019).

7

RECOGNITION, NOT REWARDS

Children should experience success and failure not as reward and punishment but as information.

Jerome Bruner (1961: 26)

THE HEADLINES

- The recognition that a child receives for behaving well is more effective in fostering, maintaining and improving behaviour than rewarding children for behaving well.

- School systems should ensure they recognise the progress children make with their behaviour, irrespective of their current situation, rather than operate systems with arbitrary benchmarks (i.e. good children and naughty children).

- Don't catch them being good, catch them being better.

- 'Good/naughty' systems swiftly recognise children who already find schools relatively easy places to feel successful. They already receive frequent affirmative messages from the adults around them that they are successful, welcome and valuable members of the school community. Those same systems make it far harder for children who find it difficult to feel successful at school to receive recognition for the effort and progress they make with their behaviour.

- Rewards and inducements appeal to self-interest and can encourage a 'What's in it for me?' attitude.

- Rewards and inducements convey the message to children that learning and behaving are a means to securing a reward, and are not valuable in their own right.

- 'Time off for good behaviour' policies, such as Golden Time, convey the same message that work or behaving well is a means to some time off.

- Such policies require, by definition, some children to fail or the perceived incentive disappears and those children must also therefore be made to do something that seems unpleasant by comparison. This is inevitably school work, which further entrenches the view that work is unpleasant.

- Public ranking of children in reward systems, such as for attendance and those for attainment, ignore the dignity of children and do more harm than good. They are based on the flawed logic that improvement is simply a matter of attitude.
- Intrinsic motivation is more effective in securing improvements in behaviour than methods relying on extrinsic motivation.
- Intrinsic motivation can be characterised by:
  - a thirst for knowledge
  - activities or learning that provide a level of satisfaction
  - activities or learning that provide a sense of accomplishment, progress or mastery.
- Extrinsic motivation can be characterised by:
  - a desire to gain something such as a reward or a desire to avoid something such as a punishment
  - rule-following behaviour (even if the rule has no value to the person it is still important to them that they don't break it)
  - following rules, doing work or behaving in a certain way because they have value (such as working hard to obtain a set of grades to get on a desired degree course even if the A-Level courses themselves are detested).

'Shouldn't children be rewarded for doing the right thing?'

Have you ever been asked this question? I have, countless times. The question almost inevitably arises somewhere in the middle of a discussion about rewards and sanctions, incentives and deterrents, praise and punishment. It is a good question because it lets us get to the heart of what we've been led to believe is important when fostering good behaviour in children. It is also an important question because reward systems are endemic in schools – a legacy of the apprenticeship of observation, I am sure – and form a largely unnecessary part of the foundation of many behaviour policies, so we should think hard about why they are there and what function they serve.

I'll nail my colours to the mast straight away and state that, no, I don't believe children should be *rewarded* for doing the right thing. I believe that children should receive *recognition* for their achievements and efforts and, crucially, the progress they make with their behaviour, but that is not the same as rewarding them. I'll elaborate lest you think I'm splitting hairs

---

REFLECTION POINTS

Let's begin by thinking hard about your reasoning when answering the following questions:

- Why should children be rewarded for behaving well in your school?

- What do you think will happen to behaviour in your school if the entice-ment of rewards wasn't there?

- Do you think that the value, monetary or otherwise, of an inducement influences how well a child behaves in your school?

---

here, but before I do I want to go back 19 years to a child and a situation from my teacher training year that has never left me.

I taught science to Ollie and his class as part of my teacher training in a secondary comprehensive school. They were in Year 7, so all fairly new to the school, and Ollie had already become an established figure across the school as a child with behaviour problems. The class was in the bottom set – a label that I happily used for all of my mainstream teaching life without a care as to how limiting it is – and contained a number of children with special educational needs and a number of children who found it difficult to behave well in school. Needless to say, I learned fast with this group of 15 or so children and teaching them was a superb experience for me as a new teacher. As someone with liter-ally only weeks of experience I had little credit with the Bank of Behaviour Expertise so I relied heavily on two things – humour and the school's behaviour policy. The school's policy essentially amounted to two things – the warning system for sanctions detailed in Chapter 2 and a lottery ticket system as an incentive to behave well. Lottery tickets were given out for good behaviour – the teacher wrote out the lottery ticket, awarded it to the child, sometimes in front of the whole class to make a fuss of them and incentivise others, and the stub would go into a raffle drum kept in the staffroom from which a dozen or so would be drawn at each end-of-term assembly with prizes on offer such as vouch-ers, chocolate, CDs and DVDs. (I used a variation of this idea a few years back, I'm sorry to say.)

I awarded Ollie a lottery ticket one afternoon for what had been a sus-tained period of good work and behaviour and thought no more about it. Weeks later, I was having a conversation with one of the school's Deputy

Headteachers about the system and it became apparent that the raffle drum was filtered before each prize draw assembly with tickets for certain students being removed, no matter how many they'd been given, Ollie being one of them. The reasoning, so said the deputy, was that, 'we can't have children like him winning prizes in front of the rest of the school'. I was bemused, sad and angry all in one go, and for three reasons. Firstly, children earned those tickets whether one agreed with the system or not (I did then, but now I don't). Secondly, my own professional judgement was being overridden. If the school leadership was concerned that some teachers were attempting to bribe children with the lure of a lottery ticket – a distinct possibility I suppose, but a lure that was doomed to fail – then there were other ways of dealing with that. And thirdly, what hope did Ollie and others affected ever have of having their improvements in behaviour recognised?

I am sure that Ollie and others were unaware that this was happening, but I'm equally sure that they knew that some adults in the school had written them off as beyond hope. This seems to me to be a very efficient way of reinforcing poor behaviour. It is pointless trying to do well if you believe the adults think you're bad and there is nothing you can do to change their minds.

As mentioned above, I used the basis of this system when I first became a Headteacher, although I now regret doing this. I remember colleagues being infuriated for the same reason as the deputy above that one student who most certainly had a number of behavioural challenges had won a prize. They hated the public recognition and felt that it sent the wrong message to the rest of the school. I know some colleagues weren't convinced with my defence: 'One of you, and it doesn't matter who, has decided that Sandy's work or behaviour was worthy of recognition in your lessons. I respect that. Secondly, he has shown significant improvements in his behaviour this year. He still isn't where we need him to be, but he is far, far better. We must acknowledge that'.

Catch them being better

This highlights a key component of behaviour improvement that can be lacking in schools' approaches, namely that we need to recognise *progress* in improving behaviour. This is doubly important when working with the children who find schools difficult places to be successful. It is why I object to the term, 'Catch them being good'. Some children find 'being good' effortless and they are routinely experiencing success and affirmation at school on a daily basis which reinforces this. They get implicit and explicit messages from many adults that they are highly valued members of the school community and we could catch them being good all day long. Other children, however, require superhuman determination to feel successful on the odd occasion and are far more used to receiving implicit and explicit messages from many adults around them that they are valued far less, or rejected even, and may well feel a very poor sense of the belonging that we covered in Chapters 1 and 2. We don't need to catch children being good; we need to catch them being *better*. Given that lasting behaviour change takes time it makes sense to me that we need to recognise progress at each and every step, rather than decide that anything below a certain level is a failure. There is a loose analogy here with the grades 1 to 8 awarded in music exams. This setup is developmental and passing each grade acknowledges progress along the way. Grade 1 has as much value as Grade 8 and it is implicit that a student who has achieved Grade 1 will now work towards the skills and knowledge needed to play at a Grade 2 level if they so wish. Grade 1 is not a failure, it is a measure of progress. Contrast this with pass/fail systems. Some, like the driving test, exist for good reason but others, such as GCSE, arbitrarily label grades 1 to 3 as failures. To be clear, I do not imply from the above that there is no minimum level of acceptable behaviour. Clearly there is. What I am saying is that we should not reserve recognition, or reward if that is still your thing, for children above a certain level.

We must recognise improvements when they occur, irrespective of where the child currently is. This is a good way of reinforcing what we want and what is good for the child. Without this, we maintain a system that refuses to acknowledge children's progress until they cross a line of acceptability that is probably unknown to them. On one side of the line are the children labelled 'good', on the other those labelled as 'bad'. (I think of this line as the Father Christmas Line.) Many of the experiences of the children on the 'bad' side, for they know on which side the adults have placed them, will reinforce their negative behaviour. We risk these children being stuck in a cycle of negative reinforcement, with a potential perverse outcome whereby children realise that they are 'bad' and therefore have no hope of being 'good' so give up trying. These children will take their successes where they can find them (perversely they can find success in misbehaving), such that walking out of a lesson, ending up in isolation or ripping up a piece of work can all be regarded as successful, especially when seeking to avoid potential failure or humiliation.

REFLECTION POINTS

- Look afresh at your school's behaviour policy and your practice and answer the following questions:

  o Are we more likely to identify for positive recognition the children who already find school an easier place to be successful?

  o Are we less likely to recognise achievements and progress of the children in our school with the biggest behavioural challenges?

  o If so, what can we do about it?

The difference between reward and recognition

Rewards are offered before the fact: 'If you do this, you will get that'. The inducement is conditional on the child doing something that the teacher deems important – behaving in a certain way or producing a piece of work to a certain standard, for example.

Recognition arises after the fact as a result of a child doing something that is noteworthy. Crucially, there is no conditionality involved. There is also nothing attached to the recognition, such as a voucher, and this too is important. I think of recognition as a form of feedback (as Bruner would say) and it needs to be more than just empty praise.

This distinction is crucial and once I'd thought deeply enough about this, it brought to light some serious reservations and convinced me to focus on recognition and forget rewards entirely.

I am concerned that rewards send a number of messages to children that are unhealthy.

Firstly, it suggests that the behaviour or work we want to see is not valuable in its own right and in order to encourage a child to behave in a certain way or do a certain task we must incentivise them to do so. The logic suggests that without the offer of the reward children would simply not comply as it wouldn't be worth their while. This is a gloomy outlook on children and one I don't recognise. For work especially, it implies that it is a chore and that the reward is the sugar that will help the unpleasant medicine go down that little bit easier.

Following on from this, the use of rewards can foster a, 'What's in it for me?' attitude. Altruism or contributing to the common good does not pay under such systems. I know that I want children to learn that doing the right thing is worth it for its own sake and offering conditional rewards does not help in that quest. The answer to, 'What's in it for me?' may well be, 'Absolutely nothing, beyond the warm, fuzzy feeling you're going to get by doing something that helps others'. Picking up litter has its own inherent value; following school rules benefits everyone; encouraging another student when they're struggling is a beautiful thing when I see it. None of these things is made more valuable or more likely to occur when something irrelevant is attached to it. It cheapens the task. If the only reason a child is picking up some litter is because there are some Vivo points dangling in front of them then I don't think we've educated them very well.

The offer of an inducement in return for carrying out a task or behaving in a certain way also carries with it a risk that the child does the bare minimum necessary or tries to finish as quickly as possible in order to secure the reward. This is quite clearly undesirable as a child is far less likely to put their heart and soul into something if they've figured out the Goldilocks formula for just the right amount of effort or work to get what's on offer.

For sure rewards can influence behaviour in the short term, but for all the reasons above you can see why they won't lead to lasting behaviour change and quite clearly that is what we really want.

In short, rewards teach children the price of everything but the value of nothing. They are also likely to contradict the values of many schools who state that they seek to produce responsible citizens who recognise the importance of service to others.

Recognition, on the other hand, is essentially feedback (as per Bruner's quote at the beginning of this chapter) and should be there to serve a number of crucial purposes. A clear aim is to reinforce good behaviour and offer encouragement to the child or children to keep going with it. This is especially important for children who may regularly find themselves in trouble for poor behaviour. Secondly, it may not be obvious to the child that they have done something well or better than before and we need to make it explicit to the child that this has happened. This is why it is more than just empty praise. When we regard behaviour improvement as a matter of education and not of retribution this becomes as natural as the formative feedback we provide to children with their academic work.

When viewed in this way, behaviour improvement does not become a competitive sport. Prizes for all implies a very low bar for earning them and no school would do such a thing for that very reason. And yet, it is of course entirely possible that every single member of the school community can be better behaved this year than last. Children shouldn't be competing to be the best behaved, as someone always has to lose and that child may be the one with the most entrenched behavioural challenges who has made the most progress that year, yet still seems to lag behind everyone else. This is where we should be on the lookout for poor proxies for behaviour that we may find ourselves using in our systems in schools.

Poor proxies for rewards and recognition

I read a lot of behaviour policies and I remain concerned that there are a number of examples of attributes that schools seek to reward that are actually poor proxies.

The humble effort sticker is one of my all-time favourites. My deep suspicion is that what is really being rewarded here are things like attainment, volume of work, neatness, task completion, compliance or quietness as opposed to true effort.

Ollie's case above is a classic case of using proxies for behaviour. Our school wanted the right kind of child up there on the stage in front of the rest of the year group winning something and so, inevitably, we had a parade of the children who already found school a far easier place to be successful than Ollie, and the lottery assembly reinforced that, both for them and Ollie. The intention that it would send a message to Ollie and others on the blacklist that they needed to buck their ideas up if they wanted to be one of those kids of course fell on deaf ears. It also entirely missed the point. We could have used the lottery system, with the entirely unnecessary prize draw at the end, as a way of giving recognition and besides, some children would have rather run a mile than go up on the stage to win a prize, such was their already entrenched view of themselves as 'bad' (which we also successfully reinforced). The act of awarding the ticket, minus the lottery, was where the power really lay if it was used as a device to convey how the child had improved.

Why are we rewarding attendance?

Nothing gets close, though, in terms of missing the point as rewards for 100 per cent attendance. This practice is not just pointless, it is counterproductive. Firstly, most children aren't in control of whether they go to school or not, their parents are. This practice penalises children who are ill, and being ill is not simply a matter of being determined enough to stay well. It isn't a straightforward matter of incentivising children to get themselves out of bed in the morning with the prospect of a trip to the cinema at the end of term. It could also encourage children to attend when they should be away from school so they can't infect others. Being too unwell to attend school is, for some, largely a matter of chance and for others with lifelong conditions such as epilepsy simply a fact of life on occasion. During the last half-term holiday, my wife, son and daughter were all ill with a vomiting virus. I spent the week waiting for it to strike me, but I escaped. All three, though, didn't miss any school and that was by sheer chance.

Should my children be rewarded by their schools for being ill at the right time? Or my wife? Rewarding staff for high attendance exists in some schools too, unbelievably.

Lastly, a defence I am often presented with is that schools take into account genuine absence. Well, all absences that are authorised by parents are, by definition, genuine unless you believe that you can tell which parents are lying. Or by 'genuine', they mean an epileptic seizure is a genuine reason whereas a cold is not. At the Department for Education's last count, authorised absences accounted for three quarters of all absences (Department for Education, 2018: 4). Even then, unauthorised absence could be down to parents not notifying the school of the reason for the absence yet it could still be down to genuine illness.

In any case, there is thought-provoking research on the effect of rewarding attendance, and its outcomes make for interesting reading. A recent study by Robinson et al. (2018: 2), involving over 15,000 students, found that, '[c]ontrary to our preregistered hypotheses, prospective awards had no impact while the retrospective awards decreased subsequent attendance'.

REFLECTION POINTS

- Give some thought to rewards and recognition in your school. Is a reward or recognition for one thing really a reward or recognition for something else? For example, are effort stickers really awarded for effort, or for a poor proxy for effort like neatness or attainment?

- Is your system based on the progress that children make with their behaviour or do they have to cross a defined line first? Essentially, is it a 'catch them being good' or 'catch them being better' system?

- If you reward 100 per cent attendance, reconsider your rationale for doing so. What are the unintended messages you are sending out to children?

Time off for good behaviour

In the same vein as rewarding attendance, reward systems that offer time off for good behaviour also send unfortunate and unintended messages to children.

Golden Time, a favourite amongst some teachers of younger children, is a prime example. It goes something like this – children can earn time during the working week for things like good work or good behaviour and this is then cashed in on a Friday afternoon for some free time. There are risks with this system.

- Work can be seen as a chore to be endured in order to obtain the dividend of free time.
- Some children must lose out as any incentive disappears if everyone in the class always qualifies for it.
- A graduated approach to Golden Time, whereby children accumulate differing amounts including some children who may earn none, must have a plan for those children whose time has run out. Whilst others are enjoying their Golden Time they will be working, and that work needs to feel at least a little bit unpleasant, otherwise the deterrent effect, if it ever existed, evaporates.
- I know of a number of Golden Time systems that claw back earned time for poor behaviour. This unwise move makes all earned time conditional upon future conduct, and for those children who regularly struggle to earn any time, this can make what time they have earned a precious and precarious commodity that could be devastating to lose.

Rankings and displays

A practice that is more concerning is the use of ranking and public displays of ranks as a motivator to students. I have seen two types – only in secondary schools in my experience – and they seem to be sadly creeping up in popularity. These are display boards in a prominent place in the school for all, visitors included, to see. Students are ranked in terms of attainment such that a student heading for a string of grade 8s and 9s at GCSE sits atop a list of 200 or so students, propped up by a child, possibly with diagnosed learning difficulties, at the bottom who may not sit any GCSEs at all. Goodness knows why anyone thinks this is a smart idea. The ham-fisted logic at play is simply that attainment is solely a matter of effort and application. If you're at the bottom it is only because you can't be bothered to put the work in so you deserve it. You could argue that it is a form of recognition, but to what purpose? Recognition of what? I contend that it is a form of shaming, and no good ever comes of public shaming of children. The second sort, less popular in my experience, is public displays of attendance percentages for children, and follows the same logic as for attainment displays. Both belong in the bin, and in any case are likely breaches of the General Data Protection Regulations.

Motivation

Whether or not you share my views on rewards and recognition, all positive systems in schools, no matter how individualistic or materialistic they seem, are attempting to motivate children to do the right thing. With that in mind it is worth taking some time to look at the ladder of motivation to see the different ways in which children can be motivated to behave better and to see where rewards are placed on that ladder.

Intrinsic motivation

You will see from what I have written earlier that I am concerned that rewards can appeal to an individualistic desire to complete a task or behave in a certain way in order to gain or avoid something. When someone is intrinsically motivated to do something no inducement or threat is necessary, and their motivation may not be entirely or at all self-centred. Intrinsic motivation can arise from a culture, environment and work that provide a sense of fulfilment, success or satisfaction such that the experience of being in school is itself rewarding.

A thirst to know

Some topics or subjects seem to capture the attention of our children (and us) more readily than others and you can see why little or no encouragement is needed for those children to throw themselves into their studies. Clearly, how we as teachers present those topics or subjects to children is important and indeed this can be the catalyst that accelerates the thirst to know. Of course, the opposite is also true, where children have little or no interest in a subject, this can make motivation a struggle.

A sense of accomplishment

It is self-evident that the experience of success or progress – what Bandura from Chapter 3 would call 'mastery' experiences – builds confidence in a student. There exists a positive feedback loop and its biggest advantage is that it allows future problems or struggles to be approached with a confidence that can be overcome. Recall also from Chapter 3 the negative feedback loop that can be overpowering if enough failure is experienced early on. This applies equally to behaviour as it does to academic work. A child who found, for example, a one-hour written exam intolerable last term receives a tremendous sense of accomplishment if they manage it next time. When the seemingly impossible becomes possible, the sense of accomplishment is huge but it also, crucially, reduces fear. Fong et al. (2019) interestingly found that the effect of negative feedback (it is a fact of life for all of us at times whether we like it or not) on intrinsic motivation could be reduced when: '(a) the feedback statement included instructional details on how to improve, (b) criterion-based standards were used to provide feedback, and (c) feedback was delivered in-person' (2018: 121). As teachers, we intuitively know this to be true. How sensitively and humanely we deliver the feedback is as important as the information we are trying to convey.

Something that the child finds inherently satisfying

I always think of physical activities such as swimming or cycling here, and this prompts me to recall that a level of proficiency is needed for many things before they can be satisfying. If you can't swim then it is anything but satisfying. Satisfaction is not limited to physical activities though. I find factorising the roots of quadratic equations satisfying, but this is only because I have attained a level of proficiency that makes this possible. What is now satisfying was once frustrating or infuriating.

Extrinsic motivation

By contrast, extrinsic motivation relies on external influencers, positive or negative, to alter behaviour. If the behaviour or work is not satisfying or fulfilling enough and does not have its own inherent value to the student then we can lean on external motivators to help. This is not inherently a bad thing. As we can see from the examples above, intrinsic motivation can rely on a certain level of skill, confidence or proficiency and this develops over time.

Rules, work or behaviour have value

This is not the same as rules, work or behaviour being inherently valuable. For example, the requirement to secure a set of particular GCSE or A-Level grades to get on to a preferred course at college or university means that they have value as a sort of currency.

Rule-following behaviour

I am a rule follower. Even for rules that are seemingly stupid I will tend to conform unless I have a strong reason not to. (I remember working as a postman during the university summer vacation and a colleague remarked that he couldn't understand why I stopped at red traffic lights at 4 a.m. when it was abundantly clear that there was no traffic anywhere to be seen and it was safe to proceed.) Below the motivation level where rules, work or behaviour have value we may find students conforming because they self-identify as conformists. They would be mortified to get into any sort of trouble and so rule following is very important to them.

Gain this or avoid that

Now we get to the most basic and least desirable form of motivation whereby we secure compliance through the attraction of gaining something desirable or through the deterrent effect of avoiding something unpleasant.

When we take a look at the different ways that motivations manifest themselves we can see that appealing to reward or deterrence is a very basic tactic and misses all of the more wholesome ways we can encourage good working habits and good behaviour. It is also clear to me that lasting behaviour change is highly unlikely under such a limiting approach and, of course, we would have long ago cracked behaviour improvement simply by offering extremely attractive rewards and equally unpleasant punishments. Well, pick a teacher at random and ask them. We haven't.

TAKING IT FURTHER – QUESTIONS AND ACTIVITIES FOR YOU AND YOUR COLLEAGUES

Let's use this end-of-chapter feature as a way to audit your current systems for reward and recognition and come up with an action plan for improvement. (For ease of reference and to avoid continual separation of the two, the phrase 'positive behaviour systems' refers to any that use reward or recognition.)

Values first

- What do you value in your students at your school?

    o   Do your positive systems encourage and recognise them?
    o   If not, or if partially, what changes could you make to ensure your positive systems support and reflect the values of your school?

Rewards

- What current practices exist in your school that use reward as an incentive to behave well?

- What current practices exist in your school that use reward as an incentive in other areas of school life, i.e. academic attainment?

(Continued)

- What do you currently know about the effectiveness or otherwise of their use in terms of improving behaviour?

- What more needs to be done or what changes could be made if rewards aren't proving as effective in improving behaviour as you would like?

- Pick three children – one child who is one of your most frequent receivers of rewards, one child from the middle of the pack and one child who has behavioural challenges – and compare their experiences of the reward systems in operation at your school.

  o Use this comparison to see if there are poor proxies for behaviour that are being rewarded (attainment, volume of work, neatness, etc.).
  o Use this comparison to see if it reflects improvement or deterioration in the behaviour of those children.

- What do you think would happen if reward was replaced by recognition in all these systems?

- If the thought of wholesale change is too much to bear, could you start with one system and gauge the difference after, say, a term or school year?

Recognition

- What current practices exist in your school that recognise the behaviour of children?

- What current practices exist in your school that recognise the achievements of children in other areas of school life, i.e. sporting achievements or volunteering?

- What do you currently know about the effectiveness or otherwise of their use in terms of improving behaviour?

- What more needs to be done or what changes could be made if recognition isn't proving as effective in improving behaviour as you would like?

Improvement

- How do your current systems recognise *improvements* in behaviour?

- Do any of your systems require children to cross an arbitrary threshold before they can 'qualify' (i.e. rewards for 100 per cent attendance)?

(Continued)

Public displays

- Do any of your positive systems rank children publicly?
- What do the children, the staff and the parents think about this practice?

Views of parents and students

- What do parents think about your current positive systems?
- What do children think about them?
- What suggestions do both have for changes to your systems?
- What will you do with this information?

Action planning

- What actions do you need to take as a result of your answers to the questions in the sections above?
- Who will be responsible for them?
- How will the school be better as a result?
- What will the children be saying and doing that is different?
- What will the adults be saying and doing that is different?

References

Bruner, J.S. (1961) 'The act of discovery', *Harvard Educational Review*, 31: 21–32.

Department for Education (2018) *Pupil Absence in Schools in England: Autumn 2017 and Spring 2018*. https://assets.publishing.service.gov.uk/government/uploads/system/uploads/attachment_data/file/749352/Absence_2term_201718-Text.pdf (accessed 23 September 2019).

Fong, C.J., Patall, E.A., Vasquez, A.C. and Stautberg, S. (2019) 'A meta-analysis of negative feedback on intrinsic motivation', *Educational Psychology Review*, 31(1): 121–162.

Robinson, C., Gallus, J., Lee, M. and Rogers, T. (2018) *The Demotivating Effect (and Unintended Message) of Retrospective Awards*. HKS Faculty Research Working Paper Series RWP18-020, July. https://scholar.harvard.edu/files/todd_rogers/files/the_demotivating.pdf (accessed 23 September 2019).

8

SANCTIONS

Goodness that depends on fear of hell or fear of the policeman or fear of punishment is not goodness at all – it is simply cowardice. Goodness that depends on hope of reward or hope of praise or hope of heaven depends on bribery.

A.S. Neill (1960)

THE HEADLINES

- Sanctions that depend on removal of time, in the form of detention or exclusion, or privileges can provide a short-term corrective, but are unlikely to lead to long-term behaviour change.

- Loss aversion – for example, the confiscation of a mobile phone for misuse – can be powerful short-term influencers on children's behaviour, but are unlikely to lead to long-term behaviour change.

- Sanctions are less likely to be effective for children with more persistent behavioural difficulties. This can result in the imposition of sanctions of ever-increasing severity in an attempt to make the child behave. This is highly unlikely to be effective and can escalate situations.

- Ross Greene's contention that children do well if they can, not if they choose, can help us to think more about working with children rather than imposing things upon them.

- Treating children differently, but equitably, is more effective in improving behaviour than treating children equally.

- Shaming a child will change their behaviour, just not in the way you intended.

One of my duties when I taught science in a comprehensive school in the first few years of my teaching life was staffing detentions with some other colleagues on a rota basis. (I note a recent development amongst some behaviour gurus to call these centralised detentions as if they are radical and new. They aren't.) I was simply armed with a list of students who were due to attend; I had no idea why they were there and I wasn't interested. I wanted the children to work in silence for the allotted time and then to be on their way. For those who disrespected the rules I always had to hand my trusty sidekick – the physics teacher's stopclock. I had one for each child in the room and any talking or messing about resulted in me stopping the clock until their behaviour was back to where I wanted it. By that method I could ensure I got my time's worth from each student. There was no purpose to the detention for the students other than for the time to be endured. For me it was important to hold the line on standards and that meant I had to win and the stopclock helped me to do that. For every winner, though, there must be a loser and plenty of those children didn't like losing, especially in front of their peers. When this happened, both of us by this time had lost sight of why the child was in there in the first place and occasionally the stopping and starting of the clock became a game to the child (see shaming denial later in this chapter). The system rested on the behaviourist principle of disincentivising through punishment by serving up something unpleasant to the child because they themselves had done something unpleasant. The inconvenience and the supposed unpleasantness was designed to act as a deterrent to prevent poor behaviour from occurring, or if it did occur, to be aversive and thus improve the behaviour of the children because they wouldn't want to experience it again. It plainly didn't do this in very many cases, but it enabled us as a school to satisfy ourselves and to justify to parents that we were dealing with situations by taking some form of tough action.

My biggest concern with the use of sanctions is not that some are too soft or too tough, but that many are simply ineffective with the children who find it toughest to behave well in schools and that we are kidding ourselves by not being more critical about this ineffectiveness. When we lack this criticality we tend to place the blame in one of two places. An external observer may decide that a school is not being tough enough or tenacious enough, and there is some mileage in this, but the problem can lie in the inconsistent application of the rule, not the sanction itself. Most behaviour advice, my own included, contends that the certainty of a sanction is more important than the severity.[1] Severity is not unimportant, though, as heavy-handed crackdowns for minor infringements are at best pointless, and are likely to escalate some situations by deepening resentment amongst some children. An internal observer may place the blame squarely at the feet of the child by claiming that, despite repeated sanctions, they are choosing not to behave better. What do we mean when we say, 'That'll teach 'em!' after imposing a sanction? We are implying that the child will learn their lesson about behaving differently in the future, but we leave the learning entirely to chance if we expect the dead time, the inconvenience or the unpleasantness of a sanction to somehow do the teaching we want. This is incredibly unlikely but the dice are loaded in our favour because this particular problem has a very easy (for the school) and predictable outcome – the behaviours recur and the child eventually ends up being permanently excluded for persistent disruptive behaviour. The child carries all of the blame (yes, they remain responsible for their actions; I'm not a free-will denier) and we claim justification because we did our bit by continuing to impose sanctions, but we maintain that the child chose not to behave differently and therefore deserves what was coming to them despite repeated warnings. Sanctions in and of themselves are simply retribution; there is no educative value to them, and this is where we go wrong for any situations that require more than mild correctives. We don't take this 'leaving learning to chance' approach when addressing literacy difficulties, for example, and I remain concerned that the blind application of sanctions and the increase in severity for failure to conform or change is not securing the improvements in behaviour we seek.

This sanctions escalator or merry-go-round highlights the obvious limitations of pop behaviourism. The focus on 'do this, get that' for rewards or 'do this, avoid that' for sanctions can foster a, 'What's in it for me?' attitude. This is entrenched when we talk of consequences for a child's behaviour because we can mean only the consequences for them and the focus on self-interest intensifies. You may, in some cases, purchase some short-term compliance but you certainly won't secure long-lasting behaviour change. The rules, the work or the desired behaviour have no value, they are simply a means to an end and that, for me, is a very limited way of working with humans, especially still-developing young ones.

REFLECTION POINTS

- Think of all the sanctions you have available to you. Which ones rely on:
    - deprivation of time?
    - loss aversion (i.e. the threat of confiscation of property influencing behaviour)?
    - loss of privileges?
- Which ones do you most commonly use?

Children do well if they can

A more productive approach to improving behaviour for children who can struggle to behave well in schools than the blunt application of sanctions can be found in the work of American clinical psychologist, Dr Ross Greene. He contends that children will do well if they can (Greene, 2014: Chapter 2). He extends this by saying that if a child (this works equally well for teachers or anyone else, by the way) is not doing well it is because they are lacking the necessary skills to do well in that situation. The moment I first heard this I was immediately attracted to it as it crystallised my experiences of over a decade, at that point, of working with children with special educational needs and disabilites (SEND) and my time prior to that in a comprehensive and a selective school. I had long since arrived at the view that negative behaviours communicate unmet needs, but I could see straight away that he had defined this in a better way. When you understand things in the way that Greene describes, it becomes obvious why children with SEND are grossly over-represented in the statistics for exclusion and are far more likely to develop behaviour problems (see Chapter 11 for more on this). It is a mistake, though, to regard both of our perspectives as pathological. Greene is not seeking to diagnose and intervene medically, and my learning from experiences in special education, and mainstream schools too for that matter, is informed by needs not conditions, syndromes and disorders.

One of the reasons I like Greene's approach so much is because it tackles head on the thorny issue of choice. If you scoff at the idea of children doing well if they *can* you are really only left with the view that children do well if they *choose*. This is a comfortable place to be for teachers and school leaders because it distils behaviour down to a matter of coercion and motivation. In order to get the behaviour you want all that is needed is the simple application of sanctions when a child chooses not to do what is required, or rewards when they do. There is no depth to the situation – the child made a choice, a poor one, and now they pay. If they continue to make poor choices then the sanctions are ratcheted up until they conform, or as stated on the previous page, the child eventually leaves your school. This may be seen as a positive development as the school may hold up the fact that the learning and safety of other students has been protected – this is a persuasive argument – but the essential problem remains unsolved by being moved elsewhere along with the child and may even be exacerbated via feelings of rejection. A school that operates in this way does not improve behaviour, it changes behaviour by changing its students.

I take Greene's thinking and bend it a little when thinking about 'kids do well if they can'. I always remember that we have to hold in our mind that when we say 'do well' we mean our definition of doing well, that is to say, what *we* want the child to do. If they are struggling to meet that expectation they may well seek their own way of doing well or being successful instead. That may involve getting out of your class as fast as possible, for example. They may swear at you, turn over a chair or rip up their work for good measure. You wouldn't regard this as 'doing well', and it may be highly inappropriate yet extremely successful. It is these kinds of situations where sanctions fail to hit home. In those moments, no threat, no matter how severe, will arrest the behaviour. Indeed, any or all of them may be preferable. If the aim of the child is to get out of a class then the threat of isolation, the Headteacher's office or exclusion ceases to be a threat, it becomes a desirable escape route.

I believe that no child sets out to do badly, to be unsuccessful, to be a failure, to risk embarrassing themselves in front of their peers and their teachers. We as teachers intuitively get this when we think of 'hard' skills like reading or conjugating French verbs, and our approach to improving these skills reflects that. No Headteacher sets out to do badly either, yet I recall the many times that I have been overcome with a crippling anxiety when trying to deal with some aspects of school leadership and I am sure I am not alone with this problem. In some of those cases I found ways to avoid doing what was really needed, even though I was clear in my mind that I was doing the wrong thing, but this was the only way I could think to be successful at those times. If I was better able to handle those situations, I would have. It wasn't simply a lack of motivation; I desperately wanted to do the right thing, but felt completely unable and therefore managed as best I could. At other times, I sought support, got through it and learned something. And sometimes I found a way to do the right thing and my confidence grew as a result, but it wasn't easy and I know this will happen to me again in the future.

No one behaves poorly all of the time or even for the majority of the time (just like no one behaves perfectly all the time), and Greene invites us to consider what it is about those situations that the child found challenging. His view is that the child is developmentally delayed in one or more of the 'umbrella' skills, as he calls them, of flexibility, adaptability, frustration, tolerance or problem-solving or in the application of one or more of these skills when they are most needed.

When considering behaviour through Greene's lens, we are left with a choice (oh, the irony):

- kids do well if they *can* means doing something *with* them in response to poor behaviour
- kids do well if they *choose* means doing something *to* them in response to poor behaviour.

The Social Discipline Window helps us to understand how the balance of control and support creates these differing conditions.

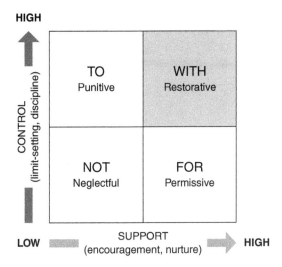

Figure 8.1 The Social Discipline Window (reproduced by permission of the International Institute of Restorative Practices, 'Defining Restorative', www.iirp.edu)

Source: Wachtel (1999)

A combination of high control and low support results in punitive, stigmatising and authoritarian environments and this is where things are done *to* people. Low control and low support indicates neglectful and irresponsible leadership (a rarity in schools in my experience). High support and low control amounts to doing things *for* people where it can prove difficult to get people to take personal responsibility for anything if they have learned that there is little or no expectation of them. High support and high control creates the conditions for, as Greene says, things to be done *with* people.

This means we as leaders need to decide how our sanctions can be truly educative. Generally, sanctions in schools are based on the temporary loss of property in the form of confiscation for misuse, the loss of privileges, or the biggest by far, the loss of time in the form of detention or exclusion. If we use this time as an opportunity to directly address and teach these skills then we are in with a fighting chance of helping the children who are finding it tough to do well at school with the skills they are lacking. If we don't, we're stuck with the detentions as dead time and the Groundhog Day of the names of the same children who simply won't learn appearing week after week until the end of time.

REFLECTION POINTS

- What are your immediate thoughts about Ross Greene's approach?

- Think of an example where a child didn't do well because you thought that they chose not to. What reasons can you think of for the child to choose not to do well in that situation?

- Does Greene's thinking have any implications for your approaches to supporting the children who find it hardest to behave well in your school?

Consistent with values, not consistency of action

With Ross Greene's advice still fresh, you can see why there will be times when we need to treat children differently. This is at odds with much of the advice out there on behaviour. In most books on behaviour you won't get past the first chapter without the advice that consistency is key – treating everyone the same so that everyone knows where they stand. I believed this to be misguided before I read Greene's work and I am doubly convinced of it now. I am perfectly comfortable with treating children differently for a number of reasons. All situations will be different, so the factors involved require different solutions and, in line with Greene's thinking, all children are different because their strengths and difficulties are different – why the child is not doing well will be different for two children in seemingly very similar situations – and will require different approaches and support to improve their behaviour. Treating children equitably is what is required, not treating children equally. Actions in response to poor behaviour that are consistent with your values as a school are more effective than consistency of action.

A common criticism of this view is that children will feel there has been an injustice if they are treated differently. It is true that children can feel injustice very keenly, but my experience has been that, if I'm asked (and I'm usually happy to explain and justify up to a point without going into personal details), they often accept that circumstances are different. This is different from making examples of children in front of others in order to show the student population what may happen to them if they overstep the mark or to demonstrate that a situation has been dealt with. This is never okay. Students can usually see that something has been resolved without there being a show trial.

The fundamental difference, then, between the consistency of action and action that is consistent with your values is that the former is focused on retribution, whereas the latter regards the follow-up to incidents, which will include sanctions by the way, as teachable moments, an opportunity to do our collective best to ensure this doesn't happen again. This is not soft. Its main aim is prevention and the repairing of harm. Furthermore, it is supportive to our colleagues. (I fail to see how sanctions that do not change behaviour are supportive to colleagues if children continue to present with the same problems over and over again.)

To help with this I prefer to put potential responses to situations into groups depending on the nature of the situation(s). This is slightly different from the standard approach to sanctions, which has been to decide on a progressively more severe set of responses depending on the seriousness of the offence(s), with senior colleagues arriving on the scene at some point if things don't desist or improve. I like to think along the following lines:

- Discussion
  - for very low-level situations that can be dealt with by a teacher's verbal correction or rule reminder.

- Supervision
  - where there is a need to make up lost learning time (as opposed to detention) or where a teacher sees a need to move seats to ensure closer supervision
  - supervision can be combined with discussion where, for example, you need to talk to a child outside of the classroom away from their peers for a few moments.

- Reparation
  - this may be suitable for responses to conflict or bullying where restorative processes could be useful.

- Deprivation
  - for rather more serious situations where the teacher requires the removal of a child from a lesson; where there is a need for detention; or where loss aversion hasn't worked and the teacher needs to confiscate property.

REFLECTION POINTS

- Do you insist that all children are treated equally?
- In what circumstances will you treat children differently?

Shaming

You may recall from Chapter 1 the regular crackdowns we had on uniform when I worked in a comprehensive school. One such effort involved an instruction that all staff police the doors into the assembly hall and we were to direct any child improperly dressed onto the stage. At the beginning of assembly there were about a dozen or so Year 10s, all boys, on the stage and they remained there, facing the whole year group but behind the back of the Headteacher, as an example to the other students as the assembly began. Unfortunately, as you can imagine, things swiftly deteriorated as one student began aping the Headteacher behind his back whilst the other students remained motionless, mortified that they appeared to be associated with this foolish act of disrespect. It ended badly for that boy, but it was a lesson in how shaming a child can escalate a situation which, in this case, resulted in him denying the shame by an outward show of insouciance.

It should seem obvious to teachers and school leaders that shaming a child into behaving well is unlikely to succeed and may well escalate a situation, yet it happens and indeed is sometimes built into school policies. Take traffic light systems, for example, or their cousins the rainbow → dark cloud → lightning charts. These are endemic in schools, especially primary schools, and some schools insist on them in every class (the secondary school equivalent is usually writing children's names up on the board). Harmless, you may think, but shaming children is their one and only purpose. They require the teacher to publicly take the laminated strip of paper with the child's name on and put them from green (usually the default setting for everyone) and place them on orange or red depending on the child's behaviour. Sometimes this is used as a warning or threat – 'Now, come on Daniel. You don't want me to put you on ORANGE do you?' whilst dangling Daniel's name tag over the orange traffic light. The logic feeding them reckons that the child will be encouraged to behave differently to enable a move back to green; the encouragement coming, presumably, from the embarrassment and public shame of being separated from their peers on the chart.

Shaming generates strong feelings which, for some children, will be internalised and held tightly until they are safe to release somewhere else and which, for others, may be immediate and violent. Shaming can aggravate a combination of behaviours, none of which is helpful or productive (Elison et al., 2006) and leaders should ensure that their policies are free of tactics and responses that could shame children. The four different types of behaviour that may be provoked are withdrawal, denial, attacking themselves and attacking others.

Withdrawal

In response to shaming, a child may become introverted in a number of different ways: head down on the desk with their arms over their head, sitting under the desk, becoming mute, or they may actually physically withdraw from your lesson by leaving the classroom or failing to arrive at all next time.

Denial (also called 'avoidance')

The Year 10 boy on the stage in the earlier example was dealing in shaming denial. With these responses a child is seeking to minimise or deny the negative experience. The outward appearance suggests the child is unbothered, so they may laugh or maintain that 'I DON'T CARE!' but the shame still hits home.

Attacking themselves

Here the child turns their negative feelings inwards, which can magnify them. You may see behaviours such as ripping up their work or refusing to eat (indirect forms of self-harm), calling themselves names or showing contempt for themselves. This is my default response to being shamed.

Attacking others

This response turns the child's negative feelings outwards and, as with denial, this can be an attempt to deflect the feeling of shame by focusing their anger at someone else, who could be the source of the shaming, but who may not even be involved in the situation. Attacking can be physical or verbal and can be direct (i.e. aimed at the person) or indirect (i.e. at their property).

REFLECTION POINTS

- Taking a fresh look at your school's practices, do you have any approaches to behaviour that may inadvertently shame children?

- Are there traffic light systems in operation in your classrooms? Why?

- Do you display individual attendance figures? Why?

- Do you have displays up in public places of league tables of individuals' academic attainment? Why do you do this?

I hope you can see that shaming is wholly counter-productive and that we should seek to humanely correct behaviour, not shame a child into changing. I fail to see how it can be consistent with the values of any school and, besides, it carries a big risk of escalating a situation so should have no part in our behaviour toolbox anyway.

TAKING IT FURTHER – QUESTIONS AND ACTIVITIES FOR YOU AND YOUR COLLEAGUES

- What were the results of the analysis of your sanctions that you did for Chapter 5?

- What does this tell you about how effective your systems of sanctions are at improving the behaviour of:
  - children with SEND?
  - the children who find it hardest to behave well in your school?

- If you use traffic lights or similar in your school, table a discussion for a staff meeting in which all colleagues can offer their views on the perceived effectiveness or otherwise of this approach.

- Are there children that you work with who are withdrawing, denying, attacking themselves or others in response to shaming and is this being mistaken for something else?

- Have a discussion with colleagues about their views on whether they believe that children do well if they can or that children do well if they choose.

Note

1. As a rule, I do not like to draw comparisons between children's behaviour in schools and the criminal justice system, especially for adults, but from a sociological point of view there is some learning to be had from interesting American research looking at the deterrent effects of certainty and severity. The Sentencing Project's 2010 report *Deterrence in Criminal Justice: Evaluating Certainty vs. Severity of Punishment* concluded that: 'research findings imply that increasingly lengthy prison terms are counterproductive. Overall, the evidence indicates that the deterrent effect of lengthy prison sentences would not be substantially diminished if punishments were reduced from their current levels'. See www.sentencingproject.org/wp-content/uploads/2016/01/Deterrence-in-Criminal-Justice.pdf (accessed 23 September 2019).

References

Elison, J., Lennon, R. and Pulos, S. (2006) 'Investigating the Compass of Shame: The development of the Compass of Shame scale', *Social Behavior and Personality*, 34: 221–238.

Greene, R. (2014) *Lost at School: Why Our Kids with Behavioral Challenges Are Falling Through the Cracks and How We Can Help Them.* New York: Simon & Schuster.

Neill, A.S. (1960) *Summerhill: A Radical Approach to Child Rearing.* New York: Hart Publishing Company.

Wachtel, T. (1999) 'Restorative justice in everyday life: Beyond the formal ritual', paper presented at the 'Reshaping Australian Institutions Conference: Restorative Justice and Civil Society', The Australian National University, Canberra, 16–18 February. www.iirp.edu/eforum-archive/4221-restorative-justice-in-everyday-life-beyond-the-formal-ritual (accessed 23 September 2019).

9

BULLYING

Childhood was the germ of all mistrust. You were cruelly joked upon and then you cruelly joked. You lost the remembrance of pain through inflicting it.

Graham Greene (1958)

THE HEADLINES

- Research consistently finds rates of bullying between 10 and 30 per cent of the student population.

- Research suggests that girls, with the exception of physical bullying, are more likely to be bullied than boys.

- The effects of bullying on victims are damaging and long term. They can affect both physical and mental health for decades.

- Being the victim of bullying can be predicted by individual characteristics and family factors.

- Children with special educational needs are far more likely to be bullied than their peers.

- Bystanders can have a powerful influence on encouraging or stopping bullying. Schools though, should guard against placing too much responsibility on children to intervene lest they escalate situations or place themselves in danger.

- Research indicates that punitive approaches to tackling bullying are less effective than attempts to work with children to change bullying behaviours.

- Restorative approaches to resolving bullying must be done carefully and with due regard to the feelings and sense of safety of victims.

Bullying is a pressing and persistent problem for schools, the children within them and for their parents. Its effects are obviously immediately damaging and widespread, but they can also persist for decades afterwards, influencing victims' mental and physical health long after the event. Parents worry that it could happen to their child, especially if their child is already vulnerable in some way (and the research detailed below shows that parents of these children are right to be worried). If it does happen to a child, parents sometimes take the agonising decision to remove their child from a school if they feel the school's response has been ineffective and they see no other way to protect them. When this happens, the trust parents place in us as school leaders is destroyed. Bullying is widespread – no study finds its absence (Noble, 2006: 68) – so for all of these reasons the eradication of bullying should always be very high on the list of school leaders' priorities.

Sadly, though, sometimes schools do not tackle bullying as effectively as they might. As I write this particular section I am reading an article in *The Guardian* about a 10-year-old child with autism who, when complaining of being bullied, was 'forced by staff to listen to classmates listing the reasons why they didn't like him – and had to write these on a hand-drawn poster that was then stuck on his classroom wall'. The peers told him that if he wanted to have better relationships with them then he needed to 'stop annoying us' and to 'be happy, not sad' (Jayanetti, 2019). According to the parent of the child, the session was described by the school's Headteacher as restorative justice. It seems to have been anything but restorative.

In this chapter, we will look at the research evidence out there on the extent of bullying, who is more likely to be a victim and some of the strategies that seem to be effective in tackling this destructive problem.

What is bullying?

The literature most commonly quotes Olweus' (1993: 9) definition of bullying, 'a student is bullied when he or she is exposed, repeatedly and over time, to negative actions on the part of one or more other students'. Olweus defines 'negative actions' as when someone intentionally inflicts, or attempts to inflict, injury or discomfort upon another. Some definitions explicitly mention an imbalance of power or a difficulty in defending oneself. 'Negative actions' allows for the inclusion of cyberbullying, additionally defined as taking place in an electronic context.

Some other behaviours are harder to fit within that definition, but can also be regarded as bullying. Professor Ian Rivers from the University of Strathclyde provides the example of social isolation where one child stops talking to another one: '[h]ow do you challenge that? Because nothing is said, nothing is done, there's no bruises. And that becomes very, very difficult. And I always give that example when I'm talking to teachers about what do you do when nothing is done. Because the entire [bullying] narrative is about somebody doing something to someone else. But what about when you withdraw all of the behaviour and you just say that I'm not engaging with that person?' (cited in Amass, 2018).

Prevalence

In what Przybylski and Bowes (2017: 24) say is, 'the largest study to date to examine the prevalence of traditional bullying and cyberbullying in adolescents in England', researchers examined self-reported experiences of bullying in over 110,000 children aged 15, with about 30 per cent, a worryingly high figure, of that group reporting being bullied in the past two months. Interestingly, they found that this split into 36 per cent of the girls in the sample and 24 per cent of the boys. They go on to say that '[w]ith the exception of physical bullying, girls reported significantly higher levels of all forms of aggressive behaviour studied. In this large-scale study, we found gender differences in self-reported prevalence rates, supporting previous studies that suggested girls might be more involved in indirect forms of bullying than boys. Gender norms regarding bullying might play a part in self-reporting. Cyberbullying was less common than traditional forms, with one in 20 girls and one in 50 boys reporting recent regular experience in the past couple of months' (Przybylski and Bowes, 2017: 24). Whereas research encompassing 25 countries found on average 10 per cent of 11- to 16-year-olds admitted bullying others in the current school term (Nansel et al., 2004).

REFLECTION POINTS

- What is the current knowledge amongst leaders and governors in your school as to the prevalence of bullying?
- How has this changed over the past five years?
- What has the school done in that time to tackle the issue?

Effects

Wolke and Lereya (2015: 879) argue that bullying should be taken far more seriously as a public health issue, detailing the strong evidence of bullying as a major risk factor for poor physical and mental health and for a, 'reduced adaptation to adult roles including forming lasting relationships, integrating into work and being economically independent'. The sections where they detail the potential adverse effects make for very uncomfortable reading. The effects can be persistent into adult life, with Evans-Lacko et al. (2017: 127) finding that, '[c]ompared to participants who were not bullied in childhood, those who were frequently bullied were more likely to use mental health services in childhood and adolescence, and also in midlife'. They also note, very worryingly, that, 'bullying victimisation may set the conditions for a cycle in which people become at risk of exposure to further abuse in later life (Dodge et al., 1990)' (Evans-Lacko et al., 2017: 133).

Early identification and prevention

Research indicates that being the victim of bullying is not a random event and can be predicted by individual characteristics and family factors. Arseneault et al. (2009) summarise the research evidence, noting that, for individual characteristics, those with, 'internalizing problems, such as withdrawal and anxiety-depression (Hodges and Perry, 1999; Arseneault et al., 2009), low self-regard and reduced assertiveness (Egan and Perry, 1998), have an increased risk of being bullied in childhood' and that, '[g]irls who are bullied showed higher levels of externalizing behaviours prior to being bullied compared to non-bullied girls of the same age (Arseneault et al., 2009). Early aggressiveness was also shown to precede chronic peer rejection and victimization in both boys and girls assessed at four time points from age 3 to 6 years' (Arseneault et al., 2009: 719).

On the subject of family factors they note that, 'child maltreatment (Shields and Cicchetti, 2001), domestic violence in the home (Baldry, 2003), parental depression (Beran and Violato, 2004) and low socio-economic status (Wolke et al., 2001)' (Arseneault et al., 2009: 720) are all associated with increased rates of bullying victimisation. There is an added complexity to this research picture, unsurprisingly, because some of these factors and characteristics are simultaneously observed in the same people and the same homes.

The school is not an entirely neutral environment either and they note that one 'study [(Bowes et al., 2009)] also showed that schools with large numbers of pupils were uniquely associated with children's risks for being bullied' (Arseneault et al., 2009: 720). On the plus side, research indicates that a strong sense of belonging (see the Introduction and Chapters 1, 2 and 4 because it is that important) can be a protective factor in reducing bullying behaviours (Slaten et al., 2019).

It should come as no surprise to anyone that children with special educational needs are at an elevated risk of being bullied (Redmond, 2011; Chatzitheochari et al., 2016), and that, specifically, children with communication difficulties are more likely than their peers to be bullied (Knox and Conti-Ramsden, 2007).

REFLECTION POINTS

- How does this list of individual characteristics and family factors compare to the children who you know have been bullied in your school over the past three years?

- Given what you now know from this section, are there children in your school that deserve closer attention to see if they are being bullied?

Bystanders

Witnesses to incidents of bullying, either in person or electronically, can influence whether those situations persist or cease depending on their responses. Supporting aggressors of bullying can happen for a number of reasons, such as fear of being targeted themselves, friendship with the bully or to sustain or improve social status. Others may not care that someone else is being bullied and simply mind their own business. The research literature names bystanders depending on their roles – either *assistants* who are active participants, or *reinforcers* who are passive approvers.

There is much advice out there on how bystanders can help. I am personally uncomfortable with the aspects of this advice that place responsibility on children to intervene in situations of bullying as they may well place themselves at risk of physical harm and escalate situations (Hawkins et al., [2001: 521] found that half the time students intervened it resulted in further aggression). I find it far better to set a firm expectation that all children will report bullying *without delay* if and when they witness it (this predisposes a good understanding on the part of the children as to what bullying is and ensures this understanding is, of course, part of a good school's strategy). This can be effective in terms of bringing adults to the scene as soon as possible, thus shortening the duration of the particular incident. It also provides hard evidence for the school to take firm action whilst protecting the witness(es) from retaliation. This requires schools to have systems that are well understood by the children in order for them to report, and this should include reporting anonymously as, despite our reassurances, some children may delay reporting or not report at all if they fear identification and retaliation.

REFLECTION POINTS

- What are your school's expectations for the behaviour of bystanders?
- What systems are in place currently for children to report bullying in your school?
- How much use has been made of these systems over the past five years?

Reaching for punitive approaches

I know as a school leader that I instinctively want to take a very hard line on bullying. I find it difficult to consider other approaches, often termed 'softer' approaches, because I want to protect victims and ensure the bullying stops immediately. That is why I am having a tough time engaging with the evidence about what can be effective in changing bullying behaviour. The more punitive approaches – three strikes and you're out, zero tolerance, etc. – have an instant appeal. If the bully keeps bullying they leave our school. We can guarantee the bullying stops, in our school at least, and this is likely to be met with support from parents, staff and students. The fact that it may start up again elsewhere is of secondary importance; maybe some bullies are changed by that treatment and in truth we will probably never know. Engaging in different approaches to stopping bullying and in trying to change the behaviour of the bully are, by definition, less likely to succeed, but the pay-off is greater – long-term behaviour change and an intact school community. I include this opening paragraph to be honest about my own internal struggles with this issue and I am confident that I am not alone as a school leader in thinking this way.

Louise Porter, in the extremely comprehensive *Behaviour in Schools: Theory and Practice for Teachers* (2014: 369), states: 'findings from a considerable and unanimous body of research [cited within the original text] with parents and in schools that a controlling, hostile and rejecting style of discipline fails to teach young people self-regulatory skills and prosocial means of solving problems, resulting in their escalating and ongoing anti-social behaviour'. And this is where some of us will immediately part company with the research, claiming that a zero tolerance approach is firm and fair, and is mischaracterised as controlling, hostile or rejecting. No matter that Porter then goes on to say, 'most researchers favour non-punitive (non-behaviourist) approaches to bullying [citation included]' (2014: 369). (This is, by the way, a neat example of the uneasy relationship that can exist between some educational researchers and teachers.)

The Anti-Bullying Alliance (2017) promote a set of 10 principles developed with children and teachers on which to underpin anti-bullying work in school, noting that a school with effective strategies: listens, includes us all, respects, challenges (i.e. disablist language), celebrates difference, understands (i.e. everyone in the school understands what bullying is), believes, reports bullying, takes action and has clear policies. This makes good sense, but doesn't get to the heart of what a school should *actually do* when bullying occurs.

The Department for Education's research report from 2011 notes that schools seem to regard sanctions and restorative approaches as effective responses to bullying incidents, with sanctions being more popular, partly because some schools were unsure what restorative approaches actually were.

REFLECTION POINT

- What sanctions-based approaches have been effective in changing bullying behaviour over the past five years?

Restorative approaches

There are a number of complementary aims of restorative approaches to resolving bullying and conflict. This way of tackling bullying seeks to:

- provide a safe and secure space for children who have been harmed to communicate the impact of that on them
- improve behaviour of those causing harm by allowing children to understand the impact of their behaviour on others
- find solutions by working with children rather than imposing solutions upon them
- help children to take responsibility for their behaviour and be accountable for their actions.

All noble aims, but it is not an easy thing to do. I confess to making concerted efforts in my first few years as a Headteacher to work in this way to tackle bullying, but I never quite managed to feel like we were doing it well enough. It was effective in a couple of cases and plainly not in a couple more. It was a failure of implementation rather than with the principle of the thing itself. I never invested sufficient time and training for everyone in our school to make it a fundamental part of how we worked. I learned two main lessons from this time: firstly, that this is not a strategy to use every single time there is a problem; and secondly, which follows from the first, this can only really be used when the victim is comfortable with this approach. In my view they cannot and must not feel compelled to engage in this process, because the process of bringing victim and perpetrator together can be very damaging.

To prevent issues such as those occurring, there is a set of underlying principles upon which effective restorative work is based.

- *Restoration*: the primary objective of restorative practice is to address and repair harm.
- *Voluntarism*: children cannot and must not be forced to participate. To gain consent children need to understand what will happen and what is expected of them.
- *Neutrality*: 'Restorative approaches need to be fair and unbiased towards participants. If they are considered to be another forum in which to hector a child, a *fait accompli*, or a thinly veiled form of court, then this risks the process breaking down or, at the very least, being less effective' (O'Brien, 2018: 104). This is a tough one for some to accept as it risks the victim feeling that giving the perpetrator equal status is unfair.
- *Safety*: 'If a child has been harmed by another then it cannot be easy for them to sit down and talk through the emotions, the hurt and the after-effects in their presence unless they can be confident that it is safe to do so. This will involve some preparation on your part as you may need to give careful consideration to the details, such as the location; for instance, the Headteacher's office can be considered to be a very intimidating place for some children' (O'Brien, 2018: 104).
- *Accessibility*: I think this is the most challenging of all the principles and one of the main reasons why my earlier attempts failed at times. The language needs to accessible, and we should also understand how difficult it can be for children to communicate their feelings, intentions and actions and to even understand their own feelings. Harder still for some children to appreciate the effects of their actions on others. This is why restorative approaches require careful planning.
- *Respect*: restorative practices must be respectful to the dignity of all participants and those affected by the harm caused. It is not a forum to shame the person causing harm as, again, this is likely to reduce the effectiveness of the process.

REFLECTION POINTS

- What is the current level of knowledge in your school about restorative approaches to resolving conflict?

- If a restorative approach has been used, how effective has it been in changing bullying behaviour?

Other approaches

The KiVA anti-bullying programme, pioneered in Finland but used extensively in other countries too, shows promise with research evidence supporting its effectiveness (KiVa, n.d.). It takes a three-pronged approach – prevention, intervention and monitoring – with a universal component aimed at whole-school education, which inevitably focuses on prevention and creating the conditions for bullying to be less likely to occur, and a targeted component, known as indicated, when instances do occur.

Paluck et al. (2016) report on a very interesting approach that takes into account how strong the effect can be of the behaviour of peers when influencing others. The programme seeks to understand how community-wide behaviours can be changed as, 'individuals attend to the behavior of certain people in their community to understand what is socially normative and adjust their own behavior in response' (Paluck et al., 2016: 566) rather than the more common approach of intense focus on an individual's behaviour.

TAKING IT FURTHER – QUESTIONS AND ACTIVITIES FOR YOU AND YOUR COLLEAGUES

- What has been the view from parents, teachers and students over the past five years as to how effective your school is in tackling bullying?

- What have been your most successful strategies in resolving bullying in recent years?

- What was it about those examples that proved so effective?

- What have been the hardest bullying problems to resolve?

- What was it about those examples that proved so difficult?

- Given the research above on predictors of children being bullied, is there further work that your school could do to identify vulnerable children from being bullied in the first place?

References

Amass, H. (2018) 'Why your anti-bullying strategy isn't working', *Times Educational Supplement*, 19 October. www.tes.com/magazine/article/why-your-anti-bullying-strategy-isnt-working (accessed 24 September 2019).

Anti-Bullying Alliance (2017) '10 key principles', 18 April. www.anti-bullyingalliance.org.uk/tools-information/all-about-bullying/preventing-bullying-and-ethos/10-key-principles (accessed 24 September 2019).

Arseneault, L., Bowes, L. and Shakoor, S. (2009) 'Bullying victimization in youths and mental health problems: "Much ado about nothing"?', *Psychological Medicine*, 40(5): 717–729.

Chatzitheochari, S., Parsons, S. and Platt, L. (2016) 'Doubly disadvantaged? Bullying experiences among disabled children and young people in England', *Sociology*, 50(4): 695–713.

Department for Education (2011) *The Use and Effectiveness of Anti-Bullying Strategies in Schools*. DFE-RR098. www.gov.uk/government/publications/the-use-and-effectiveness-of-anti-bullying-strategies-in-schools (accessed 24 September 2019).

Evans-Lacko, S., Takizawa, R., Brimblecombe, N., King, D., Knapp, M., Maughan, B. and Arseneault, L. (2017) 'Childhood bullying victimisation is associated with use of mental health services over 5 decades: a longitudinal nationally-representative cohort study', *Psychological Medicine*, 47(1): 127–135.

Greene, G. (1958) *Our Man in Havana*. London: Heinemann.

Hawkins, D., Pepler, D. and Craig, W. (2001) 'Naturalistic observations of peer interventions in bullying', *Social Development*, 10(4): 512–527.

Jayanetti, C. (2019) 'Teacher "forced special needs child to make a list of his faults"', *The Guardian*, 28 July. www.theguardian.com/education/2019/jul/28/derby-primary-school-boy-with-special-needs-blamed-for-being-bullied (accessed 24 September 2019).

KiVa (n.d.) 'Is KiVa effective?'. www.kivaprogram.net/is-kiva-effective (accessed 24 September 2019).

Knox, E. and Conti-Ramsden, G. (2007) 'Bullying in young people with a history of specific language impairment (SLI)', *Education and Child Psychology*, 24(4): 130–141.

Nansel, T., Craig, W., Overpeck, M., Saluja, G. and Ruan, W. (2004) 'Health behaviour in school-aged children bullying analyses working group: Cross-national consistency in the relationship between bullying behaviors and psychosocial adjustment', *Archives of Pediatric and Adolescent Medicine*, 158: 730–736.

Noble, T. (2006) 'Core components of a school-wide safe schools curriculum', in H. McGrath and T. Noble (eds), *Bullying Solutions: Evidence-Based Approaches to Bullying in Australian Schools*. Sydney: Pearson Longman, pp. 67–83.

O'Brien, J. (2018) *Better Behaviour: A Guide for Teachers*. London: SAGE.

Olweus, D. (1993) *Bullying at School: What We Know and What We Can Do*. Oxford: Blackwell Publishing.

Paluck, E., Shepherd, H. and Aronow, P. (2016) 'Changing climates of conflict: A social network experiment in 56 schools', *Proceedings of the National Academy of Sciences*, 113(3): 566–571.

Porter, L. (2014) *Behaviour in Schools: Theory and Practice for Teachers.* Maidenhead: Open University Press.

Przybylski, A. and Bowes, L. (2017) 'Cyberbullying and adolescent well-being in England: a population-based cross-sectional study', *The Lancet Child & Adolescent Health*, 1(1): 19–26.

Redmond, S. (2011) 'Peer victimization among students with specific language impairment, attention-deficit/hyperactivity disorder, and typical development', *Language, Speech & Hearing Services in Schools*, 42(4): 520–535.

Slaten, C., Rose, C. and Ferguson, J. (2019) 'Understanding the relationship between youths' belonging and bullying behaviour: An SEM Model', *Educational & Child Psychology*, 36(2): 50–63.

Wolke, D. and Lereya, S.T. (2015) 'Long-term effects of bullying', *Archives of Disease in Childhood*, 100(9): 879–885.

10

SUPPORT STAFF

Questions about 'what works' – that is questions about the effectiveness of educational actions – are always secondary to questions of purpose.

Professor Gert Biesta (2010: 500)

THE HEADLINES

- Have a vision for the teaching assistants (TAs) in your school that focuses on those students requiring their support attaining a level of independence and confidence that means the support is no longer required.

- Communicate this vision to TAs at recruitment and induction and regularly thereafter, and ensure that it is understood by all colleagues.

- TAs deserve paid working hours that enable them to attend staff briefings before school, staff meetings after school and training sessions.

- TAs must have a high-quality induction that contains a core syllabus common to all staff, and a role-specific element for specialist knowledge such as specific medical conditions.

- Provide appraisals for TAs; failure to do so communicates that their contribution to the school is not worth discussing and that the school is uninterested in their professional growth.

- A career structure for TAs that reflects specialisms that the school needs, such as speech, language and communication needs, aids retention and builds expertise within schools.

- Ensure TAs can easily be part of the communications systems in the school, which do not require significant amounts of their own time.

- An absence of a hierarchy helps develop a culture where children afford all adults the same respect.

In 2000, the year I started my teacher training, teaching assistants made up 13.9 per cent of the workforce in England's schools. In 2017 that proportion had precisely doubled to 27.8 per cent (Department for Education, 2018). (This reflects an increase in nursery and primary schools from 19 per cent to 35 per cent, in secondary schools from just over 5 per cent to about 14 per cent and in special schools from about 40 per cent to a shade over half the workforce.)

In all phases TAs now represent a sizeable proportion of the educators in our classrooms so careful thought needs to be given by leaders as to how we get the best out of them, how we provide them with good opportunities for professional growth and how we ensure they feel a valued part of their teams.

This chapter will explain how leaders can work most effectively with teaching assistants (see also Chapter 9 from *Better Behaviour: A Guide for Teachers* (O'Brien, 2018) for class teachers working with TAs).

Having a vision for the TA role

What are the teaching assistants actually there for in your school? What is their distinctive contribution to the children they work with? The most skilled TAs I work with know far more about special educational needs and disabilities than many teachers ever will and they are a tremendous asset, but used poorly they can become glorified and frustrated childcarers. Of course TAs are most likely to be in your classrooms to provide specific support to children often with SEND. They are not minders for the children who may find it the hardest to behave well, but they may find themselves working with those children often. With that in mind schools do need a vision for what they want their TAs to achieve. Perhaps this sounds obvious to you. What a TA ends up doing on a lesson-by-lesson, day-by-day basis can look very different depending on the expectations on them. Are they there to promote independence, to develop self-regulation skills in the child, to encourage a child to keep going when things get tough, to essentially make themselves redundant? I hope so, especially because their presence in our classrooms is precisely because some children need extra support in these areas. Without those long-term aims too often TAs become the main or only teacher for particular children. This certainly happened to most TAs who worked with me when I first qualified. I didn't really know what I wanted them to do; they seemed to know some of the children better anyway and would make my lesson work for the child or children they were with. The lazy part of me was happy with that, and I justified it on the basis that the child was probably getting a better deal from the TA than from me – what a cop out – so I enabled a form of fake inclusion. With the basic right of inclusion in the front of my mind, and a clear aim to arrange the support for the child so that in the longer term they would no longer need that support, I would have done things very differently.

This aim of promotion of independence cannot be underestimated and I encourage all school leaders to make this a major focus for the work of their TAs. Far too often I see dependency building up between TA and child, and that can certainly be in the form of dependency by the adult on the child. By that I mean an adult saying things like, 'Well, I'm the only one who can calm him down when he gets like that'. You can immediately see why this is a bad thing, no matter how good it may make one member of staff feel about their skills or influence. This is why it is worth ensuring that your system doesn't allow any one member of staff to work with a child for a number of years because a very strong emotional attachment can build up. At some point the child or the adult will leave the school and that separation can then become problematic.

With a clear vision for the work of TAs that all understand and can articulate, you stand the best possible chance of children with additional needs thriving in your school and the TAs who do sterling work with them being part of a satisfied team. I think a decent albeit imperfect indicator of a school's success is what its students are doing when they're 25, and TAs play a significant part in creating those adults who are ready to thrive in life after school. I am reminded of the surely apocryphal tale of President Kennedy visiting NASA in 1962 and, after asking a janitor about his work, receiving the response, 'Well, Mr. President, I'm helping put a man on the moon'.

An entitlement to professional growth

There is much that I find uplifting and inspirational in schools, but there is one thing that never fails to sadden me – and what is worse is that I hear this thing with depressing regularity – and that is when TAs tell me that they do not get the opportunity to take part in some or all of the various professional development activities that take place in schools. If this is the case, it seems that their ability to contribute meaningfully to your vision is compromised.

Terms and conditions

School leaders are undoubtedly under financial pressures, but it is a false economy when the working hours of TAs prevent them from being part of after-school training sessions and staff training days. This must be the only reason that TAs are not routinely involved in training and so I encourage all school leaders to work out what it would actually cost to make this necessary change in your school and find ways to afford it. I am also aware of practices where TAs are present on training days and evenings, but they are sent off to laminate, do displays, make resources and wash paint pots. This sends an unfortunate message to TAs that training and development does not apply to them.

Induction

The entitlement to professional growth begins with a good quality induction programme when a TA first takes up a role. Again, I remain stunned that some schools do not offer an induction programme for TAs. This is poor practice and could, in some cases, be regarded as negligent. TAs are usually employed to work with some of our most vulnerable children, typically children with SEND, and will often carry out very demanding work for poor pay, so expecting them to figure it out as they go along is plainly unfair on both adult and child. TAs deserve the same standard induction that the teaching staff receive and, just like all other colleagues, they should also receive induction training that is specific to their role, such as that necessary to support certain medical conditions like epilepsy or diabetes, or to teach certain aspects of the curriculum like phonics. This applies equally to behaviour training. All staff should have the same standard behaviour training and if certain TAs are working with children who are experiencing behavioural difficulties then it is vital that they have further sufficient training to feel confident to meet the child's needs well.

Appraisal

This is another aspect of support for colleagues (and I accept that the process of appraisal or performance management sadly may not always feel supportive) that is a given for teachers, but sometimes missing for TAs. Why, I do not know. I have long held the view that a failure to offer a colleague appraisal, in the developmental sense, communicates to them that their contribution to the school isn't worth discussing. The fact that there is no pay decision to make at the end of the year is not a reason not to do this. TAs, like all other members of the team, deserve a forum in which to discuss how they want to be better at their job and how we as a school can help them to achieve that. I recommend that all schools use the *Professional Standards for Teaching Assistants* (Department for Education, 2016) that was commissioned by the DfE (who then decided not to publish them) as a useful tool to support their appraisals.

REFLECTION POINTS

- What does the current induction programme for TAs look like? Could it be improved? Do TAs who have been through the programme have a view on potential improvements?

- Are TAs included in training and development opportunities at your school?

- If not, what would the cost be to ensure that they were?

- Are TAs included in your appraisal process? If not, why not? What needs to happen for this to change?

Developing the workforce through specialisms

One common criticism from TAs is that there is no career structure for them. I think this is a fair comment and it is something that we as leaders can do something about. Special schools provide a model for mainstream schools to learn from here. Many special schools have a career structure that reflects the fact that TAs often develop significant knowledge and skill in certain areas such as speech and language therapy support, behaviour support or specific literacy or numeracy strategies, and they become the resident expert in the school on such matters. This is partly down to the fact that, as we saw above, TAs make up more than half of the special school workforce. All of these areas of school life make contributions either directly or indirectly to how good behaviour is in the school. It is immediately obvious for TAs with expertise in behaviour support, perhaps via roles such as ELSA (emotional literacy support assistant) or through the Thrive Approach, but it also applies to those with expertise in support of the therapies (speech and language, occupational, physiotherapy) given what we know about the correlation between SEND and behaviour (see Chapter 11 for more on this).

There does not have to be a massive overhaul in how TAs are organised and deployed, but it can start with a recognition that the expertise already exists within the school. The cost of creating a couple of more senior TA roles would not be significant, would undoubtedly improve retention and would make a positive statement about the value of TAs within your school.

REFLECTION POINTS

- Is there a career and pay structure for TAs in your school to aspire to and to work towards?

- What specialisms do you consider to be of most benefit to your school?

    o Speech, language and communication needs?
    o Occupational therapy support?
    o Physical difficulties support?
    o Sensory impairment?
    o Literacy and numeracy support?
    o Behaviour support?

- What steps would you need to take to make these roles a reality?

Communication

I recall that after a couple of daily staff briefings in my first week as a Headteacher I asked a colleague where all the TAs were. I had assumed that their working hours meant that they started work after briefing ended, but I was wrong. Daily staff briefings were for teachers only for reasons that I could not understand. Teachers used to leave the briefing and then repeat anything of note to the TAs in their tutor group. Obviously I changed that without delay, but talking to the TAs reminded me once more how ill-informed they can be as a group in schools through no fault of their own. If the working hours of TAs are largely set around the school opening hours for children then they will miss out on most if not all of the set pieces where information is shared – regular staff briefings before school, staff meetings after school and INSET days and evenings. 'We have an "All Staff" email bulletin that goes round every week and then we email updates as and when other things happen, though', you may say. That's good, but TAs will instantly remind us that they do not have any time in the week to check emails and will also very reasonably remind us that their terms and conditions are not the same as teachers, so we shouldn't expect them to catch up in the evenings (we shouldn't really with teachers either), just because they are nice people committed to working with children who will go the extra mile week in, week out.

Leaders do need to give careful thought as to how TAs know everything they need to know to do their job well and to stay well informed. For example, our office staff had a list of colleagues who preferred the weekly bulletin in paper form (which could include teachers too, by the way), so this went into their pigeonholes on a Monday morning. My wife's school has a weekly TA meeting during assembly time. There are ways to make it happen, but failure to do so results in TAs regularly and rightly exclaiming, 'How am I supposed to know that? I'm not a mind reader!'.

This lack of space in the working day for TAs can create other problems too in terms of TAs supporting behaviour as well as they can. Take the paperwork that we often have to fill in if there has been an incident. These days this 'paperwork' can be an electronic form on a school-wide system such as SIMS. Teachers often use planning, preparation and assessment (PPA) time, break or lunch time, the end of the day or evenings or weekends to catch up on these things. How manageable we make our systems is of course a key part of our management responsibilities, but at the very least teachers are better placed to find the time to complete them than TAs. One solution that often arises is that the teacher benevolently and understandably tells the TA that they will do the admin at the end of the day. Admirable and noble, but not a great solution as something will be lost by the reporting being completed by a third party if the TA was the person dealing with a situation.

This is not a minor point because we as leaders rely on our staff to get us the right information quickly so we can deal with it and support them too. It also ensures we have a good overall amount of information to back up what we see is happening in our schools. Our systems are only as good as the information that are put into them, and whilst paperwork and data entry aren't the be all and end all, they do form an important part of a school running smoothly.

REFLECTION POINTS

- How, how often and what do you communicate to your TAs?
- What do they say about how effective communication is in your school?
- Do your systems allow TAs to complete behaviour paperwork efficiently?

The absence of hierarchy

When we have a confident, well-trained and trusted team of TAs in our schools we then have a critical mass of adults who can and will nip many situations in the bud before they escalate and become problems for teachers and then leaders. Because they will know some of your children inside out they will recognise the rapid clicking of the pen, the swinging on the chair or the deep sighing for what it is and then swiftly redirect, distract or remind and prevent things getting worse. They are able to constantly reinforce the expectations and values of the school in numerous ways that keep children on track. They can assist in recognising all the little things that children do that are worthy of recognition, but that might get missed, thus reinforcing what you do want from them. To fully enable this, we as leaders need to create a culture in our schools that means that children respond to any and all adults in the same way. There is a limit to what can be achieved by any colleague if we get to, 'Mrs Norman won't be happy with you. I'm going to have to get her to come and sort this out!'. (There will, of course, be situations that require support from managers, but you'll see that that is not what I mean.) The absence of a hierarchy should support the values of our schools; we're all aiming for the children to do the right thing because it is the right thing to do, not because it depends on who is in front of them, or the threat of the Headteacher's ire or because we demand blind compliance. The children understand that respect isn't a function of position, power or privilege, but an essential ingredient for a healthy, thriving community. This is an easy position to agree with, but it does require school leaders to ensure that our own behaviour in front of the children communicates this too. By that I mean we can't be seen to over-rule TAs in front of children or wade in, superhero style, to take over in situations that are difficult. In those times when we do have to support our colleagues or take over, we need everyone to be able to see and hear that it is being done in a supportive way. (This also applies when colleagues come to support us and on occasion take over too.) Scripts – agreed phrases that are essentially code – are helpful in such situations. There are many ways of doing this. For example, one training provider Team Teach recommends a simple two-stage script:

'Help is available' – this is understood by the adults to mean that, if the person currently managing the situation would like to, the new colleague can take over. If not, they will remain nearby for a time in case that change of face (as they call it) is needed. Essentially they are saying, 'We can swap if you'd like'.

'More help is available' – this follow-up is non-negotiable. The supporting adult has decided that, irrespective of the opinion of the colleague still dealing with the situation, they must swap as things have escalated. It has been agreed beforehand that colleagues will not dispute this at the time, but meet later if they need to talk it through. You will see that it is not professional to have an argument in front of the children, and the script helps to prevent that occurring. A fellow Headteacher of mine has agreed with all of her staff that 'There's a telephone call for you in Reception' carries the same meaning.

Timetabling

Lastly, a plea to all timetablers out there. I know that you have an almost thankless job, but it is worth paying close attention to what a full timetable with no PPA and some duties at breaks and lunchtimes means in real life for some TAs. Too often TAs, especially in secondary schools, are pinballing from lesson to lesson across the school site without so much as a few minutes to go to the toilet. They are desperate to get to lessons on time, even a little early if possible, so that they are in with a fighting chance of working out what the lesson is about and what their role will be, but occasionally timetabling makes this tough.

TAKING IT FURTHER – QUESTIONS AND ACTIVITIES FOR YOU AND YOUR COLLEAGUES

- What has been the turnover of TAs at your school over the last five years?

- In exit interviews, what did TAs say about what could have kept them at the school?

- Are there any lessons in there for how to improve:
  o induction?
  o communication?
  o training and development?
  o deployment?

- What is the longest period of time any of your TAs has spent supporting the same child? Did that generate any dependency issues?

- How does the information from the appraisals of TAs feed into the overall continuing professional development (CPD) plan of the school?

- Over the last five years, how much of the CPD budget has been spent on TAs?

References

Biesta, G.J.J. (2010) 'Why "what works" still won't work: From evidence-based education to value-based education', *Studies in Philosophy and Education*, 29(5): 491–503.

Department for Education (2016) *Professional Standards for Teaching Assistants*. http://maximisingtas.co.uk/assets/content/ta-standards-final-june2016-1.pdf (accessed 24 September 2019).

Department for Education (2018) *National Statistics: School Workforce in England: November 2017*. www.gov.uk/government/statistics/school-work-force-in-england-november-2017 (accessed 24 September 2019).

O'Brien, J. (2018) *Better Behaviour: A Guide for Teachers*. London: SAGE.

Team Teach (2020) 'Developing and supporting positive behaviour management with transformative training'. www.teamteach.co.uk (accessed 20 February 2020).

11

SPECIAL EDUCATIONAL NEEDS AND DISABILITIES

The image of the ideal human as powerful and capable disenfranchises the old, the sick, the less-abled.

Jean Vanier (1998: 45)

THE HEADLINES

- Nationally, children with special educational needs and disabilities (SEND) are grossly over-represented in the statistics for children subject to fixed-term and permanent exclusion.

- Schools should be aware of how their own cohort of children with SEND compare to their peers at every level of the behaviour information that the school holds.

- School leaders should conduct internal reviews when a child with SEND leaves their school at a time other than the expected end of their statutory schooling there, with an explicit aim to elicit if behaviour was a factor, and governing bodies should demand this information.

- The Equality Act (2010) places legal obligations on schools to ensure that people with protected characteristics, including children with SEND and their parents and prospective students and their parents, are not subject to discrimination.

- To meet their obligations, schools must make reasonable adjustments to remove or reduce sources of discrimination.

- What is considered reasonable can be affected by the interaction of:

  o the nature of the disability itself
  o how practicable the changes are
  o and the context of the school.

- In making reasonable adjustments schools may:

  o change the way things are done
  o change the environment
  o provide extra services or aids.

- The public sector equality duty requires schools to publish equality information at least annually to demonstrate compliance with the equality duty and to publish equality objectives at least every four years.

- When reviewing existing policies or writing new ones, schools must consider the effects on people with protected characteristics, ensuring that they do not discriminate.

- Children with particular conditions and difficulties are more likely to go on to experience behavioural difficulties if their needs are not well met. These include speech, language and communication, literacy and sensory difficulties.

- Schools can better support children with these needs by ensuring that all staff know the basics in supporting these needs well, work with therapists or their assistants where possible and receive good quality induction and ongoing training on such matters.

Any book on behaviour in schools that does not explicitly devote significant space to looking at how behaviour intersects with SEND is incomplete. Anyone who is even vaguely familiar with the national statistics for children excluded from schools in England either for fixed periods of time or permanently (Department for Education, 2018a) – and I'm willing to wager that this is true in many other countries too – will know why. It is because children with SEND are grossly over-represented. The scale of this problem is jaw-dropping. For the academic year 2017/18:

- Children with identified SEND[1] accounted for just under half of all permanent exclusions and fixed-term exclusions.
- Children with identified SEND were around five times more likely to be permanently excluded from school than their peers with no SEND.
- Children with identified SEND were around five times more likely to receive a fixed-term exclusion than their peers with no SEND.

This set of statistics is concerning in and of itself and the trends are persistent over time, but it must be remembered that fixed-term exclusion (what used to be called 'suspension' in old money) and permanent exclusion (aka expulsion) are at the extreme end of the sanctions imposed for poor behaviour (or they should be). There are no statistics available on the use of sanctions and interventions below this level, such as internal isolation, detention, etc., but I would be very surprised if the patterns are remarkably different.

In addition, there is a worrying trend, not explicitly related to behaviour, but likely in my view to be associated, in the world of SEND and that is the change in relative proportions of children with SEND that are educated in mainstream and special schools (Department for Education, 2018b).

Table 11.1 details a clear trend over a number of years of the proportion of children with education, health and care plans (EHCPs) educated in secondary schools dropping from well over a quarter to barely over a fifth (interestingly, in the same time period the proportion in primary schools hasn't strayed far from the 26 per cent mark). Whilst this was happening, the proportion of children with EHCPs attending state-funded special schools rose by a similar amount. This is concerning because we may become less skilled as a profession over time in teaching children with SEND if we encounter them less frequently in our classrooms. This nation-wide trend reflects my personal experience as the Headteacher of a secondary special school during that time (2011 to 2017). All of our students had been to mainstream primary schools and the idea was that, for those that required it, a secondary school placement in a special school was available from Year 7 onwards. At one point, however, a quarter of all of our students had started their secondary school lives in mainstream schools, only to have to leave, almost always because of their behaviour, and this was something new for our school. As Table 11.1 shows, we clearly weren't the only ones.

Table 11.1   Percentage of students with a statement or EHC plan by type of school in England (January 2010–January 2018)

School type	2010	2011	2012	2013	2014	2015	2016	2017	2018
Maintained nursery	0.1	0.1	0.1	0.1	0.1	0.1	0.1	0.2	0.1
State-funded primary	25.8	25.8	25.9	26.0	26.2	26.2	25.5	25.8	26.3
State-funded secondary	28.8	28.4	27.7	26.9	25.7	24.6	23.5	22.2	20.9
State-funded special	38.2	38.7	39.0	39.6	40.5	41.4	42.9	43.8	44.2
Pupil Referral Units	0.9	0.8	0.7	0.7	0.7	0.7	0.6	0.7	0.7
Independent	4.2	4.3	4.7	4.9	5.1	5.3	5.7	5.8	6.3
Non-maintained special	2.0	1.9	1.9	1.8	1.7	1.6	1.6	1.5	1.4

Source: School Census and School Level Annual School Census 2010–2018 (as at January each year)

It would be very easy to come to the conclusion from the initial statistics above regarding exclusion that children with SEND must be pre-disposed to poorer behaviour than their peers. This is no more true than it is that black children are more poorly behaved than white children. Strand and Lindsay (2009) found that Caribbean and mixed white and black Caribbean students are over twice as likely to be identified as having behavioural, emotional and social difficulties at the old School Action Plus level or above (today's SEN Support or EHCP) as white British students, even after adjustment for socio-economic deprivation. A finding that is sadly, but unsurprisingly, comparable to the situation in the USA where black students and those with disabilities are similarly 'disproportionately disciplined' (United States Government Accountability Office, 2018). As leaders we should be very concerned by this and be determined to do what we can to improve the situation.

EHCP? Is this greater than would be expected given their numbers in your school?

- Do you have similar statistics for detentions, isolation and other sanctions? What do they tell you?

This chapter is devoted to issues facing leaders in schools and their role in the intersection of behaviour and SEND, so I will not go into great detail about specific conditions such as autism or ADHD and how teachers can support children with those conditions; you will find much more on that in Chapter 10 of this book's companion publication, *Better Behaviour: A Guide for Teachers* (O'Brien, 2018). To that end my aims are to highlight the central importance of the Equality Act (2010), what I believe teachers and support staff should know about SEND in order to help minimise behavioural issues that commonly arise due to communication, sensory or literacy difficulties, the hazards associated with labelling, and what information I think school leaders should monitor to ensure they are working to eliminate discrimination where it occurs.

The Equality Act (2010)

All school leaders need to be intimately familiar with this vital piece of legislation. There were a number of different pieces of legislation that existed previously to tackle discrimination, including the Disability Discrimination Act (1995), the Race Relations Act (1976) and the Sex Discrimination Act (1975), but this brought them all together to protect people from discrimination in the workplace and elsewhere. You will appreciate that when discussing SEND and behaviour, understanding your duties in respect of this law is a key part of getting things right.

For the purposes of this book we will focus solely on how this law applies to our students and, equally importantly, prospective students. I make this explicit because it is a common complaint from school leaders who are doing their utmost to be as inclusive as possible that they know of other schools that make statements to prospective parents that other schools are better than they are with children with SEND in an attempt to sway parents' decisions. The Children's Commissioner of England's 2014 report *It Might Be Best If You Looked Elsewhere* is damning, finding good evidence of schools actively dissuading parents from applying, with egregious examples such as:

I explained [my daughter's] learning and the situation and that she has memory lapse, she has ADHD, she can't sit still and that's why she has one-to-one. I asked the school if they could take her and they just said 'Ooh, ahh, we're not sure how she will fit in, her learning is not really good enough for her to be accepted into the school'. I asked if they actually meant that [my daughter] couldn't go to this school and they said, 'She wouldn't be offered a place because we can't meet her needs'. I thought, 'You made that decision based on just a ten-minute conversation'.

Indeed, I recall showing a parent around my school as she told me of a Headteacher of a supposedly comprehensive secondary school who brazenly proclaimed to the audience in an open evening speech that, 'If your child has special needs then this is not the school for you [sic]'. The Act is clear that it is illegal to discriminate against a person or people because of protected characteristics, defined as: age, sex, sexual orientation, gender reassignment, being married or in a civil partnership, being pregnant or on maternity leave, race including colour, nationality, ethnic or national origin, religion or belief, or the focus for this chapter, disability (and this includes special educational needs).

It is less well known that the Act also protects from discrimination towards people who are associated with someone who has a protected characteristic or if they have complained about discrimination or supported someone else's claim. This plainly applies to the parents of students at our schools and the parents of prospective students too.

There are two main aspects of this law that school leaders must know well – their responsibilities towards individuals and what they must do to support them to ensure they are not discriminated against (so called 'reasonable adjustments'), and their overarching duty to ensure the organisation as a whole is actively working to eliminate all potentialities for discrimination (the public sector equality duty).

Reasonable adjustments

Failing to make sufficient reasonable adjustments is in my experience one major factor that explains why children with SEND have higher incidences of behavioural issues in schools than their peers. The phrase 'reasonable adjustments' is well known amongst school leaders, but is not always well understood, or in some rare cases, it is vehemently rejected – as Sir John Townsley, Chief Executive Officer of a multi-academy trust of schools, disturbingly said, 'Others won't say this, but I will: reasonable adjustment destroys positive discipline and destroys effective schools' (cited in Parker, 2018).

Much of the problem rests with the definition of 'reasonable'. Inevitably the context within which the child finds themselves heavily influences what could be deemed reasonable, and that context includes:

- the nature of the disability or difficulty itself – a single storey school may well find it far easier to support certain mobility difficulties than a multi-storey school
- how practicable the adjustments are – rightly or wrongly I was unable to guarantee when questioned at a tribunal once that all of my staff would be competent users of Paget Gorman signed speech, but I'm sure there are other schools where this, rarely, can be guaranteed
- the circumstances of the school, including its size, available resources and existing expertise and facilities – at the same tribunal (I learned a lot that day) I was admonished by a barrister for not, at that time, having an accessible toilet. 'Call yourself a special school!' he'd bellowed. I'd been a Headteacher a matter of weeks and, deeply embarrassed, ensured on my return that we had one built without delay.

There are three key areas to study when considering reasonable adjustments.

Changing the way things are done

In terms of schools and behaviour, this can mean treating someone deliberately differently in order to ensure their needs are met. I know that some school leaders find this difficult, not least the colleague quoted earlier, and some adjustments seem easier to accept than others. You may, for example, need to allow a child to eat somewhere other than a designated area as this may be too crowded which, if another child did so, would find them in trouble. That shouldn't be too troublesome for schools to manage. Similarly, a child with mobility issues may be excused the need to stand up when an adult enters the classroom if that is a rule of yours, or be excused the need to have their top button done up if they have a tracheostomy. All easy ones to let go. However, my experience is that issues arise when there is a sense in the school that a reasonable adjustment is, in their view, unreasonable and is actually letting a child get away with something that they really can manage, but are choosing not to. For example, are you OK with a child being provided with a chewy (a therapeutic tool that comes in many forms, but most often is a cylindrical piece of rubber tubing, the ends of which are placed in the mouth and chewed or sucked)? Chewies, common in special schools and recommended by occupational therapists, can help by providing a calming, organising and focusing effect on a child, and for some who can ingest inedible items, they can provide a safer sensory alternative.

I know a number of schools that refuse to allow them and, sadly, I know why. The adults are uncomfortable about the look of them, worrying about their image as a school, and with the volume of saliva that sometimes gets produced. I have often heard the opinion that they are glorified dummies and therefore for babies. Without the chewy the child will need (not choose) to satisfy that sensory craving somehow. One student I worked with sometimes ate Blu Tack and the graphite innards of pencils, but the inedible materials can be much more difficult to cope with, including – and this happened in my classroom once – their own faeces. Not so bothered about the chewy now, eh?

More commonly there will be things that schools do that are inherently discriminatory, such as providing rewards to children for 100 per cent attendance that we covered in Chapter 7. Children with SEND are far more likely to be off school as they are not well enough to attend or because they have regular and frequent hospital appointments, often with many different medical professionals, that cannot be moved (my daughter can only see her consultant on one specific afternoon a month, for example). The fact that their attendance is less than 100 per cent is not simply a matter of them not being bothered to come in, and no amount of incentivising will change the fact that a child with Down syndrome may need to see heart, eye, ear and paediatric specialists regularly thus missing school.

REFLECTION POINTS

- How well does your current behaviour policy ensure that the needs of children with SEND are accommodated? (Refer back to Chapter 2 for more on this.)

- What more needs to be done to remove potential sources of discrimination such as 100 per cent attendance rewards?

Changing the environment

This is the most commonly known and least controversial aspect of the reasonable adjustments under the Equality Act – apart from the frequent arguments between schools and councils about who will pay. It could mean alterations to the physical infrastructure such as step-free access to buildings, widening certain doorways or corridors (it will surprise you to know how many parts of many schools are inaccessible to a person using a wheelchair), the provision of a lift to enable access to upper floors, changing toilets (or in my case above, building new ones), but it could also mean work on rooms to improve the acoustics. These changes are often done piecemeal as a child is admitted to a school, more often than not in buildings that are decades old, and therefore the school has to work swiftly to ensure the child is not disadvantaged. The section below on the public sector equality duty explains how schools can instead plan in advance to ensure their estate is as inclusive as possible.

Providing extra aids or services

Sometimes a child may need a specific piece of equipment or support to help them access the school, the curriculum or to do something, or they may need additional services – the Equality Act calls these 'auxiliary aids and services'. This could be a mobility aid such as a posture walker with a pelvic stabiliser, a device to support a child's ability to communicate such as a proxy talker or eye-gaze machine, specialist support such as from a speech and language therapist or occupational therapist or extra adult support, usually in the form of a teaching assistant (TA) or similar. In the vast majority of cases these support aids or adults are provided and funded through the formal process whereby children's needs are assessed, and the provision is then detailed in the child's EHCP.

Public sector equality duty

The reasonable adjustments detailed above refer to supporting specific children and are inevitably considered on a case-by-case basis. The public sector equality duty places responsibilities on schools to be proactive in considering how they can eliminate discrimination in all its forms. There are specific duties that schools must comply with, namely that they:

- Publish equality information at least annually to demonstrate how they've complied with the equality duty:
  - When considering SEND and behaviour I suggest that this duty can be met by publishing information detailing how children with SEND are represented in the behaviour statistics (both positive and negative) the school holds compared to their relative presence in the general population. This can be a powerful indicator as we saw at the start of this chapter and there are national and regional statistics available to allow schools to compare how they fare against other schools.[2]

- Prepare and publish equality objectives at least every four years:
  - When considering SEND and behaviour this may involve identifying what training is needed amongst the staff to better meet the needs

of children with, for example, speech, language and communication, sensory or literacy difficulties. These objectives should be informed by the equality information gathered above, highlighting where the school needs to do more or work differently.

In addition, schools should do two things to ensure they eliminate unlawful discrimination, advance equality of opportunity and foster or encourage good relations – the three things the law says schools should have due regard for (Equality Act, 2010). This means that schools must, firstly, actively consider the effects of any new policies on people with protected characteristics, ensuring that they do not discriminate, and secondly, analyse existing policies and practices for evidence of discrimination. When considering SEND and behaviour, I suggest that the following questions in the Reflection Points box below may help.

REFLECTION POINTS

- When you review your behaviour policies annually (including allied policies such as those for anti-bullying, physical intervention, etc.), is this informed by good information about how children with SEND are faring compared to their peers?

- When you develop new policies to do with behaviour, do you rigorously assess them for their potential impact on children with SEND? (These used to be called 'equality impact assessments' and you can find more resources to help with this from the Equality and Human Rights Commission, 2019.)

- Look at your current single equality scheme or similar document that details your equality information and equality targets. Is behaviour and SEND included? If not, what needs to be added when it comes up for renewal?

The limitations of labelling

We met labelling in Chapter 1 when looking at the dangers of faulty thinking. I raised it in the context of writing children off by describing them in destructive ways – 'Ed is a nightmare' – but labelling extends much further than that.

When I was first a Headteacher I had the privilege of being in post when our school celebrated its 50th anniversary and I learned that when it opened in 1964 it was a school for the educationally sub-normal. Shocking, but a product of its time when we had for a long time described children with SEND as uneducable idiots, mentally defective, feeble-minded or dull and backward (see the Wood Report, 1929). Even official, state-sanctioned labels can be horrendously damaging.

There are times when all of us are in a situation where a child is joining our school with a set of needs that we may not have come across before. At that school we had a large number of children with Down syndrome and we were commonly asked by schools for help, which we were happy to provide. 'We've never had a child with Down syndrome in our school before' was a common refrain. There is no curriculum, toolkit, set of resources or teaching style that is needed to teach a child with Down syndrome, no more than there is for boys as opposed to girls. There is, however, good research that SENCos should be aware of which can steer department heads and teachers in the right direction, for example when teaching children with Down syndrome to read (see Buckley and Bird [1993], which includes a useful list of further references) (and how reading links into their speaking skills, which is a common issue for children with Down syndrome too), but this is not the same thing as a toolkit or checklist. It's not the same thing because a diagnosis or label is not *the* defining characteristic of any person. Yes, it may be an important one in the context of learning, but conditions have a habit of coming along in groups.

There is recent research indicating that more than half of autistic people have four or more co-occurring conditions – medical issues such as epilepsy, gastrointestinal problems or sleep disorders, developmental disorders such as a language delay or a learning difficulty, mental health conditions such as attention deficit hyperactivity disorder (ADHD), obsessive compulsive disorder (OCD) or depression, or genetic disorders such as fragile-X syndrome (Soke et al., 2018). This research also noted that, '[o]ver 95% of children had at least one co-occurring condition/symptom', which suggests that co-occurrence is the norm rather than the exception. Approximately 60 to 80 per cent of children with ADHD have at least one other condition such as a speech, language and communication need or a literacy or motor difficulty (Great Ormond Street Hospital NHS Foundation Trust, 2016), and this intersection is likely to be true to a greater or lesser extent for most conditions we care to name.

Given that, you will see why it is vital we consider each child's needs for what they are – unique to that child – and decide on the best way, informed by their diagnoses but not led by them, to proceed, ensuring we work with parents (experts in their own child) as closely as we can. As *Better Behaviour* (O'Brien, 2018) describes, there are some pieces of advice that are common to many conditions (but not all – visual support is no good to a child who is blind), which are a good start and all teachers need to be aware of:

- use clear, concise language
- give positive, explicit expectations and rules
- get children to repeat back instructions and expectations
- provide structure and routine
- use visual support to break up complex tasks
- provide regular developmental feedback.

The main message regarding the limitations of labelling, though, is for us to guard against lowering our expectations of that child and this can be an important role for us as school leaders when fostering the culture we want in our schools. Who, if they were completely honest, would admit to expecting behavioural problems from a child if they were told before they met them that they had ADHD? Sadly, I know I would, and I have to fight hard against this and, further, I must ensure my colleagues do the same.

Professionals who can help

Clearly the SENCo plays the central role in all things SEND in your school, but their task is a significant one and they cannot do it alone, particularly when it comes to SEND and behaviour. Fortunately, there are a number of professionals who can support the SENCo, especially with training your staff in certain key areas where it is well known that, if needs are not well met, behaviour problems are more likely to occur.

Speech, language and communication needs (SLCN)

There is significant evidence that children with SLCN are at higher risk of developing behavioural difficulties than their peers, with prevalence rates as worryingly high as 35 to 50 per cent (Lindsay et al., 2007; Van Daal et al., 2007; St Clair et al., 2011). This seems obvious when we give it some thought as difficulties in being understood (expressive language) or in understanding what is being said to you (receptive language) can be very frustrating, so anything we can do to ensure such needs are well met is worthwhile. However, the field as a whole is complex, is likely to be bi-directional (children with communication difficulties developing behavioural difficulties and vice versa) and there is more to it than children with SLCN developing behaviour problems. There is evidence that shows preschool children with behavioural difficulties also have issues with receptive language (Cohen and Medez, 2009); there is evidence that the issues change over time, with younger children with communication difficulties more likely to exhibit hyperactivity and attention problems (Lundervold et al., 2008) and older children moving away from exhibiting frustration to more anxiety, lower self-esteem and withdrawal behaviours (Haynes and Naidoo, 1991; Rutter and Mawhood, 1991); and there is evidence of large numbers of children with recognised behavioural issues who also have communication difficulties that have gone unrecognised (Cohen et al., 1998). The research literature is extensive and I recommend Melanie Cross' excellent *Children with Social, Emotional and Behavioural Difficulties and Communication Problems: There is Always a Reason* (2001) for a thorough appraisal of the field and for superb advice for SENCos and teachers in this area. Cross provides a neat example of the negative feedback loop that can exist for some children with these difficulties – that communication difficulties cause a child to miss out on, or be excluded from, interactions with others. They may then be less likely to join in or initiate something in the future or be less able to respond to invitations. You will immediately see where this can lead, with research indicating that children with communication difficulties can be rejected and bullied by others (Conti-Ramsden and Botting, 2004) or find it challenging to interact in a positive way themselves (Rice, 1993).

There are two things that I think as leaders you could do to improve staff skill and knowledge in this area of SEND:

- Where you have speech and language therapists (SALT) in your school doing direct work with children – and I understand that for some this will be a rarity – enable them to carry out that work in class as much as they want. Some schools do not allow this and children miss classes for therapy sessions, sometimes unnecessarily. When I first became a Headteacher I was asked by a SALT assistant if she could do some sessions in class and I readily agreed. I was struck once by the pointlessness of a child missing a cooking lesson for a therapy session where the child could have practised sequencing in the context of a recipe, but instead practised sequencing dry, as it were. The added bonus, a big one, is that TAs and teachers are able to have some live CPD, picking up techniques from the SALT or assistant as the session progresses, which seems to me to be a far more powerful way of learning than being told how to do it later on.
- Ensure there is some form of training for teachers and TAs by a SALT, including as part of the induction package for new staff. In my

experience SALTs are more than willing to do this and a couple of hours goes a long way to enabling all staff to understand the basics and how they can help children with SLCN difficulties.

REFLECTION POINTS

- How many children in your school have a recognised SLCN?

- Of that group, how many concern you or have concerned you in terms of their behaviour?

- What would you say is the current level of general knowledge amongst the staff about how best to support children with SLCN?

- What more could be done in this area?

Literacy difficulties

The link between literacy difficulties and behavioural difficulties (Meltzer et al., 1999) has already been made in Chapter 2, so I will not labour the point much further here. I do want to stress, though, the importance of screening children whose behaviour is causing you concern for literacy difficulties as these can be missed and well masked as children get older. This is where the support of a language and literacy support teacher will be invaluable both to screen the child and decide on what support is required if there are literacy issues (and this is likely to be so), but also to train the teachers and support staff, especially in secondary schools, on what they can best do to help the child too.

The critical importance of improving the abilities and confidence of children with literacy difficulties is put into stark relief when I read the research from the Prison Reform Trust, summarised in *No one Knows – Offenders with Learning Difficulties and Learning Disabilities* (2007). It makes for sobering reading and it makes clear just how extensive the problems of learning and literacy difficulties are in the prison population:

> Rack found that 40–50% of prisoners were at or below the level of literacy and numeracy expected of an 11-year old (Level 1), 40% of whom required specialist support for dyslexia. He concluded that dyslexia is three to four times more common amongst offenders than amongst the general population, with an incidence of 14–31%. The general agreement in prison-based studies is a rate of about 30%

dyslexia, though rates of serious deficits in literacy and numeracy in general reach up to 60%. Deficits in literacy and numeracy are often defined as abilities below the age of an 11-year old (Level 1; Rack 2005; Bryan et al. 2004). By 'serious', however, Herrington (2005) reported that the Basic Skills Agency Initial Assessment recorded 60% of prisoners with a reading ability equivalent to or less than that of a 5-year old child.

REFLECTION POINTS

- How many children in your school have a recognised literacy difficulty?

- Of that group, how many concern you or have concerned you in terms of their behaviour?

- What would you say is the current level of general knowledge amongst the staff about how best to support children with literacy difficulties?

- What more could be done in this area?

Sensory difficulties

Well over a decade working in special education has taught me that some of the biggest unmet needs amongst children with SEND that contribute to behaviour difficulties are related to sensory issues. This is partly down to insufficient knowledge amongst the adults working with these children – it isn't simply about children wearing ear defenders because they don't like noise – and the lack of availability of occupational therapists (OTs) contributes to this. Having an OT in my science lessons doing their therapy work with students was superb live professional development for me. I learned very quickly how I could subtly incorporate OT activities into my science practical work and how this could support the behaviour of children with sensory sensitivities.

Some children can be hyper- or hypo-sensitive to information coming in from one or more of their senses and this can be a major influence on a child's ability to behave well, feel settled and to learn. Sensory-seeking and sensory-avoiding behaviours are attempts by children to have their needs met, whether subconsciously or deliberately. For example, children who are habitually loud, bang doors and are generally heavy-handed or who find buttons, labels and zips intolerable can be better understood as children

who are seeking or avoiding sensations as opposed to children who are setting out to flout rules. Once I got to grips with scientist William Powers'
(1998) angle – instead of assuming that brains control behaviour based on
sensory stimuli, it makes more sense to assume that brains adapt behaviour
to control what stimuli they get from the world – I found it easier to work
out how to help children with sensory difficulties.

In common with the advice above for children with SLCN, any work that
OTs can do in classes with teachers and support staff will be beneficial. I
am, though, painfully aware that the presence of OTs in mainstream classrooms is rare and so this is just a pipe dream for most schools. Including
sensory difficulties as part of your staff training is not a pipe dream though.
OTs can and do provide this for schools and a session on this subject should
be a standard item in induction training for new staff.

REFLECTION POINTS

- How many children in your school have a recognised sensory need?

- Of that group, how many concern you or have concerned you in terms of
  their behaviour?

- What would you say is the current level of general knowledge amongst
  the staff about how best to support children with sensory needs?

- What more could be done in this area?

TAKING IT FURTHER – QUESTIONS AND ACTIVITIES
FOR YOU AND YOUR COLLEAGUES

- Take a fresh look at your current public sector equality duty targets.
  Are any of them related to SEND?

- When you come to write your newest set of equality targets what does
  your school need to do in terms of SEND? How will this contribute to
  better behaviour?

- Carry out an equality impact assessment when you next review your
  school's behaviour policy and present this to the governing body or
  trustees when it is tabled for ratification.

(Continued)

- Lay out all of the information you currently hold on the behaviour of children in your school, both positive and negative. Do you have sufficient information within that on how children with SEND fare? If not, what further analysis do you need to do to be sufficiently informed? What does the information you do have tell you about SEND and behaviour in your school?

- What training on SEND is currently available to your staff? Is the link between meeting a child's SEND needs and the effect on their behaviour made clearly enough? Do staff know the basics about how to support speech, language and communication, literacy and sensory difficulties?

Notes

1. In England, children with identified SEND are classified as follows: a) SEN Support – from 2015, the School Action and School Action Plus categories were combined to form one category of SEN support. Extra or different help is given from that provided as part of the school's usual curriculum. The class teacher and special educational needs coordinator (SENCO) may receive advice or support from outside specialists. The pupil does not have an EHCP. b) Education, Health and Care (EHC) Plan – a child has an EHC plan when a formal assessment has been made. This is a legally enforceable document that sets out the child's need and the extra help they must receive. Adapted from https://assets.publishing.service.gov.uk/government/uploads/system/uploads/attachment_data/file/729208/SEN_2018_Text.pdf (accessed 24 September 2019).

2. Information that allows English schools to compare their rates of fixed-term and permanent exclusion, including for children on SEN Support and for those with EHCPs, is available at www.gov.uk/government/collections/statistics-exclusions (accessed 19 September 2019).

References

Buckley, S. and Bird, G. (1993) 'Teaching children with Down syndrome to read', *Down Syndrome Research and Practice*, 1(1): 34–39. https://library.down-syndrome.org/en-gb/research-practice/01/1/teaching-down-syndrome-read/ (accessed 24 September 2019.)

Cohen, J.S. and Medez, J.L. (2009) 'Emotion regulation, language ability and the stability of preschool children's peer play behaviour', *Early Education and Development*, 20(6): 1016–1037.

Cohen, N.J., Barwick, M.A., Horodezky, N.B., Vallance, D.D. and Im, N. (1998) 'Language, achievement, and cognitive processing in psychiatrically disturbed children with previously identified and unsuspected language impairments', *Journal of Child Psychology and Psychiatry*, 39(6): 865–877.

Conti-Ramsden, G. and Botting, N. (2004) 'Social difficulties and victimization in children with SLI [specific language impairment] at 11 years of age', *Journal of Speech, Language and Hearing Research*, 47: 145–161.

Cross, M. (2011) *Children with Social, Emotional and Behavioural Difficulties and Communication Problems: There Is Always a Reason*. London: Jessica Kingsley.

Department for Education (2018a) *Permanent and Fixed Period Exclusions in England: 2017 to 2018*. www.gov.uk/government/statistics/permanent-and-fixed-period-exclusions-in-england-2017-to-2018 (accessed 24 September 2019).

Department for Education (2018b) *Special Educational Needs in England: January 2018*. https://assets.publishing.service.gov.uk/government/uploads/system/uploads/attachment_data/file/729208/SEN_2018_Text.pdf (accessed 24 September 2019).

Equality Act (2010) 'Public sector equality duty', Section 149. www.legislation.gov.uk/ukpga/2010/15/part/11/chapter/1 (accessed 24 September 2019).

Equality and Human Rights Commission (2019) 'Public sector equality duty'. www.equalityhumanrights.com/en/advice-and-guidance/public-sector-equality-duty (accessed 24 September 2019).

Great Ormond Street Hospital NHS Foundation Trust (2016) *Information for Families: Attention Deficit Hyperactivity Disorder (ADHD)*. Ref 2016F1282. www.gosh.nhs.uk/medical-information/attention-deficit-hyperactivity-disorder-adhd (accessed 24 September 2019).

Haynes, C. and Naidoo, S. (1991) *Children with Specific Speech and Language Impairment* (Clinics in Developmental Medicine 119). Oxford: MacKeith Press/Blackwells Scientific.

Lindsay, G., Dockrell, J. and Strand, S. (2007) 'Longitudinal patterns of behaviour problems in children with specific speech and language difficulties: Child and contextual factors', *British Journal of Educational Psychology*, 77: 811–828.

Lundervold, A.J., Heimann, M. and Manger, T. (2008) 'Behaviour: Emotional characteristics of primary-school children rated as having language problems', *British Journal of Educational Psychology*, 78(4): 567–580.

Meltzer, H., Gatward, R., Goodman, R. and Ford, T. (1999) *The Mental Health of Children and Adolescents in Great Britain*. The Office for National Statistics. London: The Stationery Office.

O'Brien, J. (2018) *Better Behaviour: A Guide for Teachers*. London: SAGE.

Office of the Children's Commissioner (2014) *It Might Be Best If You Looked Elsewhere*. www.childrenscommissioner.gov.uk/wp-content/uploads/2017/07/It_might_be_best_if_you_looked_elsewhere.pdf (accessed 24 September 2019).

Parker, K. (2018) 'Big rewards and "really harsh" punishments – meet the man who says he has a behaviour silver bullet', *Times Educational Supplement*, 4 February. www.tes.com/news/long-read-big-rewards-and-really-harsh-punishments-meet-man-who-says-he-has-behaviour-silver (accessed 24 September 2019).

Powers, W.T. (1998) *Making Sense of Behaviour: The Meaning of Control*. New Canaan, CT: Benchmark Publications.

Prison Reform Trust (2007) *No One Knows – Offenders with Learning Difficulties and Learning Disabilities: The Prevalence and Associated Needs of Offenders with Learning Difficulties and Learning Disabilities*. www.prisonreformtrust. org.uk/uploads/documents/noknl.pdf (accessed 24 September 2019).

Rice, M.L. (1993) 'Don't talk to him he's weird: A social consequences account of language and social interactions', in A.P. Kaiser and D.B. Gray (eds), *Enhancing Children's Communication: Research Foundations for Intervention*. Baltimore, MD: Brookes Publishing, pp. 139–158.

Rutter, M. and Mawhood, L. (1991) 'The long-term sequelae of specific development disorders of speech and language', in M. Rutter and P. Casear (eds), *Biological Risk Factors in Childhood and Psychopathology*. Cambridge: Cambridge University Press, pp. 233–259.

Soke, G.N., Maenner, M.J., Christensen, D., Kurzius-Spencer, M. and Schieve, L.A. (2018) 'Prevalence of co-occurring medical and behavioral conditions/ symptoms among 4- and 8-year-old children with autism spectrum disorder in selected areas of the United States in 2010', *Journal of Autism and Developmental Disorders*, 48(8): 2663–2676.

St Clair, M.C., Pickles, A., Durkin, K. and Conti-Ramsden, G. (2011) 'A longitudinal study of behavioral, emotional and social difficulties in individuals with a history of specific language impairment (SLI)', *Journal of Communication Disorders*, 44: 186–199.

Strand, S. and Lindsay, G. (2009) 'Evidence of ethnic disproportionality in special education in an English population', *Journal of Special Education*, 43(3): 174–190.

United States Government Accountability Office (2018) *Report to Congressional Requesters: K-12 EDUCATION – Discipline Disparities for Black Students, Boys, and Students with Disabilities*. GAO-18-258. www.gao.gov/ assets/700/690828.pdf (accessed 24 September 2019).

Van Daal, J., Verhoeven, L. and van Balkom, H. (2007) 'Behaviour problems in children with language impairment', *Journal of Child Psychology and Psychiatry*, 48: 1139–1147.

Vanier, J. (1998) *Becoming Human*. Mahwah, NJ: Paulist Press.

Wood Report (1929) *Report of the Mental Deficiency Committee: A Joint Committee of the Board of Education and Board of Control*. London: His Majesty's Stationery Office.

12

EXCLUSION

If the structure does not permit dialogue the structure must be changed.

Paulo Freire (1970: 93)

THE HEADLINES

- There are explicit laws surrounding the use of exclusion in schools, both for a fixed-term and permanently, and school leaders who don't follow these are at risk of excluding children illegally.

- Only Headteachers have the power to exclude children from schools and this power cannot be delegated.

- There is a legal limit of 45 days as to how long a child can be excluded for a fixed-term in any one academic year. This is cumulative, so represents the maximum amount of days of all fixed-term exclusions added together over the course of one academic year. Exclusions from previous schools in any one academic year count towards the 45-day limit.

- There are certain instances when a school's board of governors or trustees will review a Headteacher's decision to exclude for a fixed-term, and in some cases, that decision can be overturned.

- There is strong research evidence that vulnerable groups are disproportionately affected by fixed-term exclusion.

- Boards of governors or trustees are duty-bound to review all cases of permanent exclusion.

- Parents have the right to request an independent review panel to examine the decision by a school to permanently exclude their child. This panel does not have the power to reinstate the child, but can quash the original decision and direct a board of governors or trustees to reconsider their decision, and this carries a financial penalty.

- The use and effectiveness of isolation in schools is not well understood.

- School should keep detailed records of the use of isolation, analyse the data for effectiveness and report findings to governors or trustees regularly.

- Schools are not required to inform parents if their child has been placed in isolation, but it is clearly best practice to do so.

- Schools should avoid using isolation rooms for extended periods of time and should aim for supporting children to return to learning as soon as possible.

It was said in Chapter 1 that behaviour and school leaders' responses to it are two of the most emotive and controversial topics in the teaching profession. Within that crowded field, exclusion provokes the fiercest discussions and arguments, producing the most heat, but often very little light.

In this chapter I aim to make clear what the law says school leaders must do when excluding children and who in the school can exclude children, and to offer advice on how leaders can ensure their schools are monitoring the usage and effectiveness of exclusion. I will also point to where exclusion can be misused and comment on how schools must review its effectiveness and ensure that exclusion really is a last resort.

The power to exclude children from school temporarily or permanently is a very serious one and I worry about the misuse and abuse of this power as I have seen first-hand many times when children have been excluded from schools illegally – the power to exclude being covered by legislation. Children and their parents are afforded certain rights when a child is excluded and a failure to stick to the law robs the child and their parents of these rights. Those rights are inalienable and we as school leaders don't get to decide that a child, and their parents, has fewer rights just because the child has behaved badly, nor are these rights therefore more important than those of any victims. I shall lay out those rights, and what schools must do, later on in this chapter.

Late last year I was approached by a national training provider to ask if I would put together a course to help, and I quote, 'Headteachers avoid illegally excluding children'. I instantly refused, replying that any Headteacher who illegally excludes a child is either incompetent because they do not know the law, or a wilful lawbreaker because they do know the law, but broke it anyway. I have no sympathy for the well-worn excuse that accountability pressures force some Headteachers (highly qualified, well-paid professionals remember) to behave in such a way, especially from commentators who simultaneously maintain that children should be afforded no such mitigation for their behaviour. Sadly, they didn't take the hint and found someone else to run the course instead.

I want to be clear on the definitions from the outset of this chapter as most discussions I have – and I have a lot – involve people using the term 'exclusion' without specifying what they really mean. I want to define four terms: fixed-term exclusion, permanent exclusion (both defined by the Department for Education [2017] and covered by legislation [The School Discipline (Pupil Exclusions and Reviews) (England) Regulations 2012] and statutory guidance); internal exclusion and illegal exclusion.

- Fixed-term exclusion: when a child is barred from attending school for a defined period of time. Commonly known as 'suspension'.
- Permanent exclusion: when a decision is made that a child can no longer attend a school. Also known as 'expulsion'.
- Internal exclusion: when a child is removed from their timetabled lessons for a period of time and placed elsewhere in the school. There are many variations on this theme in operation in schools and many names for it too, including isolation, referral, reflection or internal inclusion (an oxymoron if ever I heard one). It is a form of exclusion, but not one that is covered by any legislation or government statutory guidance.
- Illegal exclusion: when a child is prevented from attending school for a period of time, but the law regarding exclusion has not been followed.

Who has the power to exclude a child?

It is the Headteacher and the Headteacher only (this includes colleagues in the role of Acting Headteacher) who has the power to exclude a child for a fixed-term. This power cannot and must not be delegated to other members of staff.

For cases of permanent exclusion the initial decision is made by the Headteacher, and this cannot be delegated either, but each and every decision to permanently exclude must be reviewed by a governing body or board of trustees (for an academy). This body retains the power to reinstate a child, essentially overturning a decision to permanently exclude, or to decline to reinstate, effectively endorsing the initial decision of the Headteacher. This means that the decision actually rests with the governing body and the Headteacher's role is to make a recommendation to the board, and to justify it with compelling evidence.

What can a child be excluded for?

A child can only be excluded for disciplinary reasons. This may sound obvious, but there are examples of children being forced to leave schools because of their (lack of) academic attainment. The most recent high-profile case to come to light concerned a grammar school's policy, formal and published amazingly, of forcing students to leave at the end of Year 12 if the school decided that their grades weren't good enough (BBC News, 2018). The Headteacher, who resigned over the incident, offered the inexcusably thin defence that, 'no one ever told him [the policy] was illegal'.

Another example is where a child is prevented from returning to school following a fixed-term exclusion because a parent cannot attend a reintegration meeting. This too is unlawful. A school cannot extend a fixed-term exclusion under any circumstances (a further fixed-term exclusion can begin after a first one if further evidence comes to light) and punishing a child by preventing their return to school because of the unavailability of an adult is ridiculous, but I have come across it many times.

The statutory guidance states that, '[t]he behaviour of a pupil outside school can be considered grounds for an exclusion' (Department for Education, 2017: 8), such as when they are travelling to and from school in their uniform.

Fixed-term exclusion

I stated above that exclusion, both for a defined period of time and permanently, should be a last resort option for Headteachers. With that in mind, I want you to choose one of the options to the question below.

What percentage of children get at least one fixed-term exclusion at some point in their secondary school life?

a.   0–5 per cent
b.   6–10 per cent
c.   11–15 per cent
d.   16+ per cent

Strand and Fletcher (2014) carried out a five-year longitudinal study on the cohort of children that went through the English secondary school system from September 2006 to the summer of 2011. This study followed well in excess of 500,000 children and they found that 16.3 per cent of that group experienced at least one fixed-term exclusion during their time in secondary school. This is one in six of *all* children – a stunningly high number. More than half of those children also went on to receive a second or further fixed-term exclusion. This immediately suggests a couple of things that schools should be monitoring closely (granted, the above statistics are for secondary schools where exclusion is far more frequent, but the point stands): 1) Is fixed-term exclusion really a last resort in your school? 2) Does it have the deterrent effect that many claim it does? With those questions in mind, this seems like a natural place for some reflection points.

REFLECTION POINTS

- Look at the fixed-term exclusion information from the last five years in your school.

    o   What percentage of your student population received at least one fixed-term exclusion in that time? (Be careful with the maths here because of leavers and joiners.)
    o   What percentage of the children receiving fixed-term exclusion received more than one in that time?
    o   How many of those receiving multiple exclusions were for the same issues?

Alarmingly, Strand and Fletcher (2014) found that over 30 per cent of the black Caribbean and mixed white and black Caribbean students in their study received at least one fixed-term exclusion in their time in secondary school. I shall expand upon this at the end of this section as I detail what we as leaders must do to ensure we're alert to the signs of potential systemic discrimination in our policies and systems. 'Not at my school!' I hear you cry, but we all need to be live to the fact that our schools can be institutionally discriminatory and we should be actively gathering evidence either to rule that out or to inform ourselves of where we must do better. The research by Figlio (2006) is both disturbing and fascinating in equal measure and serves as a warning sign to us all. After analysing tens of thousands of incidents in which two students were suspended (i.e. excluded for a fixed-term) he found that, 'schools always tend to assign harsher punishments to low-performing students than to high-performing students throughout the year' and that, 'this gap grows substantially during the testing window' (Figlio, 2006: 837).

Duties on schools

If a Headteacher decides in response to a behavioural incident in school to exclude a child or children for a period of time then there are a number of things that the law states must be done (The School Discipline [Pupil Exclusions and Reviews] [England] Regulations, 2012). Failure to do any of these can render the exclusion illegal. The Headteacher must:

1. Establish if, by excluding the child, the child would be excluded in total for more than 45 school days in that school year. (This includes any fixed-term exclusions the child may have received in another school or schools within that academic year.) If this were to be the case then the Headteacher is prevented by law from issuing a fixed-term exclusion as the law explicitly caps fixed-term exclusions at 45 days in total within any school year.

2. Inform parents of the decision to issue a fixed-term exclusion without delay.

    • Inform the parents of the child of the reason(s) for the exclusion and of its duration. A phone call is always preferable here. I am always concerned when I hear from parents that they have been told by text or email that their child has been excluded as this offers no immediate chance of a conversation.

    • Write to the parents stating the following:

        ○ the duration of the exclusion and the reason(s) for it (schools are required to categorise the main reason for a fixed-term exclusion under one of the following 12 headings: verbal assault against a pupil, verbal assault against an adult, theft, sexual misconduct, racist abuse, physical assault against a pupil, physical assault against an adult, persistent disruptive behaviour, drug and alcohol related, damage, bullying, other)

        ○ that they may make representations about the decision to the governing body (or equivalent in a pupil referral unit or academy), that their child may also be involved in the process of making representations and how they and their child can do this (a parent can ask a school's governing body to hear their views, but for exclusion of five days or fewer, and where the cumulative total of exclusions in any one term does not exceed five days, the decision cannot be overturned. See point 3 below for more on this)

        ○ where and to whom the representations should be sent (this person should be the chair of the governing body or equivalent and the contact details of the clerk to the board should be provided).

3. Inform the governing body (or academy equivalent) and the local authority in all cases where a fixed-term exclusion is for six or more days, or if the fixed-term exclusion would take the cumulative total to 15 days or more in any one term, or if a fixed-term exclusion would result in a child missing a public examination or a national curriculum test. This is because the governing body has a statutory duty to review such decisions and may direct a Headteacher to reinstate the child.

When I first became a Headteacher I developed a habit of using fixed-term exclusion. It was a habit that resulted directly from a lack of confidence in how to deal with the situation that had just happened. I could very easily suspend a child from our school for a period of time in response to an incident and I could be certain that I would be met with unanimous support from the staff and the rest of the students. I was also able to convince myself that I was taking a tough line on behaviour, sending a strong message to the students and their parents and that I was supporting my colleagues. There was, however, one significant problem. It became glaringly obvious to me over time that it wasn't improving behaviour. In some cases, it was simply respite and in the most difficult cases it actually contributed to making things worse. It entrenched resentment and fostered feelings of rejection that I was then unable to undo. I am reminded of the secondary analysis of the 2004 and 2007 British Child and Adolescent Mental Health Surveys carried out by Ford et al. (2018: 629) that, 'detected a bi-directional association between psychological distress and exclusion'. I do not have a blindly ideological opposition to the use of fixed-term exclusion in schools, I have just come to the conclusion that it is largely ineffective, its use is poorly evaluated and that, in cases like mine above, it becomes a crutch to lean on. This is supported by Professor Linda Graham's work (2018) where she notes that, '[r]esearch from different international contexts consistently finds that students with a disability, minority students, Indigenous students, students from disadvantaged backgrounds, and students in out-of-home care are significantly overrepresented in both suspensions and repeat suspensions (Beauchamp 2012; Dyson and Gallannaugh 2008; Losen and Gillespie 2012). In other words, these are the students for whom suspension does not work, yet schools continue to use it even when suspension has previously proven ineffective with that student. Taken together, the bulk of the research evidence indicates that suspension does not help to address the reasons for student disengagement and may in fact accelerate vulnerable students' disconnection from school (Valdebenito et al. 2018)'. Furthermore, recent American research from Bacher-Hicks et al. (2019) makes a very controversial contribution to the ongoing debate about whether exclusion is a contributor to the so-called school-to-prison pipeline. They note that 'we find that schools with stricter discipline practices have substantial negative long-run impacts. Students who attend a school with a 10 percent higher number of suspensions are 10 percent more likely to be arrested and 12 percent more likely to be incarcerated as adults. We also find negative impacts of school suspension on high school graduation and four-year college attendance. The impacts are largest for males and minorities' (Bacher-Hicks, Billings and Deming, 2019: 2).

In my case, exclusion was inaction brought on by a lack of knowledge and confidence in knowing how to improve behaviour masquerading as firm, decisive action. I stopped doing it and forced myself to work out how to improve the behaviour of the children who were struggling. The introduction to this book explains what happened – it wasn't plain sailing, of course, but it cured me of that habit and has made me far more discerning about my responses to poor behaviour ever since.

In the last set of Reflection Points above you looked at some of your school's statistics around fixed-term exclusion. Let's go a little deeper to see if any further trends arise.

REFLECTION POINTS

- Strand and Fletcher (2014: 3) noted that, '[t]he probability of experiencing one or more [fixed-term exclusions] is strongly related to gender, ethnicity, poverty (as indicated by entitlement to a Free School Meal and by local neighbourhood deprivation), scores in national attainment tests (particularly English) at age 11 and early patterns of attendance in Year 7'. Compare the characteristics of the children in your school receiving one or more fixed-term exclusions against the student profile in your school overall. Are there any characteristics that stick out? Why might that be?

- Pay particularly close attention to ethnicity, as Strand and Fletcher (2014: 3) also note that, '[t]he relationship between ethnicity and the odds of experiencing one or more [fixed-term exclusions] remains large and significant even after controlling for all these other variables'.

- Add in the information that you have already obtained on your students with SEND in Chapter 11 to give you a rich picture of what is happening in your school:

  o What proportion of your fixed-term exclusions over the past five years have been issued to children on SEN Support? And to children with an EHCP? Is this greater than would be expected given their numbers in your school?

  o What proportion of your permanent exclusions over the past five years have been issued to children on SEN Support? And to children with an EHCP? Is this greater than would be expected given their numbers in your school?

- What does all of this rich information that you now have to hand suggest you need to do to improve things?

Permanent exclusion

There is no decision in a school that carries with it a greater responsibility than the one that results in a child having to leave a school. Permanent exclusion, also commonly referred to as expulsion, is therefore rightly considered to be an absolute last resort and is something that most leaders I know will go to great lengths to avoid.

The justification for deciding that, because of their behaviour, a child must leave a school and can no longer return should be, to quote the Department for Education (DfE), 'in response to a serious breach or persistent breaches of the school's behaviour policy; and where allowing the pupil to remain in school would seriously harm the education or welfare of the pupil or others in the school' (Department for Education, 2017: 10). Whilst this may sound like a high bar, what is regarded as 'serious' or 'persistent' is open to interpretation by Headteachers. A child can persistently breach a school's behaviour policy by refusing to follow the school's uniform code and it could be argued that permanent exclusion could be a disproportionate response from a school – although I have had colleagues argue that open defiance must be eliminated and if a child cannot conform to uniform expectations then they must leave their school.

Recall from earlier in the chapter that the decision to permanently exclude a child from a school effectively rests with a board of governors or trustees as each and every decision to permanently exclude by a Headteacher must be reviewed by them, with their task being to either uphold the initial decision – essentially a recommendation – or to order reinstatement. This should not be a rubber-stamping exercise and should therefore be the safeguard against poor interpretation by Headteachers of the words 'serious' or 'persistent' from above. Boards of governors or trustees apply the civil standard of proof – on the balance of probabilities, as opposed to beyond reasonable doubt – when testing the evidence.

Boards also have a further significant responsibility when reviewing cases of permanent exclusion. They must satisfy themselves that the school has met its duties under the Equality Act 2010 not to discriminate against children on the basis of protected characteristics (see Chapter 11 for more on this) and this includes the exclusion process. I detailed in Chapter 11 that children with SEND are far more likely to be excluded, both for a fixed-term and permanently, than their peers, so this responsibility for boards is a serious one. Indeed, DfE's guidance explicitly states that schools, 'should, as far as possible, avoid permanently excluding any pupil with an EHC plan or a looked after child' (Department for Education, 2017: 11).

With the Equality Act in mind, the research by Strand and Fletcher (2014: 18) also worryingly notes that, '[n]early every ethnic minority group reaches a permanent exclusion on average after fewer FTEs [fixed-term exclusions] than White British students and all but the Irish students reach a permanent exclusion having experienced FTEs of longer average duration than the White British students. These data are consistent with a degree of systemic discrimination'.

Independent review panels

If a board of governors or trustees decides not to reinstate a student, i.e. they uphold the initial decision of the Headteacher, they must inform the parents that they have the right to request an independent review panel be arranged by the local authority or academy trust to review the decision to permanently exclude their child. Parents have 15 days from the date on which notice in writing was given to them from the board of the decision not to reinstate their child to apply for a review. In addition, DfE advises that, 'if parents believe that there has been unlawful discrimination in relation to the exclusion then they may make a claim under the Equality Act 2010 to the First-tier Tribunal (Special Educational Needs and Disability) in the case of disability discrimination, or the County Court, in the case of other forms of discrimination' (Department for Education, 2017: 22).

Independent review panels consist of three or five members and a clerk to administer the process. The members must be trained within the past two years and must clearly be impartial and free from any perception of bias. A lay member, without paid experience working in schools, chairs the panel. The other two or four members comprise one or two governors or Headteachers, or former governors or Headteachers, who have held those posts within the past five years.

There are three outcomes open to an independent review panel, which can be reached by a majority vote so do not need to be unanimous:

- the panel can uphold the governing body's decision
- it can recommend that the governing body reconsiders reinstatement
- or it can quash the decision and direct that the governing body reconsiders reinstatement.

The final option comes with a power to order a local authority to adjust the school's budget to the tune of £4,000, or in the case of an academy, the trust must pay that amount to the host local authority unless within ten school days of receiving notice of the panel's decision, the governing body decides to reinstate the student. Clearly, this last option is a very serious one, and one I have made myself as part of a review panel, and must be justified by deciding that the original decision was flawed when considered in the light of the principles applicable on application for judicial review:

- Illegality – did the governing board act outside the scope of its legal powers in deciding that the pupil should not be reinstated?
- Irrationality – did the governing board rely on irrelevant points, fail to take account of all relevant points, or make a decision so unreasonable that no governing board acting reasonably in such circumstances could have made it?
- Procedural impropriety – was the governing board's consideration so procedurally unfair or flawed that justice was clearly not done? (Department for Education, 2017: 38)

As mentioned above, I am a trained panel member and my experiences have given me a further insight into how the law is applied, or misapplied in some cases, by schools. I have also benefited from the presence of a barrister whose role has been to provide legal advice to the panel. My experiences have taught me that understanding of the law around exclusions by Headteachers and boards of governors and trustees is often incomplete and occasionally ignored, and I have seen a number of cases that were entirely avoidable but became extremely stressful for everyone involved because the law hadn't been followed in the first place.

Illegal exclusion

The illegal exclusion of children from schools is one of my biggest worries. Beyond my own experience, which has mounted over the years such that it can't now be brushed off as simple anecdote, there is ample evidence from disparate sources that this is happening in our schools, including, to name but a few: Ambitious About Autism's report *When Will They We Learn?* (2016), from Ofsted's inspection of schools report (2017); the Children's Commissioner for England's report *Always Someone Else's Problem* (2013), and through investigative journalism such as that of Warwick Mansell (2018).

However, sadly little has been done to date to tackle the problem. Every few months or so a case of misconduct comes up in the press where a school leader is struck off from the profession for either financial malfeasance or exam malpractice, but I have yet to see a case of misconduct brought before the Teaching Regulation Agency for the illegal exclusion of a child despite the fact that it is, in my view, a far more serious offence than tampering with exam papers.

The explanations above of the law on fixed-term and permanent exclusions are not technically complex, but are detailed and they, rightly, place many responsibilities on schools. There are, though, a number of weaknesses in the system, which mean that if the law isn't followed, either inadvertently or deliberately, it is very unlikely to be picked up.

Parental knowledge of the law

Why should parents know anything about the law on exclusions from schools? There should be no expectation that they do, nor should there be any responsibility on them to ensure the law is followed. Parents, quite reasonably, trust us to act with integrity and probity. If a school rings a parent and tells them that their child has been poorly behaved and has been suspended for three days I can see why many parents will be supportive of the school, keep their child at home and then bring them back in for a reintegration meeting. There will be few that know the law well enough to know the duties placed on the school, and even fewer who will then challenge the school if they suspect the law is not being followed. Even when they do, as in the case of a friend of mine who is a highly experienced teacher and knows the law well, the scale of the challenge for one lone, vulnerable parent against a school is a daunting one. Parker et al. (2016) research paper on the parental experience of exclusion – a field of sadly limited research – is an important one as it highlights the importance of communication and the wider impact of exclusion on families.

Perverse incentives

The law on exclusions has one thing in common with all laws – it is vulnerable to unintended consequences, and unfortunately there are perverse incentives for school leaders to ignore these laws, enabled by the understandable lack of knowledge of the details by other teachers, school staff and parents. For example, the law limits the amount of time in any one academic year that a child can be excluded for a fixed-term at 45 days. You will immediately see that if a school leader excludes children without following the proper procedures this limit can be breached. The incentive to knowingly illegally exclude, safe in the knowledge that the chance of detection is low, can deter some leaders from having to address some behavioural issues in the school in a different way.

There is a myth out there, too, that a relatively high number of exclusions is automatically regarded as a bad thing by Ofsted. This is not so, but it should automatically secure attention and scrutiny from inspectors. Keeping exclusion numbers artificially low, therefore, can be regarded as an attractive thing to do.

Staff knowledge of the law

Lastly, the rest of the staff team in a school will probably never see any of the paperwork, meetings or administration that should accompany lawful exclusions, so there is virtually no way for them to know if the law has been followed. If the Headteacher says that a child is to be excluded for three days, no one is going to ask to see the paperwork or to ask if the law has been followed correctly, assuming they know it. Likewise with governors and trustees, they are only likely to see the administration of lawful exclusions, making it very difficult to spot illegal exclusions at all.

Isolation (aka internal exclusion)

I mentioned the use of isolation – the removal of a child from a lesson to another part of the school for a period of time – at the start of this chapter. It is not a matter that is covered under legislation, but it is mentioned in the DfE's advice on behaviour in schools where they state that, 'schools must act reasonably in all the circumstances when using such rooms' and that children should be kept in isolation, 'no longer than is necessary and that their time spent there is used as constructively as possible' (Department for Education, 2016: 12).

It is unarguable that there are occasions when a child can no longer remain in a lesson because, despite our best efforts, their behaviour is preventing others from learning. What is up for debate is how long the child spends out of that lesson (and others), where they go and what they do whilst they are there. (The use of structured isolation is largely confined to secondary schools, mostly because the numbers involved require something more organised than sending a child to sit outside the Headteacher's office, but the principle remains the same.)

I see the use of isolation based broadly on one of two differing aims – either punishment or de-escalation.

In my first few years as a teacher, our science department team made good use of each other's classrooms to temporarily relocate a child who was disruptive in our lessons. It was often enough to place a child in the classroom next door or nearby to remove the fuel from conflict with another child or the teacher, or from peers egging them on – this is *de facto* isolation. They were loosely supervised and unfortunately may have completed little further work, but the initial situation was defused and the rest of the day could continue for everyone once the lesson ended. The child may end up back with the teacher for a detention and/or to catch up on the missed work, but it seemed like a reasonable and effective response in many cases and its primary aim was de-escalation.

A more formal use of isolation, where a child is taken to a room designated and staffed precisely for that, can still achieve the aim of de-escalation and for preparing the child to return to learning if it is set up with that aim in mind. When done in this way a child is likely to spend the rest of the lesson there and, in most cases, can be supported to be ready to return to their next lesson. We can see that there may be some exceptions to that, such as a fight between two students or something similarly serious or worse, where some investigation is required by school staff or a longer cooling off period is needed.

If, however, the aim is to punish, then these rooms can begin to look different, and the time that children spend in them can grow. The experience needs to be an unpleasant one and rules are created to ensure discomfort such that the only behaviours allowed require facing into a booth in silence. There has to be a decent length of time, too, to provide enough of that discomfort because, so the logic goes, the experience needs to be so unpleasant that it is a major deterrent. Sir John Townsley, CEO of the Gorse Academy Trust (we met him in Chapter 11), supports this view, stating that, '[i]solation ... has to be "really, really harsh"' (cited in Parker, 2018). These rooms then run the risk of becoming dumping grounds, or perversely, places some children seek out because they can virtually guarantee silence, minimal interaction and, despite the tough rhetoric, low expectations because the work needs to be able to be done without adult input, so can end up being flurries of worksheets or questions from textbooks. When this happens disturbing reports surface, such as the harrowing one that the BBC's *Victoria Derbyshire* programme reported on in 2019 with the headline: 'I was put in a school isolation booth more than 240 times', adding, 'A girl who tried to kill herself after spending months in an isolation booth at school has said she felt, "alone, trapped and no-one seemed to care"'. The report went on, 'The 16-year-old spent every school day from mid-January to March this year in the room, the family say' (Hynes, 2019). Examples such as these show how schools can lose sight of what they are trying to achieve. They end up deepening resentment and fostering feelings of rejection, increasing the chances of children isolating themselves, emotionally and sometimes literally, even further.

I recall visiting a child in a secondary school after being asked to consider him for a place in our school because his behaviour was putting his place in their school at risk. I spent a good three hours there and had some very helpful conversations with teachers about this child, but one remains with me. The child had recently sworn at a teacher and as a result was given five days in isolation. One could argue that this was an alternative to excluding the child for five days, but I've already argued why this is a poor substitute as there is no law covering its use and it doesn't count towards the 45-day legal limit. The child stopped attending for a time, and the school simply waited for him to return each time, eventually squeezing out the five days in isolation from him in chunks. Of course, its effectiveness, if it was ever effective with him, had long since evaporated and it became a war that the school had to win. There was no way the school was going to back down, so the child clung to what power he had left by trying to win a battle or two by staying away from school. The original incident had ceased to be the issue; it simply became something that had to be won, no matter how long it took. In all zero sum games, for you to win I have to lose, and I don't like losing, especially not in front of my peers.

There can be only one real aim when isolation goes beyond a few hours and that is to inflict misery. 'Quite right!' you might say. 'The child inflicted misery on others, so now it's their turn!' Stick to that if you wish, but don't expect any improvements in behaviour.

My other major concern with the use of isolation is its use as an alternative to exclusion. To protect against misuse of isolation schools should record when and for how long children are isolated because of their behaviour, and parents should be informed each and every time it happens. Further, the use of isolation should be reported as a standard element of the information provided to governors or trustees. Boards of governors or trustees could then, if they wished, adopt a similar approach to reviewing its use that the law demands of them for fixed-term exclusion. For example, if a child ends up in isolation for 15 or more days in a term then the governors should review the situation with the school's leadership team to see what leaders plan to do next.

REFLECTION POINTS

- What quantitative information do you currently have on the use of isolation in your school?

- What is the maximum number of days any one child has spent in isolation in each of the last five years?

- What proportion of the children that have been in isolation are on SEN Support?

- What proportion of the children that have been in isolation have an EHCP?

- Do you currently inform parents when children are placed in isolation?

(Continued)

- If not, why not?
- What information do you currently provide to governors or trustees on the use of isolation?
- Can this reporting be improved?

TAKING IT FURTHER – QUESTIONS AND ACTIVITIES FOR YOU AND YOUR COLLEAGUES

- Fixed-term and permanent exclusion:

  o With all the information that you have gathered above, what do you now know about the effectiveness, or otherwise, of both fixed-term and permanent exclusion in your school over the past few years?
  o What needs to be different in your school as a result of this knowledge?

- Isolation:

  o Have you clearly defined what isolation is for in your school?
  o Is that definition consistent with your values that we discussed in Chapter 1?
  o If not, what needs to be different to ensure that it is?

- Illegal exclusion:

  o Ensure that all of your senior leaders and governors or trustees know the law with regard to exclusion in sufficient detail.

- The potential for discrimination:

  o Do you have sufficient information to satisfy yourselves that, despite the evidence on the national scale that systemic discrimination is a concern, your school is not contributing to that?
  o If not, what further information do you need to gather and from whom? Who will do this?

References

Ambitious About Autism (2016) *When Will ~~They~~ We Learn?* www.ambitiousabout autism.org.uk/sites/default/files/AAA%20When%20Will%20We%20 Learn%20REPORT%20LORES%20FINAL.pdf (accessed 25 September 2019).

Bacher-Hicks, A., Billings, S. and Deming, D. (2019) 'The school to prison pipeline: Long-run impacts of school suspensions on adult crime', paper presented at the National Bureau of Economic Research Summer Institute, Boston, 24 July. http://papers.nber.org/conf_papers/f124381.pdf (accessed 25 September 2019).

BBC News (2018) 'London grammar school's exclusion policy was illegal, report finds', 12 July. www.bbc.co.uk/news/uk-england-london-44793707 (accessed 25 September 2019).

Department for Education (2016) *Behaviour and Discipline in Schools: Advice for Headteachers and School Staff*, January. https://assets.publishing.service.gov. uk/government/uploads/system/uploads/attachment_data/file/488034/ Behaviour_and_Discipline_in_Schools_-_A_guide_for_headteachers_and_ School_Staff.pdf (accessed 25 September 2019).

Department for Education (2017) *Exclusion from Maintained Schools, Academies and Pupil Referral Units in England – Statutory Guidance for Those with Legal Responsibilities in Relation to Exclusion*. DFE-00184-2017. https:// assets.publishing.service.gov.uk/government/uploads/system/uploads/att achment_data/file/641418/20170831_Exclusion_Stat_guidance_Web_ver sion.pdf (accessed 25 September 2019).

Freire, P. (1970) *Pedagogy of the Oppressed*. New York: Herder and Herder.

Figlio, D.N. (2006) 'Testing, crime and punishment', *Journal of Public Economics*, 90(4): 837–851.

Ford, T., Parker, C., Salim, J., Goodman, R., Logan, S. and Henley, W. (2018) 'The relationship between exclusion from school and mental health: A secondary analysis of the British Child and Adolescent Mental Health Surveys 2004 and 2007', *Psychological Medicine*, 48(4): 629–641. doi:10.1017/S003329171700215X.

Graham, L.J. (2018) 'Questioning the impacts of legislative change on the use of exclusionary discipline in the context of broader system reforms: A Queensland case-study', *International Journal of Inclusive Education*. DOI: 10.1080/13603116.2018.1540668.

Hynes, C. (2019) 'I was put in a school isolation booth more than 240 times', *BBC News*, 15 April. www.bbc.co.uk/news/education-47898657 (accessed 25 September 2019).

Mansell, W. (2018) 'Are schools flouting the exclusion laws to protect their reputations?', *Times Educational Supplement*, 14 February. www.tes.com/news/ are-schools-flouting-exclusion-laws-protect-their-reputations (accessed 25 September 2019).

Office of the Children's Commissioner for England (2013) *Always Someone Else's Problem: Office of the Children's Commissioner's Report on Illegal Exclusions*. www.childrenscommissioner.gov.uk/wp-content/uploads/2017/07/Always_ Someone_Elses_Problem.pdf (accessed 25 September 2019).

Ofsted (2017) Inspection report of The Brookfield School, *Hereford*. https://files. api.ofsted.gov.uk/v1/file/2730459 (accessed 25 September 2019).

Parker, C., Paget, A., Ford, T. and Gwernan-Jones, R. (2016) '".he was excluded for the kind of behaviour that we thought he needed support with ...": A qualitative analysis of the experiences and perspectives of parents whose children have been excluded from school', *Emotional and Behavioural Difficulties*, 21(1): 133–151. DOI: 10.1080/13632752.2015.1120070.

Parker, K. (2018) 'Big rewards and "really harsh" punishments – meet the man who says he has a behaviour silver bullet', *Times Educational Supplement*, 4 February. www.tes.com/news/long-read-big-rewards-and-really-harsh-punishments-meet-man-who-says-he-has-behaviour-silver (accessed 24 September 2019).

The School Discipline (Pupil Exclusions and Reviews) (England) Regulations 2012. www.legislation.gov.uk/uksi/2012/1033/made (accessed 25 September 2019).

Strand, S. and Fletcher, J. (2014) *A Quantitative Longitudinal Analysis of Exclusions from English Secondary Schools*. Oxford: University of Oxford.

13
GOVERNANCE

It is meaningless to talk about effective teaching or effective schooling; the question that always needs to be asked is 'Effective for what?'

Professor Gert Biesta (2007: 8)

THE HEADLINES

- Governors should ensure that there is meaningful consultation with staff, students and parents in the formation and review of behaviour policies.

- Governors should receive a breadth of information on behaviour, including on:

  - o permanent exclusions
  - o fixed-term exclusions
  - o use of isolation or similar
  - o detentions and other sanctions
  - o use of restrictive physical intervention (i.e. restraint)
  - o managed moves via in-year fair access panels
  - o information from the positive side of the school's behaviour systems.

- This information should be contextualised by the addition of comparative information on behaviour in previous years in the school, and on comparative information on a local, regional and national level.

- Governors should request information from school leaders on how children with protected characteristics, as defined by the Equality Act (2010), fare under the school's behaviour policies to ensure there is no systemic discrimination in the school.

- The governor with oversight of behaviour should receive underlying information in a much greater depth and report back the main headlines to the board.

- The governor with oversight of behaviour should be provided with an opportunity to see and understand the systems in use to report, collect and analyse behaviour information.

- Governors should consider being more proactive in the school's drive for equity by adopting a policy to review fixed-term exclusions at a lower threshold for children with protected characteristics (for example, after the tenth day of fixed-term exclusion in a term) than for their peers (the law demands review after 15 days).

- Governors could go further and extend the review system to a school's use of isolation (effectively internal exclusion). Governors should consider adopting a policy to review all cases where a child spends more than 15 days in isolation in any one term (as per fixed-term exclusion). This could be reduced to 10 days for children with protected characteristics.

- In order to combat the practice of off-rolling, governors should consider adopting a policy of reviewing all cases of children leaving their school roll at a time other than their expected leaving date.

At various points throughout this book I have given snippets of my first few years as a Headteacher through the lens of behaviour improvement. What I failed to mention at all was the crucial role that governors played during that time. This is typical for governance; the largest volunteer force in the country who mainly go about their important work unseen and, in my opinion, under-appreciated. (For the purposes of simplicity, I will use the terms 'governor' and 'governance' throughout this chapter to represent both governors in maintained schools and trustees from academies, for whilst their roles have technical differences, they are essentially the same in terms of their contribution to the leadership of behaviour.)

REFLECTION POINTS

- What roles do governors currently play in respect of behaviour in your school?

- What information do you currently provide to governors on behaviour in your reports?

- Is there a designated governor for behaviour on your board? What do they do?

There are some aspects of leadership where the role of governance seems obvious – setting budgets and reviewing spending immediately springs to mind. Governors make a vital contribution here, and it is common to find governors with transferable financial expertise of one sort or another on boards, which is of obvious benefit to the school. When I was first a Headteacher we had a health and safety professional on our board, so the decision as to who would be the chair of the Health and Safety Committee every year was less of a debate and more of a coronation. But how governors can contribute to good behaviour in our schools and what they do is far less clear, and the aim of this chapter is to improve this.

The role of governance in behaviour policy creation and review

I have benefited from working with some brilliant governors since I became a senior leader. One in particular had a great habit of quizzing me on policies. 'You're giving us this policy to ratify, but how do we know if it's any good? How do we know that you haven't just knocked this up yourself?' he would ask. (Great governor questions, by the way.) The answer to the first question is covered below in the 'Providing information' section, but the answer to the second question is, in terms of behaviour, well within the remit of governors because they can, and should, insist that information from the staff, the students and their parents informs policy development. Indeed, in 2009 Sir Alan Steer produced the second of his reports on behaviour commissioned by the government entitled *Learning Behaviour: Lessons Learned – A Review of Behaviour Standards and Practices in Our Schools* and it reinforces this: 'The legal requirement on school leaders and governing bodies to ensure that their behaviour policies are reviewed regularly and that staff, pupils and parents are involved in the process is extremely important and must be observed' (Department for Children, Schools and Families, 2009: 9). I remain concerned that this does not happen and that, too often, governors first become involved when they are expected to simply sign off on policies at the back end of the process. I confess to having done this myself numerous times.

With Steer's prompt fresh in our minds, here is the place to commit to involving governors earlier in the process. When we involve staff, students and parents we should inform governors in advance so that they have a chance to influence (I nearly wrote steer) what information is sought, and then be included in analysing the responses. I recall in the past writing home to parents asking for their views on our current behaviour policy, and providing a link to the policy on the school's website. No replies came back, so I regarded my consultation as complete. Hardly thorough is it?

You may well also seek information and views from staff, students and parents in a general annual questionnaire. However, given that parents are busy and filling in one of our questionnaires is not always top of their list of priorities, which can lead to low rates of completion, it seems sensible to avoid asking all of these people the same or similar questions twice. This means that some care needs to be given to the questions you are asking.

When I was first a Headteacher and our school was struggling with behaviour (i.e. I was struggling with behaviour) I simply used the Ofsted questionnaire in its entirety. This tells you all you need to know about my mindset and twisted priorities at the time. The questionnaire was not really being used to inform our thinking and improve our evidence base at all; it was used blatantly as a source of evidence for an Ofsted inspection. I didn't involve governors in this and if I had I'm sure they would have helped me to formulate better questions.

Governors need to be involved in the construction of the questions so that the information gleaned from them adds to the already existing body of knowledge on behaviour in the school and on the board. It can be used to triangulate other sources of evidence such as what governors see and hear when they visit the school, and the harder sources of information that school leaders provide governing bodies, such as information on the use of exclusion and isolation or policies on the use of mobile phones.

REFLECTION POINTS

- What is the current extent of governor involvement in policy creation and review at your school?

- What information do you currently obtain from staff, students and parents when reviewing your behaviour policies?

Providing information to governors

I learned quickly as a school leader that the information I provided to governors, and the clarity with which I communicated it, could make it easier, harder or impossible for them to do their job well. Our governing body at the time – a superb bunch – didn't know what they didn't know in the field of behaviour and were totally reliant on what little information they did get, so in the absence of any other concerns – when they visited the school it seemed calm enough – there wasn't an urge to ask for more.

There are two things that are important to enable governors to process the information you give them:

- presenting the information so that the governors can see how this year compares to previous years where possible in this school

- providing any local, regional and/or national comparisons that are available to see how the school measures up against other schools (see Chapter 5 for references on some of these).

Neither source is perfect – schools change over time and no two schools are the same – but it does give governors the chance to put the school into some sort of context. I recall when I started to provide governors with some detailed information on staff absence I was, rightly, asked by governors to come back with information from other schools as they had no way of knowing if they should be worried about our levels of absence.

Below are the suggested areas to cover when providing information to governors. The level of detail needs to be considered carefully to avoid the governors getting bogged down, so I suggest that the governor for behaviour gets the main outcomes in greater depth, and a distilled version with the headlines can then be provided for the rest of the board. You will notice that this list essentially amounts to the headlines from your detailed analysis from Chapter 5. There should be no new analysis just for the governors as this is information that you should already have and of which you make good use:

- permanent exclusions
- fixed-term exclusions
- use of isolation or similar
- detentions and other sanctions
- use of restrictive physical intervention (i.e. restraint)
- managed moves via in-year fair access panels
- information from the positive side of the school's behaviour systems.

When this information is presented well, challenge from governors is inevitable. A well-prepared senior leader will have the answers ready too, as the initial analysis should inform the work that is to be done to improve behaviour. It is no use informing governors that there has been a spike in fixed-term exclusions without knowing why and what you're doing about it. This can suggest to a governing body that they are dealing with a leader who is not on top of their brief.

Systems

Part-way through my first headship we invested in an electronic system for recording, storing and analysing behaviour incidents. It proved extremely useful, not least because the design allowed us to tailor it specifically to our requirements. The governing body asked to be given a guided tour of the system by the senior leader responsible for behaviour in the school. This was a superb idea, so I reserved 15 minutes of the next full governing body meeting for this. It took over 90 minutes as the governors were so engrossed in the system that my colleague was bombarded by brilliant questions. At the end of that hour and a half the governors were reassured about the system, that it wasn't too onerous for the staff to complete and that they could see how the information from individual incidents was collated and analysed to become the information they saw on our reports to them.

I highly recommend this to any school leader. In most cases, though, it only really needs the governor responsible for behaviour to be involved and they can report back to the board. In our case, though, because behaviour was the cause of our adverse Ofsted judgement, the whole board felt the need to see it for themselves.

REFLECTION POINT

- What is the current depth of knowledge amongst the governors about the systems in use by the school to record, store and analyse behaviour incidents?

Ensuring equity

Governors can also play a proactive part in the drive to ensure a school's policies and procedures are as equitable as possible. Take, for example, the use of isolation in schools. I mentioned in Chapter 12 that this is unregulated so there is no limit to the time a child could spend in there. I have long thought it wise that governors take the same view of the use of isolation as the law does on fixed-term exclusion. We saw in Chapter 12 that governors must review fixed-term exclusions once they have reached 15 days in any one term for a child. I would take the view that governors adopt this practice with the use of isolation. Once a child has spent 15 days in isolation in any one term (the quantum of a period of isolation being regarded as half a day), which is a lot incidentally, the governors could mandate that they review the situation with that child with the senior leadership team and parents in the same way they would when fixed-term exclusions reach that level. In addition, I would take the decision to review fixed-term exclusions (and isolation based on the policy suggested above) sooner for children with protected characteristics. Given that we know children with SEND and children from many ethnic minority backgrounds are grossly over-represented in exclusion statistics it makes sense to review their situations earlier, so instead of reviewing after 15 days of fixed-term exclusions (or in isolation) in a term, a governing body could do so after 10 days for children in certain groups, which would be defined by the board.

The other area that governors need to be alert to is off-rolling (mentioned in Chapter 1, this is a gutless practice whereby schools force children that they judge to be a risk to the school's performance measures to leave). With that in mind, governors can insist that they are informed each and every time a child leaves the school roll at times other than at the end of their statutory schooling. This is especially important in secondary schools at the end of Year 10 and the start of Year 11 because the exam results of a child who is on the roll of a school at the time of the January census count in the school's overall performance measures. Governors can then review cases where off-rolling may have occurred, such as for children with EHCPs, those on SEN Support, children looked after and those from other vulnerable groups. Of course, it is entirely normal for children to move school for understandable reasons, moving house, for example, and the process will pick this up, but it will add a layer of reassurance and safety for vulnerable children and their families. Further, and this is the point really, it will influence school leaders who have engaged in this shameful practice to cease as it increases the chance of being caught (Roberts, 2019).

Visiting the school

In the same way that governors do not and must not carry out lesson observations, they should not make formal assessments of behaviour whilst they are in school. That said, they will clearly see and hear a lot whilst they are in the building during the school day, and this can help them to round off the other sources of information they receive from senior leaders.

I strongly encourage school leaders to ensure governors visit any areas of the school used for isolation (or similar) so that they can satisfy themselves of the use of the facility. This visit should include talking to any students and staff who are in there. For governors reading this, please don't wait to be invited by the senior leaders from your school, insist that someone from the board visit on at least an annual basis and that they write a report for the board.

Governors' formal role in reviewing exclusions

The role of governors in reviewing exclusions, both fixed-term and permanent, was mentioned in Chapter 12, so I signpost that here in case this chapter is being read in isolation. (It also provides me with a chance to direct governors to the excellent resources available for governors from the National Governance Association – NGA, n.d.)

TAKING IT FURTHER – QUESTIONS AND ACTIVITIES FOR YOU AND YOUR COLLEAGUES

- For school leaders:
  - o Ask governors what they would really like from school leaders in terms of information on behaviour in their regular reports that they receive from you.
  - o Set up a time for a governor with delegated oversight for behaviour to visit the facility you use for isolation, and to talk to the staff and students whilst they are there.
  - o Sit down with your governor for behaviour to look in detail at the evidence you have on behaviour in your school to search for signs of systemic discrimination (see Chapters 5 and 12 for more on this).

- For governors:
  - o Discuss with fellow governors if there is a desire to lower the threshold to review fixed-term exclusions for children with protected characteristics.
  - o Discuss with fellow governors if your board would consider adopting a similar review system for the use of isolation (perhaps with lower thresholds for children with protected characteristics as per the previous suggestion).
  - o Consider adopting a policy of reviewing all cases of children leaving your school roll at a time other than their expected leaving date. Pay particularly close attention to children with protected characteristics and those who are low attainers to satisfy your board that off-rolling is not occurring in your school.
  - o Ask school leaders that the board be alerted to any cases that occur in the academic year before the January census, especially from Year 6 or Year 11.

References

Biesta, G.J.J. (2007) 'Why "what works" won't work: Evidence-based practice and the democratic deficit of educational research', *Educational Theory*, 57(1): 1–22.

Department for Children, Schools and Families (2009) *Learning Behaviour: Lessons Learned – A Review of Behaviour Standards and Practices in Our Schools*. DCSF-00453-2009. https://webarchive.nationalarchives.gov.uk/20130321074534/ https://www.education.gov.uk/publications/standard/publicationDetail/Page1/ DCSF-00453-2009 (accessed 25 September 2019).

NGA (National Governance Association) (n.d.) Admissions and exclusions. www. nga.org.uk/Knowledge-Centre/Pupil-success-and-wellbeing/Admissions-and-Exclusions.aspx (accessed 25 September 2019).

Roberts, J. (2019) 'Spielman: Ofsted has identified off-rolling at three schools', *Times Educational Supplement*, 5 February. www.tes.com/news/spielman-ofsted-has-identified-rolling-three-schools (accessed 23 September 2019).

AFTERWORD

Times are bad. Children no longer obey their parents, and everyone is writing a book.

Marcus Tullius Cicero

If you are leading behaviour in your school, or are aspiring to do so, I take my hat off to you. It is no mean feat and you deserve great credit for taking on the challenge. You also deserve great support for no woman or man can do this job alone.

I encourage you to make friends with colleagues doing your job in other schools. Visit them and ask *critical* questions about what they are doing – do not be afraid to ask for evidence of effectiveness. Invite them to your school to do the same. Time pressures mean that too often we don't allow colleagues to see anything other than a brief tour of our schools so their understanding will always be limited. Get involved in proper peer review of each other's work, examining the evidence of what is working and, more importantly, what is not working, in schools. These people will become great allies, especially those in other phases where your students either go to from your primary school or come from if you work in a secondary school. Don't just nick other schools' shiny new ideas. Pick them up and play with them. Discuss them in staff meetings, knock them around a bit and then think deeply about your context before deciding what your school is going to do.

Sooner or later you're going to be confronted with your own Cicero telling you that behaviour has never been worse and asking you what you're going to do about it. When this happens, have a read of a superb article by Adrian Elliott (2009) in which he recalls this apparent golden age with some deeply alarming examples where some children were trying to drown their Headmaster, others shot dead a teacher, only to express regret that they got the wrong one – they were aiming for the Headmaster – and other equally horrifying reports. Comparisons with days gone by are pointless. What matters is how your school is getting on today, and how it has progressed over the past few years, both with reference to itself and to its fellow schools.

And lastly, stick with it. We all want behaviour to be better and we all want it now. Lasting behaviour change, though, takes time, just as losing weight or training for an ultra-marathon takes time. I hope that this book has given you plenty of food for thought, clarified areas for improvement but has also allowed you to reflect on the great work that you're already doing. I'm keen to hear how you get on.

Thanks for spending this time with me.

Jarlath

Reference

Elliott, A. (2009) 'Behaviour and discipline in schools today are far worse than in the past', *Times Educational Supplement*, 6 November. www.tes.com/news/ myth-behaviour-and-discipline-schools-today-are-far-worse-past (accessed 25 September 2019).

INDEX